Advance Praise for *Fabricating Jesus*

"*Fabricating Jesus* exposes the misinformed nonsense that has confused the reading public over the past few years. Craig Evans is a well-read and thoughtful scholar who knows all the ancient texts. In this well-written book, he exposes the misguided assumptions and dubious sources that lie behind the wild theories that have plagued the public. He has also presented Jesus and the Gospels in their proper historical context. With enthusiasm, I recommend this book for scholars and all interested in Jesus and Christian origins."

JAMES H. CHARLESWORTH, George L. Collord Professor of New Testament Language and Literature, Princeton Theological Seminary; Director and Editor of the PTS Dead Sea Scrolls Project; and author of *Jesus and the Dead Sea Scrolls* and *The Beloved Disciple*

"Craig Evans is a prolific and distinguished scholar whose many books and articles are well known to his colleagues in the academy. *Fabricating Jesus* adds another fine work to the list of his accomplishments. For decades now, the unsuspecting American public has been subjected to dubious academic claims about the historical Jesus that hardly raise above the level of sensationalistic novels. In particular, the Coptic *Gospel of Thomas* has been misused as a privileged route to the historical Jesus, when in fact it is an interesting and valuable source for knowledge of the patristic period. Especially in regard to the *Gospel of Thomas,* Prof. Evans's arguments against the misuse of apocryphal Gospels are especially cogent. This book is a healthful antidote to a great deal of what claims to be the quest for the historical Jesus in the United States today."

JOHN P. MEIER, William K. Warren Foundation Professor of Theology, University of Notre Dame, and author of the multivolume work on the historical Jesus titled *A Marginal Jew*

"This powerful and persuasive book is a much-needed antidote to the outrageous distortions about Jesus and the Gospels that have been popularized in recent years. It's authoritative while still being accessible, and well-argued without being mean-spirited. I strongly recommend this outstanding resource to both Christians and spiritual seekers."

LEE STROBEL, author of *The Case for Christ*

"Many recent studies of Jesus are arguing that evidence requires a Jesus redo. Some works are written by well-known academics, while others are written by less well-known authors. Enter Craig Evans, who has given his life to the historical study of Jesus. Mincing no words, he calls most of these efforts what they are—fabrication. However, his tone is irenic, the style is accessible, his argumentation is sound, and his scope is comprehensive. This book is a necessary exposé of many recent works, taking us from the hype to the historical Jesus. Eminently qualified, Evans has done us all a great service."

DARRELL BOCK, Research Professor of New Testament Studies, Dallas Theological Seminary, and author of *The Missing Gospels*

"Craig Evans is well known in academic circles for his expertise in Judaism and the history of early Christianity. In this new book he brings a refreshing mixture of scholarly erudition and critical common sense to an evaluation of the various documents that have been thought to undermine the credibility of the New Testament and demonstrates convincingly that they cannot bear the burden of proof that has been placed upon them. Such documents as the *Gospels of Thomas* and *Peter* have no significant new light to shed on the historical Jesus. At a time when much baseless fiction is being developed by novelists on the basis of such dubious sources, it is good to have this exposé of just how fictitious such writings are."

I. HOWARD MARSHALL, Honorary Research Professor of New Testament, University of Aberdeen, and author of **I Believe in the Historical Jesus** and **The Origins of New Testament Christology**

"This book belongs with the excellent work Craig Evans has already published on the historical Jesus. Professor Evans consistently uses evidence in a truly scholarly and properly balanced manner to reach convincing conclusions—so different from some sensationalist claims about Jesus that quickly turn out to be based on mere wishful thinking. This is contemporary Gospel apologetics at its very best."

GERALD O'COLLINS, S.J., Professor Emeritus of the Gregorian University (Rome), and author of **Jesus Our Redeemer**

"Craig Evans has written a necessary book on historical Jesus research. His book is exemplary for a 'conservative enlightenment.' It is aptly critical as scholarship—but it is also critical of sensational modern approaches in Jesus research that do not live up to the standards of academic research. In this well-written, lucid book, Evans informs readers of exciting new developments in Jesus research which outdate some hypotheses that were once in vogue. He knows academic scholarship from within—and also the very human aspects of all those who are engaged in Jesus research. So it is not only a very good scholarly book, but also a noble and fair book."

GERD THEISSEN, Professor of New Testament Theology, University of Heidelberg, and author of **The Shadow of the Galilean** and **The Gospels in Context**

"Few scholarly debates are more controversial or more vulnerable to distorted views from right and left than the discussion about the historical Jesus. The increased attention given to extracanonical texts such as the recently published *Gospel of Judas* and even the fictional vapors of *The Da Vinci Code* can seem in the eye of the casual reader to put the historical and theological credibility of the New Testament materials themselves in question. That is why Craig Evans's thoughtful, well-informed and balanced review of the debate is so welcome. *Fabricating Jesus* is not a reaction to modern biblical scholarship but a judicious guide through the evidence—and a fair-minded and careful assessment of how scholars have dealt with it."

DONALD SENIOR, President and Professor of New Testament, Catholic Theological Union in Chicago, and author of **Jesus: A Gospel Portrait**

"The quest of the historical Jesus has been seriously misled by much poor scholarship and distorted almost beyond recognition by recent pseudoscholarship. But now Craig Evans out-skeptics the historical skeptics, demonstrating from his own intimate familiarity with the biblical texts and his mastery of ancient sources how unfounded are many of the claims made and how ridiculously bizarre are the hypotheses thought to give some support to *The Da Vinci Code* and its like. The mature judgment of such an accomplished and front-rank scholar cannot be ignored or lightly gainsaid—a welcome draft from a clear spring after all the muddied waters of recent years."

JAMES D. G. DUNN, Lightfoot Professor of Divinity Emeritus, University of Durham, and author of *Jesus Remembered* and *Christology in the Making*

"Few scholars are as well positioned, well trained and well informed as Craig Evans to critique the recent spate of books that have hit the stands, touting a new Jesus for a new day. In a scholarly world where almost anything can pass for knowledge of the historical Jesus or earliest Christianity no matter how far-fetched, it is comforting to have someone like Craig Evans as a sure guide through the maze of books on Jesus and supposedly lost Christianities. *Fabricating Jesus* is simply the best and most well-informed popular-level book ever written on the Gnostic and apocryphal Gospels, as well as on a host of other early traditions that in some way touch on the story of Jesus. Along the way, Evans also provides us with a sane and sober reconstruction of Jesus and his aims and the history of earliest Christianity. I hope this book will gain the wide audience it so richly deserves."

BEN WITHERINGTON III, Professor of New Testament, Asbury Theological Seminary, and author of *The Jesus Quest* and *What Have They Done with Jesus?*

"In *Fabricating Jesus,* we have one of the greatest talents in biblical studies applying his skills to one of the biggest problems in popular culture—the eclipse of the true Jesus, to whom history gives abundant witness. Craig Evans does a masterful job of exposing the sort of tabloid scholarship that captures headlines and confuses the general public. He returns us to the clear-headed analysis of genuine historical inquiry, demonstrating the reasonableness of the Gospel accounts. This book will clarify matters for ordinary readers, yet satisfy scholars too."

SCOTT HAHN, Professor of Theology and Scripture, Franciscan University of Steubenville

FABRICATING JESUS

How Modern Scholars
Distort the Gospels

CRAIG A. EVANS

IVP Books

An imprint of InterVarsity Press
Downers Grove, Illinois

InterVarsity Press
P.O. Box 1400, Downers Grove, IL 60515-1426
World Wide Web: www.ivpress.com
E-mail: mail@ivpress.com

InterVarsity Press® is the book-publishing division of InterVarsity Christian Fellowship/USA®, a student movement active on campus at hundreds of universities, colleges and schools of nursing in the United States of America, and a member movement of the International Fellowship of Evangelical Students. For information about local and regional activities, write Public Relations Dept., InterVarsity Christian Fellowship/USA, 6400 Schroeder Rd., P.O. Box 7895, Madison, WI 53707-7895, or visit the IVCF website at <www.intervarsity.org>.

Scripture quotations are based on the Revised Standard Version of the Bible, copyright 1946, 1952, 1971 by the Division of Christian Education of the National Council of the Churches of Christ in the U.S.A., and modified by the author where necessary to bring out certain things more clearly.

Design: Cindy Kiple
Images: Burstein Collection/CORBIS

ISBN-10: 0-8308-3318-8
ISBN-13: 978-0-8308-3318-4

Printed in Canada ∞

Library of Congress Cataloging-in-Publication Data

Evans, Craig A.
  Fabricating Jesus/Craig A. Evans.
    p. cm.
  Includes bibliographical references and index.
  ISBN-13: 978-0-8308-3318-4 (cloth: alk. paper)
  ISBN-10: 0-8308-3318-8 (cloth: alk. paper)
  1. Jesus Christ—Historicity. I. Title.
  BT303.2.E93   2006
  232.9'08—dc22
                                                    2006030075

| P | 19 | 18 | 17 | 16 | 15 | 14 | 13 | 12 | 11 | 10 | 9 | 8 | 7 | 6 | 5 | 4 | 3 | 2 | 1 |
| Y | 21 | 20 | 19 | 18 | 17 | 16 | 15 | 14 | 13 | 12 | 11 | 10 | 09 | 08 | 07 | 06 | | | | |

To Merrick,

grandson extraordinaire

CONTENTS

FACT:

The *Gospel of Thomas*—in comparison with the New Testament Gospels—is late, not early; secondary, not authentic. Contrary to what a few scholars maintain, the *Gospel of Thomas* originated in Syria and probably no earlier than the end of the second century.

The *Gospel of Peter*, which describes a talking cross, is late and incredible. In fact, the fragmentary document that we have may not be the *Gospel of Peter* at all. The document that we have may date to the fourth or fifth century.

The "secret" version of the Gospel of Mark, allegedly found in the Mar Saba Monastery, is a modern hoax. Analysis of the hand-writing betrays the tell-tale signs of forgery.

The distinctive conclusions of the Jesus Seminar are rejected by most scholars in North America and Europe.

There is absolutely no credible evidence that Jesus had a wife or a child.

The evidence is compelling that the New Testament Gospels—Matthew, Mark, Luke and John—are our best sources for understanding the historical Jesus. The New Testament Gospels are based on eyewitness testimony and truthfully and accurately relate the teaching, life, death and resurrection of Jesus.

Jesus was not a Cynic; in all probability he never encountered a Cynic.

No killer monks (albino or otherwise) number among the membership of Opus Dei.

All descriptions of documents, literature and archaeology in this book are accurate.

PREFACE

In high school I assumed that I would be a lawyer, so I went to a very fine liberal arts college in southern California, where I majored in history and minored in philosophy, in preparation for law school. But in my senior year in college I had become a committed Christian, which led me to seminary, instead of law school ("from law to grace," as one minister remarked).

I went to seminary for the purpose of training in Christian ministry. I was fascinated with Jesus of Nazareth and wanted to learn more about him and his teaching. I looked forward to a lifetime in pastoral ministry. But in seminary I discovered the academic side to theology and biblical studies. I loved it. Greek and Hebrew came easily; exegesis was fun; historical and background studies were stimulating. While other students were attempting to avoid these subjects, I engaged them enthusiastically.

In my second year I took an advanced course in Greek in which we read the Gospels of Matthew, Mark and Luke—in one semester! That did it; I was hooked on the life, teaching and world of Jesus. I was fascinated with the Gospels themselves and the questions scholars grappled with: What are the sources of the Gospels? How do they relate to one another? How much of the Gospels is history, and how much is interpretation? I enjoyed it so much I decided to pursue a Ph.D.

I had the good fortune of entering Claremont Graduate University at a time when its biblical studies faculty was at its greatest. CGU, along with the nearby Claremont School of Theology, boasted a powerhouse faculty in New Testament and related fields of study. In this faculty were Hans Dieter Betz, William Brownlee, Burton Mack, James Robinson, James Sanders and John Trever.

Professor Betz chaired the Hellenism and the New Testament Seminar, which was favored with visits from Ronald Hock and Edward O'Neill, both on the faculty of the University of Southern California. During this time the seminar was finishing its work on Plutarch and just launching its work on the Greek magical papyri. Betz impressed me greatly with his high standards and attention to detail. His commentaries on Galatians and the Sermon on the Mount in the Hermeneia commentary series are impressive and well respected.

Professor Robinson chaired the Nag Hammadi Seminar, dedicated to the publication and study of the Coptic Gnostic codices found in Nag Hammadi, Egypt. I found his enthusiasm for fresh research, discovery and publishing infectious. Entering Claremont was like walking into a publishing factory. I was overwhelmed by the activity. During my time with the Nag Hammadi Seminar, I became acquainted with Charles Hedrick (who taught me Coptic) and Marvin Meyer, who now is the research director for the Coptic Magical Texts Project at Claremont Graduate University and an expert on Gnostic texts.

Professor Mack was in those days engrossed in Philo and Jewish wisdom traditions. He was at that time a warm-hearted Christian scholar. I distinctly recall him in 1977 telling me how happy he was that I was serving on the staff of a nearby church. "That is really good," he said. "What we need are more doctors of the church." Times change and so do some people.

Professor Brownlee was wonderful to work with. He was quiet, gentle and unassuming. Yet he was one of the very first scholars to lay eyes on the Dead Sea Scrolls. He was in Jerusalem, doing a year of postdoctoral studies in 1947-1948, when the first cave containing scrolls was discovered. His studies in the book of Ezekiel and the ancient Ugaritic language were set aside. Brownlee brought one of the scrolls back with him to Duke University in the fall of 1948 so he could use it in teaching Hebrew. (That of course is no longer allowed!) He published an early study of the Rule Scroll (1QS) and spent much of his career analyzing Qumran's commentary (or pesher) on the book of Habakkuk. I found him delightful to work with and eventually finished my doctoral dissertation under his supervision. It was from Brownlee that I learned much about the Dead Sea Scrolls, and it was with him that I studied Aramaic and Syriac. His sudden death in 1983 left me an academic orphan and ended plans that we had made for collaborative studies in Isaiah and Daniel.

I also had the privilege of making the acquaintance of John Trever, Bill Brownlee's longtime friend. Trever was with Brownlee in Jerusalem in 1947-1948, and it was he who took the very first—and quite excellent—photographs of the Dead Sea Scrolls. Trever was also happy to give me a guided tour of his collection of photographs and artifacts, explaining where they were found and their significance.

Although I was very close to Brownlee, the person who influenced me the most at Claremont was Professor Sanders, who joined the faculty in 1977, the year my doctoral studies commenced. It would be almost impossible to exaggerate the significance of his contribution to my understanding of biblical literature and its full context. Sanders introduced me to the versions of Scripture, such as the Old Greek (or Septuagint) and the Aramaic (or Targum). He led me through the rabbinic literature, taught me to appreciate rabbinic midrash and transformed textual criticism—the study of ancient manuscripts and their diverse readings and variants—into a joy. Under his instruction my appreciation of Scripture grew. Over the years we have collaborated on a number of publishing projects and jointly chaired from 1989-1996 a program unit in the Society of Biblical Literature.

Although I started out at Claremont as a New Testament student, I was so deeply influenced by Brownlee and Sanders that I wrote my dissertation on the book of Isaiah. There are New Testament components in the dissertation, to be sure, but at the conclusion of my doctoral studies I was as much interested in a career in Old Testament as I was in New Testament. One of the ironies of my life is that twenty-five years ago I interviewed for a position in Old Testament at Acadia Divinity College. I was passed over on account of my youth and ended up at Trinity Western University instead—as an assistant professor of New Testament! This appointment guided me back to the New Testament, and after twenty-one years at Trinity I was appointed to Acadia Divinity College as the Payzant Distinguished Professor of New Testament. It seems I was destined for Acadia after all—but in New Testament not Old.

As I taught New Testament at Trinity, I of course began to shift my research and publishing away from Isaiah and the Old Testament to the New Testament. I focused on Jesus and the Gospels, which had been the focus of my interest back in seminary. An interesting thing happened. I realized that my work in Isaiah, the Greek and Aramaic versions of the Old Testament, the Dead Sea Scrolls and early rabbinic literature was an enormous asset in the study of Jesus and the Gospels. As I became acquainted with more and more New Testament scholars (at regional and national Society of Biblical Literature meetings), I became aware that many of them lacked training in the Semitic background of the New Testament. I was bumping into New Testament scholars who had studied Greek and knew something of the Greco-Roman world, but had only the feeblest ability with Hebrew and Aramaic (if at all). Most knew little of early rabbinic literature and the Aramaic paraphrases of Scripture.

This deficiency on the part of so many New Testament scholars helps explain the oddness of much of the work of the Jesus Seminar, founded by Robert Funk in 1985. Whereas many of the Seminar's members have been exposed to Greek literature and Greco-Roman culture and conventions, not many of them appear to have competence in the Semitic (Jewish) world of Jesus. Few seem acquainted with the land of Israel itself. Few have done any archaeological work. Few know rabbinic literature and the Aramaic paraphrases of Scripture. As a consequence of these deficiencies, it is not surprising that the Jesus Seminar has come to so many odd and implausible conclusions. For example, the Seminar does not understand what Jesus meant by his reference to "kingdom of God." The Seminar has completely misunderstood the meaning of eschatology and holds to a skewed idea of the meaning of Jesus' favorite self-designation "Son of Man." Moreover, the Seminar finds no meaningful place for Israel's Scripture in Jesus' self-understanding and teaching. The Seminar's errors are egregious and legion. Unfortunately, the Seminar has gained a great deal of media attention and has cultivated a series of books that advance misguided and mistaken views of Jesus and the Gospels—both those in the New Testament and those outside the New Testament. *Fabricating Jesus* will address just these sorts of issues.

I am a Christian. I was a Christian before going to seminary and graduate school, and I still am after completing school and teaching and publishing for more than a quarter century. When some of my friends at seminary learned that I would be entering Claremont to pursue a doctorate, I was warned that critical study would not be good for my faith. Of course, I had heard of some who after becoming involved in critical research had given up faith. I will speak to that topic in the first chapter.

My academic life has not resulted in the loss of faith. Aspects of my faith have changed, to be sure. Not everything is as cut and dried, black and white, as it once was. There are aspects of theology that remain uncertain, historical details that remain unclear. But then again, I have found that that was the way it was for Jesus and his earliest followers. Maybe not having pat answers for everything is what faith is all about.

At first, I must admit, I found aspects of biblical criticism unsettling. But in time I realized that what biblical criticism challenged was not the essence of the Christian message, but the baggage that many think is part of the message. Typically this baggage includes views of authorship and dates of given biblical books (for example, the idea that biblical books must be early and written by apostles even when they make no such claim), as well as assumptions regarding the nature of biblical literature (for example, the belief that the Gospels are history and nothing else) and the nature of Jesus' teaching (for example, the view that everything Jesus said was wholly unique and never before heard). In time I was able to distinguish the baggage from the message. In fact, I can say that biblical criticism rescued the message and helped me see it and appreciate it more fully.

I have found careful, searching study of the historical Jesus rewarding. I love to lecture. I love to preach. I love to tell the stories of the Gospels. I love to see the look in the faces of people in the congregation when they first understand what Jesus meant—what he really meant—when he said or did something. I am always touched when I see how the story of Jesus affects people and brings positive change to their lives. The story of the sinful woman (Luke 7), or the good Samaritan (Luke 10), or the prodigal son (Luke 15), if proclaimed in proper context, results in forgiveness, reconciliation and even self-reproach. It seems that none of the power Jesus exuded has diminished in the passage of time.

I have found that the better we come to understand who Jesus was, what he said and how he was understood by his contemporaries, the more we appreciate him and the movement that he inaugurated. When Jesus' actions or words are misunderstood, problems begin. I have found that lying behind assertions to the effect "Jesus could not have said this" are mistakes in interpretation, usually due to a failure to view the saying in its proper context and setting.

Fabricating Jesus is a book that takes a hard look at some of the sloppy scholarship and misguided theories that have been advanced in recent years. I am appalled at much of this work. Some of it, frankly, is embarrassing.

Fabricating Jesus is written at a popular level and is primarily intended for nonexperts who find much that has been said about Jesus in recent years terribly confusing. Notes are kept to a minimum and are gathered at the back of the book. I have tried to define terms common in biblical studies but unfamiliar to general readers as I introduce them; in addition, I have appended a glossary at the back for quick reference. A list of recommended books is provided for any readers who want to look in more depth at the documents and scholarly literature that stand behind my arguments and conclusions.

I want to thank Jim Hoover of InterVarsity Press, who invited me to write this book and provided me with many great ideas and insights. I also thank my wife, Ginny, who graciously read through the whole manuscript, one chapter at time, and asked me those important questions, such as, "What does this mean?" Because of her care and attention, the book is much easier to read. And finally, a word of thanks is due Danny Zacharias, who assisted with the preparation of the indexes.

Craig A. Evans

INTRODUCTION

Did Jesus have a child by Mary Magdalene? Was he a Cynic? Or was he a mystic, perhaps even a Gnostic? Did he fake his death and sneak out of the holy land? Did he escape to Egypt? Did he write letters to the Jewish court and explain that it was all a mistake, that he never claimed to be the Son of God? Did he celebrate the Last Supper with friends—twenty-five years after his crucifixion? Has the grave of Jesus been found? Has the grave of his father been found? Are the New Testament Gospels reliable? Are there better sources for the life and teaching of Jesus? Do the Dead Sea Scrolls talk about Jesus? Is the gospel story true? Is there a conspiracy to hide the truth? Indeed, did Jesus ever really exist?

When I first began academic study of Jesus and the Gospels some thirty years ago, I could never have guessed that I or anyone else would find it necessary to write a book addressing such questions. Surely no one in all seriousness would advance such theories. Surely no credible publishers would print them. Yet, all that has happened.

Have you wondered why it is that modern scholars (especially the ones who make it into the popular press) seem so prone to discount the evidence of the Gospels, looking to other sources for information? In several books scholars argue that it is necessary to rely on second- and third-century sources, because our first-century New Testament Gospels are not reliable. Does this make sense? Others claim that there are conspiracies to suppress the evidence. Evidence of what? Why?

We live in a strange time that indulges, even encourages, some of the strangest thinking. It is a time when truth means almost what you want to make of it. And in these zany quests for "truth," truth becomes elusive. In fact, a book published a few years ago appeared under the title *Truth Is Stranger Than It Used To Be*. Quite so.

What I find particularly troubling is that a lot of the nonsense comes from scholars. We expect tabloid pseudoscholarship from the quacks, but not from scholars who teach at respectable institutions of higher learning.

Modern scholars and writers, in their never-ending quest to find something new and to advance daring theories that run beyond the evidence, have either distorted or neglected the New Testament Gospels, resulting in the fabrication of an array of pseudo-Jesuses. A variety of influences have led to these results, whether (1) misplaced faith and misguided suspicions, (2) cramped starting points and overly strict critical methods, (3) questionable texts from later centuries, (4) appeals to contexts alien to Jesus' actual environment, (5) skeletal sayings devoid of context altogether, (6) failure to take into account Jesus' mighty deeds, (7) dubious use of Josephus and other resources of late antiquity (8) anachronisms and exaggerated claims, or (9) hokum history and bogus findings. In short, just about every error imaginable has been made. A few writers have made almost all of them.

The chapters that follow take up these issues one by one, spending two chapters on questionable texts. The book concludes with an eleventh chapter in which I offer my assessment of important aspects of genuine progress in the study of the historical Jesus, and in which the Gospels inside the New Testament and the Gospels outside the New Testament are treated properly and other relevant primary materials are given their due.

Fabricating Jesus inquires into the thinking and the methods of scholars and popular writers. What presuppositions do they hold? What methods do they use? Why do they move from valid observations to audacious conclusions? Indeed why and how do they fabricate a Jesus different from the one we find in the New Testament? Are these scholars actually using sound historical method? These are some of the questions this book explores.

Fabricating Jesus is designed to speak to a variety of readers. First, this book is written to assist anyone who is confused by the wild theories and conflicting portraits of Jesus, the claims that he really didn't see himself as the Messiah or as God's Son, or that the New Testament Gospels are not trustworthy, or that other sources are better or at least equally valid, and so forth.

Second, the book is written for people who are interested in Jesus and the New Testament Gospels and want to learn more but are baffled by the strange books that have appeared in recent years. I hope you haven't given up.

Third, it is written for skeptics, especially those prone to fall for some old nineteenth-century philosophical hokum that almost no one today holds.

Fourth, *Fabricating Jesus* is written for the guild, for the scholars whose profession is to investigate the Gospels and the life and teaching of Jesus, in hope that it may call us not to a lesser standard of scholarship but indeed to a higher one, one which doesn't presume that skepticism equals scholarship.

Finally, this book is written to defend the original witnesses to the life, death and resurrection of Jesus. When put to the test, the original documents hold up quite well. Despite their having been maligned, even ridiculed, and pushed into the background, it is time to give them a fresh hearing.

1

MISPLACED FAITH AND MISGUIDED SUSPICIONS

Old and New School Skeptics

In recent years several books have appeared, written by scholars who at one time or another in their lives regarded themselves as traditional, even conservative, Christians but who later came to define themselves as far to the Christian left or even outright agnostics, especially with regard to the traditional portrait of Jesus and the historical reliability of the Gospels. One or two of them are no longer sure Jesus ever existed at all.

My impression is that the majority of biblical scholars, archaeologists and historians who start out as Christian believers continue on in Christian faith and active involvement in the church. Their views on this issue or that may change as they study; most of us who enter the world of biblical scholarship become less rigid and more open to new perspectives. But why do some scholars depart the faith and become hostile to believers? The popular media, of course, love to exploit and sensationalize these kinds of "coming-out" stories.

A big part of the problem starts with conservative Protestant Christianity itself, especially of the Western variety. Due to controversies, such as the modernist-fundamentalist debacle at the end of the nineteenth and beginning of the twentieth centuries, lines were drawn in the sand and detailed statements (or confessions) of faith were drawn up. These statements sometimes came to function as litmus tests regarding who was in and who was out. Learn the statement and agree with it, and all was well. Fail to agree and find yourself on the outside. Indeed, some of these statements seemed to take priority over Scripture itself.

It is not surprising that negative reactions to this sort of rigidity have occurred. Learned study of Scripture that addresses serious questions—such as who wrote the books of the Bible, under what circumstances, with what purposes and, with respect to historical issues, how accurately—invariably works against rigid fundamentalism. My purpose here is not to revisit this larger question, but it is necessary to bring it up because I think it plays a significant role in why some scholars and clergy experience a crisis of faith and make radical shifts.

When it comes to evaluating Jesus, popular Christian apologists often appeal to the triad of options proposed by C. S. Lewis half a century ago: Jesus was either liar, lunatic or Lord. The appeal makes for good alliteration, maybe even good rhetoric, but it is faulty logic. Without further qualification, those who adhere to this line of argument commit the fallacy of excluded middle. That is, they overlook other viable alternatives. At least two other alternatives are possible; both relate to how Scripture is understood, and both come into play in the books that *Fabricating Jesus* criticizes.

A *fourth alternative* is that Jesus is neither liar, lunatic nor Lord (in the traditional, orthodox sense); he is something else. He may be Israel's messiah, the Lord's servant and perhaps the greatest prophet who ever lived. He could even be called God's son, but not in the trinitarian sense, in which Jesus is seen as fully God and fully human. As far as we know, this more or less agrees with Ebionite Christianity, a form of Jewish Christianity that emerged in the second century and eventually disappeared sometime in the fifth century. The Ebionites possessed one or more edited versions of the Gospel of Matthew, which tended to enhance the status of the law and minimize the divine nature of Jesus. They believed Jesus was Israel's messiah and fulfillment of prophecy. They believed that in the sense King David could be called God's "son" (as in Ps 2:7) Jesus also could be called son of God. But Ebionites did not hold to what theologians call "high Christology"—that is, the view that Jesus is divine. The Ebionite understanding of Jesus is pretty close to the view of two of the scholars considered later in this chapter.

A *fifth alternative* is that we really don't know who Jesus was, what he really said and did, what he thought of himself, or what his companions thought of him, because the New Testament Gospels and other sources we have are not reliable. The New Testament Gospels may well present Jesus as Israel's Messiah and as God's Son, but for all we know, that is nothing more than the theology of Christians who lived in the second half of the first century, Christians who had never met Jesus and had never heard him teach. This form of skepticism sometimes runs even deeper, arguing that not only were the original Gospels unhistorical and unreliable, we are not sure if the manuscripts we possess today accurately reflect the Gospels in their original form. So goes the argument. This is the view of another set of scholars we will consider in this chapter.

In reading some of the more radical books on Jesus, I find that loss of confidence in the historical reliability of the New Testament Gospels is often occasioned by misplaced faith and misguided suspicions. By *misplaced faith* I mean placing one's faith in the wrong thing, such as believing that the Scriptures must be inerrant according to rather strict idiosyncratic standards and that we must be able to harmonize the four Gospels. If our faith depends on these ideas, especially in rigid terms, then scholarly study may well lead to a collapse of faith.

By *misguided suspicions* I mean the unreasonable assumption that Jesus' contemporaries (that is, the first generation of his movement) were either incapable of remembering or uninterested in recalling accurately what Jesus said and did, and in passing it on. What we have here is a form of hypercriticism that is all too common in scholarly circles and sometimes seems to arise from confusing criticism with skepticism—that is, thinking that the more skeptical the position, the more critical it is. Radical skepticism is no more critical than is credulity.

We can see how this view of things works out by looking briefly at the work of four scholars whose Christian views at one time were fairly conservative and more or less evangelical. The first two I call "old school skeptics" and the second two I call "new school skeptics." The first two opt for something approximating the fourth alternative I have outlined; the second two opt for the fifth alternative.

I have chosen these scholars because they have discussed their personal views and their respective pilgrimages of faith, especially with regard to their understanding of Jesus and the Gospels. I could have discussed a number of other scholars, but have not done so because they have not made their views public.

I also want to make clear that I am not criticizing these scholars for taking the positions that they have taken. Their personal journeys are their business. I cite and discuss a few of their comments because I think they illustrate the issue that is being addressed in this chapter, an issue that I think lies behind many of the problems and controversies that will be considered in the other chapters of this book. I am, nonetheless, critical of some of the conclusions that they have reached.

OLD SCHOOL SKEPTICS—MINIMIZING JESUS

The two old school skeptics I wish to discuss briefly are Robert Funk (1926-2005) and James Robinson (1924-). Their skepticism of the New Testament Gospels is not as radical as some think. Yes, they are quick to point to this Gospel saying and that deed and pronounce them inauthentic, deriving from the early church, not from Jesus. I disagree with their understanding of the formation, age and transmission of the Gospels; I disagree too with the high value and early date they assign to some of the Gospels that are outside the New Testament. But even so, Funk and Robinson believe that a good amount of useful, reliable material emerges from the Gospels, so that a coherent, even edifying portrait of Jesus emerges. Both scholars appear to admire Jesus and regard him as a spiritual benchmark. Their complaints tend to be directed against an ossified church housing a Christianity preoccupied with doctrine but not with social justice. They may paint with a broad brush, but I have no doubt there are churches that would do well to consider this criticism.

Robert Funk. In *Honest to Jesus* Funk says of his youthful education:

If the creationists had their way I . . . would have been stuck with a literalist reading of Genesis 1 and 2, which I had already acquired from attending Sunday school. . . .

[My pastor] sent me to a Bible college located in the hills of eastern Tennessee. I promptly became a teenage evangelist, using my rhetorical skills to make my audiences laugh and cry.

But I was uneasy. Learning at the college was mostly by memorization and rehearsal. Truth was already encoded in the simplistic creed of the school. A doctrinal straitjacket did not suit me.[1]

Funk goes on to describe his later education, which led to a Ph.D. in New Testament and an academic career. He says that he increasingly found teaching in theological institutions frustrating, so he was glad when he relocated to the University of Montana. But even there he grew discouraged, feeling as much out of place in the university as in the church. He relocated to California, founded the Westar Institute and Polebridge Press, and launched the Jesus Seminar.

What strikes me is how Funk began his Christian experience with a "literalist reading of Genesis 1 and 2," went on to attend a "Bible college," becoming "a teenage evangelist" and learning "by memorization and rehearsal." I don't want to read into this too much, but it sure sounds as if a rigid, fundamentalist understanding of Scripture laid the foundation of his formative years. Funk goes on to say that learning was an agonizing experience. I have heard that before—how breaking away from a fundamentalist understanding of Scripture can be emotionally devastating.

James Robinson. James Robinson was one of my professors in graduate school. I found him fascinating and was much impressed by his productivity. From time to time he remarked on his upbringing and early years in theological education. Not long ago he published an insightful "Theological Autobiography." In it he spends little time describing his pilgrimage, racing on to narrate at length the frustrations and vicissitudes he experienced in gathering and eventually publishing the Gnostic codices from Nag Hammadi. But here and there in his autobiography Robinson says a few things that pertain to his pilgrimage:

> Before going on to graduate studies, I taught for a year at my college (Davidson) . . . a quite literal Old Testament. My students were mostly returning veterans, who must have experienced me as hopelessly naive. Whether or not they actually believed anything I said, by the end of year I no longer did. I had tried to make sense of my childhood theology to myself, and had failed.

> In effect, my theological trajectory over half a century has moved step by step from right to left.

> I am often asked by Christians who are not academics the leading

question as to how a lifetime of critical biblical scholarship has affected my faith as a Christian. The implied answer is that such "higher criticism" obviously destroyed it.[2]

Robinson says that at Davidson College he taught "a quite literal Old Testament." He imagines that his students viewed him as "hopelessly naive." Here again, we likely have a rigid, fundamentalist understanding of Scripture. Having taught the Old Testament, while probably reading scholarly literature along the way and trying to respond to students' questions, Robinson says he "no longer" believed what he had taught. But *what* did he no longer believe? He goes on to say, "I had tried to make sense of my childhood theology to myself, and had failed." What was this "childhood theology"? As best I can extract from his autobiography, Robinson is talking about Calvinist theology and a conservative view of Scripture.

Unable to make sense of his conservative theology, Robinson began moving "step by step from right to left." Near the end of his autobiography he acknowledges that "higher criticism" destroyed his faith as a Christian. Robinson also asserts that traditional Christianity's failure to deal with injustice would have destroyed his conservative Christian faith in any case, quite apart from higher criticism.

By saying that higher criticism destroyed his Christian faith, I take it that Robinson means the Christian faith of his childhood. Robinson seems to hold to an appreciative view of Jesus. He is skeptical to be sure, but what he says about Jesus, so far as it goes, would be appreciated by most Christians.[3] But in my estimation, what he says is comparable to a watered-down version of Ebionite Christology.

NEW SCHOOL SKEPTICS—MISUNDERSTANDING JESUS

The two scholars I mention as "new school skeptics" are far more extreme and more radical than the likes of Funk and Robinson. Indeed, they make Funk and Robinson look like Billy Graham. I have in mind Robert Price and Bart Ehrman.

Robert Price. Robert Price has recently written books in which he argues that the Jesus Seminar is far too optimistic in thinking that as much as 18 percent of the sayings and deeds attributed to Jesus in the Gospels actually go back to Jesus. Price thinks the evidence is so weak for the historical Jesus that we cannot know anything certain or meaningful about him. He is even willing to entertain the possibility that there never was a historical Jesus.[4] Is the evidence of Jesus really that thin? Virtually no scholar trained in history will agree with Price's negative conclusions.

Price is a graduate of Gordon-Conwell Theological Seminary, a conservative evangelical school. Previously he was involved with a fundamentalist Baptist church and was a leader of a chapter of InterVarsity Christian Fellowship. Not long after seminary, where he was exposed to biblical criticism, Price began rethinking his faith. He returned to school, earning a Ph.D. in systematic theology from Drew University. In the years that followed he began moving to the left, leaving one pastorate for another. He returned to school, this time earning a degree in New Testament. Influenced by nineteenth-century New Testament critics, Price moved further to the left, eventually adopting an agnostic position. His own views of the New Testament Gospels became increasingly radical.

In my view Price's work in the Gospels is overpowered by a philosophical mindset that is at odds with historical research—of any kind. For him parallels in other ancient texts mean that Jesus could not have said what is attributed to him or the event described did not happen. Moreover, because there is evidence that the sayings and stories of Jesus were edited and contextualized, nothing can be trusted. Price uncritically embraces the dubious methods and results of the Jesus Seminar, adopts much of the (discredited) Christ-Myth theory from the nineteenth century (in which it was argued that Jesus never lived), and so forth. Price's procedure strikes me as an atavistic grab bag or a throwback that seems out of touch with genuine progress in critical studies in the last 150 years. What we see in Price is what we have seen before: a flight from fundamentalism.

Bart Ehrman. Bart Ehrman became a believer as a teenager and after his conversion was nurtured in a conservative setting. He enrolled at Moody Bible Institute in Chicago, went on from there to Wheaton College and Wheaton College Graduate School, where he earned degrees in New Testament, and later completed M.Div. and Ph.D. degrees at Princeton Theological Seminary under the direction of Bruce Metzger, the venerable dean of

New Testament textual criticism.

I want to spend more time with Ehrman, for his books have sold widely and have had far more influence than the publications of the other scholars considered in this chapter. It was the study of textual variants—the usual myriad scribal errors and glosses that are found in handwritten books from

OLDEST SYNOPTIC GOSPELS PAPYRI

The earliest copies of manuscripts of the Greek New Testament (the language the New Testament was written in originally) are found on fragments of papyrus (pl. *papyri,* often abbreviated 𝔭), a type of paper made from reeds that grow along the Nile River in Egypt. Much, but not all, of the Greek New Testament survives in the papyri. All of the Greek New Testament survives in the later codices (sg. *codex*), which are ancient books usually made of vellum, or leather, pages. The oldest Greek papyri containing the text of the Synoptic Gospels are listed below along with the Gospel passage(s) or fragments they contain.

Papyrus 67 (P.Barcelona 1) A.D. 125-150
Matthew 3:9, 15; 5:20-22, 25-28

Papyrus 103 (P.Oxy. 4403) A.D. 175-200
Matthew 13:55-57; 14:3-5

Papyrus 104 (P.Oxy. 4404) A.D. 175-200
Matthew 21:34-37, 43, 45 (?)

Papyrus 77 (P.Oxy. 2683 + 4405) A.D. 175-200
Matthew 23:30-39

Papyrus 64 (P.Magdalen 17) A.D. 125-150
Matthew 26:7-8, 10, 14-15, 22-23, 31-33

Papyrus 4 (P.Paris 1120) A.D. 125-150
Luke 1:58-59; 1:62–2:1; 2:6-7; 3:8–4:2; 4:29-32, 34-35; 5:3-8

Papyrus 75 (John Bodmer) c. A.D. 175
Luke 3:18-22; 3:33–4:2; 4:34–5:10; 5:37–6:4; 6:10–7:32; 7:35-39, 41-43; 7:46–9:2; 9:4–17:15; 17:19–18:18; 22:4–24:53

antiquity and the Middle Ages—that caused Ehrman to question his faith. In short, he found what he took to be errors in Scripture. Errors in Scripture, thinks Ehrman, mean that the words of Scripture can no longer be viewed as God's words.

Rather rigid ideas about the verbal inspiration and inerrancy of Scripture underlie Ehrman's problem, as he says in the autobiographical section of his introduction:

> For me, though, this [the loss of the original manuscripts of the New Testament] was a compelling problem. It was the words of scripture themselves that God had inspired. Surely we have to know what those words were if we want to know how he had communicated to us, since the very words were his words, and having some other words (those inadvertently or intentionally created by scribes) didn't help us much if we want to know *His* words.
>
> The Bible began to appear to me as a very human book. . . . This was a human book from beginning to end. It was written by different human authors at different times and in different places to address different needs. . . .
>
> Those of us at Moody, believed that the Bible was absolutely inerrant in its very words.[5]

Because for Ehrman the Bible became a human book and therefore no longer could be viewed as God's words, he lost confidence in it. Having lost confidence in the Bible, including the Gospels that tell the story of Jesus, Ehrman lost his faith. He now regards himself as an agnostic.

I must admit that I am puzzled by all this. If not at Moody Bible Institute, then surely at Wheaton College, Ehrman must have become acquainted with a great number of textual variants in the biblical manuscripts. No student can earn a degree in Bible and not know this. Yet Bible students are not defecting in droves.

I am also puzzled by Ehrman's line of reasoning. For the sake of argument, let's suppose that the scribal errors in the Bible manuscripts really do disprove verbal inspiration and inerrancy, so that the Bible really should be viewed as a *human book* and not as *God's words*. Would we lose everything as

OLDEST GREEK CODICES

Coincident with the emergence of Christianity was the development of the codex, the forerunner of the modern book, with bound pages printed on both sides. Several early codices of the Greek Bible have survived.

Codex Sinaiticus (abbreviated ℵ): produced by three scribes in the fourth century

Codex Vaticanus (abbreviated B): produced by two scribes in the fourth century

Codex Alexandrinus (abbreviated A): fifth-century codex; first to fall into the hands of Western scholars, leading to quest for more manuscripts, presented to England's Charles I in 1627

Codex Beza (abbreviated D): late-fourth-century codex, containing numerous unique readings

Codex Ephraemi Rescriptus (abbreviated C): called the "rewriting of Ephraem" because a twelfth-century monk scraped, then copied over this sixth-century Greek codex with the discourses of Ephraem Syrus

Codex Washingtonianus (abbreviated W): late-fourth/early-fifth-century codex, containing an interesting gloss at Mark 16:14-15

a result? No. Moderate and liberal Christians have held essentially this view for a century or more. The real issue centers on what God accomplished in Jesus of Nazareth.

Let me put it this way: What did Peter and the other original followers of Jesus proclaim following the experience of the resurrection? Peter's preaching is summed up in the Pentecost sermon:

Men of Israel, hear these words: Jesus of Nazareth, a man attested to you by God with mighty works and wonders and signs which God did through him in your midst, as you yourselves know—this Jesus, delivered up according to the definite plan and foreknowledge of God, you crucified and killed by the hands of lawless men. But God raised him up. . . . This Jesus God raised up, and of that we all are witnesses. (Acts 2:22-24, 32)

Peter and the rest of the apostles proclaimed the resurrection of Jesus. For them this was the good news, this was conclusive evidence that God was at work in the ministry and person of Jesus of Nazareth. Peter didn't stand up and proclaim, "Men of Israel, I have good news; the Bible is verbally inspired and therefore inerrant and, moreover, the Gospels can be harmonized." Had that been Peter's message, then Ehrman would have a valid point.

The message that runs throughout the New Testament writings and the earliest Christian communities was that God had raised Jesus, to which Peter and many others (including one or two noncommitted persons, such as Jesus' brothers James and perhaps Jude, and at least one opponent, Paul) bore witness. It was the reality of the resurrection and its impact on those who heard and responded to it in faith that propelled the new movement forward, not "mistake-free" Scripture.

The witness of (Old Testament) Scripture was very important to the early Christian movement, of course. Throughout his sermon Peter appeals to Scripture. Almost every New Testament writer does. But the proofs adduced from Scripture are clearly subordinate to the message itself, which is the miracle of Easter. Nonexperts perhaps need to be told that in the first ten to fifteen years of the existence of the church, not one book of the New Testament was in existence. Nevertheless, the church grew fast and furious, without benefit of a New Testament or the Gospels (inerrant or otherwise).

And finally, I am puzzled by the examples of "errors" that Ehrman puts forward as evidence that Scripture is not trustworthy. Because *Fabricating Jesus* focuses on Jesus and the Gospels and not the rest of the New Testament, I will limit my discussion to the Gospel passages that Ehrman discusses.

Ehrman makes much of passages that he and most textual critics rightly deem as later, inauthentic scribal glosses. He calls attention to Luke 22:41-45, Luke's version of Jesus' prayer in the garden on the night of his betrayal and arrest. The original text consisted of verses 41-42 and 45. Verses 43-44, which describe Jesus' perspiration as great drops of blood, are almost certainly an insertion. Not only are these verses absent from the oldest manuscripts, the portrait of an emotional Jesus is out of step with Luke's tendency to downplay Jesus' emotions.

The story of the woman caught in the act of adultery (Jn 7:53–8:11) appears only in later manuscripts of the Gospel of John, and sometimes in different locations. The last twelve verses of the Gospel of Mark (Mk 16:9-20) are not the original ending; they were added at least two centuries after Mark first began to circulate. These passages—one from Mark, one from Luke and one from John—represent the only major textual problems in the Gospels. No important teaching hangs on any one of them (unless you belong to a snake-handling cult; see Mk 16:18).

Ehrman thinks he has uncovered an example that demonstrates an important theological difference between the Gospels. In some manuscripts Matthew 24:36 reads: "But of that day and hour no one knows, not even the angels of heaven, but the Father only." But earlier manuscripts read: "But of that day and hour no one knows, not even the angels of heaven, nor the Son, but the Father only." What is conspicuous is the presence of the phrase, "nor the Son." Ehrman rightly suggests that the verse originally included "nor the Son," but later scribes probably deliberately omitted it, to avoid the impression that Jesus' knowledge was limited. Fair enough. But Ehrman draws an unwarranted conclusion when he argues that a significant New Testament teaching—in this case Christology—hangs on the scribal addition. This is simply not true. The limitation of Jesus' knowledge is plainly stated in the parallel passage in Mark 13:32: "But of that day or that hour no one knows, not even the angels in heaven, nor the Son, but only the Father." Therefore, with or without "nor the Son" in Matthew 24:36, nothing is changed theologically. Ehrman's reasoning here is faulty and misleading.

For Ehrman personally, however, the smoking gun that drove him toward the abandonment of his confidence in Scripture is Jesus' comment in Mark 2:25-26:

> And he said to them, "Have you never read what David did, when he was in need and was hungry, he and those who were with him: how he entered the house of God, when Abiathar was high priest, and ate the bread of the Presence, which it is not lawful for any but the priests to eat, and also gave it to those who were with him?"

Jesus has alluded to the story of David's receiving consecrated bread (or "bread of the Presence") from Ahimelech the priest (1 Sam 21:1-10). David was fleeing from Saul, and when Saul learned that Ahimelech had assisted David and his men, he murdered Ahimelech and most of his family. Abiathar escaped and eventually succeeded his father as priest (1 Sam 22:1-10).

Because Ahimelech—not his son Abiathar—was the priest when David and his men ate the consecrated bread, we have a mistake, technically speaking, either made by Jesus himself or by Mark (or perhaps by someone who passed on the story). Ehrman says he finally admitted to himself that this passage contains a mistake: "Once I made that admission, the floodgates opened. For if there could be one little, picayune mistake in Mark 2, maybe there could be mistakes in other places as well." Ehrman then cites a few more candidates, such as Jesus' comment that the mustard seed is the smallest of seeds or the apparent discrepancy between the Synoptic Gospels and John about which day Jesus died.

And so everything began to unravel for Ehrman. But observe the line of reasoning; it is so typical of brittle fundamentalism. I have heard fundamentalists say, "Show me one mistake in the Bible and I will throw out the whole thing." I suspect Ehrman heard that more than once in his Moody Bible Institute days. His reasoning today, even as a professing agnostic, still has a fundamentalist ring to it.

I repeat: The truth of the Christian message hinges not on the inerrancy of Scripture or on our ability to harmonize the four Gospels but on the resurrection of Jesus. And the historical reliability of the Gospels does not hinge on the inerrancy of Scripture or on proof that no mistake of any kind can be detected in them. Ehrman's struggle with faith—and I feel for him—grows out of mistaken expectations of the nature and function of Scripture, mistaken expectations that he was taught as a young, impressionable fundamentalist Christian.[6]

THE FIRST CHRISTIAN WITNESSESS

Emphasizing the central role of the resurrection brings me back to the importance of the first Christian witnesses. It also brings me back to Robert Funk. In his zeal to direct attention to the authentic Jesus as opposed to the Christ of ecclesiastical dogma and creed, Funk goes so far as to assert: "We

THE OLDEST GREEK MANUSCRIPTS OF JOHN'S GOSPEL

The oldest surviving fragments of the Greek new Testament are found written on papyrus. The following are the oldest papyri that preserve portions of the Gospel of John.

$\mathfrak{p}^5$ Papyrus 5 (housed in the British Library in London), also designated P.Oxy. 208 + 1781, dates to the early third century. It contains John 1:23-31, 33-40; 16:14-30; 20:11-17, 19-20, 22-25.

$\mathfrak{p}^{22}$ Papyrus 22 (housed in the Glasgow University Library), also designated P.Oxy. 1228, dates to the middle of the third century. It contains John 15:25–16:2, 21-32.

$\mathfrak{p}^{28}$ Papyrus 28 (housed in the Palestine Institute Museum of the Pacific School of Religion in Berkeley, California), also designated P.Oxy. 1596, dates to the late third century. It contains John 6:8-12, 17-22.

$\mathfrak{p}^{39}$ Papyrus 39 (housed in Ambrose Swasey Library, Rochester Divinity School), also designated P.Oxy. 1780, dates to the early third century. It is a small fragment, containing John 8:14-22.

$\mathfrak{p}^{45}$ Papyrus 45 (housed in the Chester Beatty Collection, in Dublin), also designated P. Chester Beatty I, dates to the late second century. This is one of the major papyri. It contains large portions of the four Gospels and Acts. Of John it contains 4:51, 54; 5:21, 24; 10:7-25; 10:30–11:10, 18-36, 42-57. P46 (P. Chester Beatty II) contains significant portions of several of Paul's letters

$\mathfrak{p}^{52}$ Papyrus 52 (housed in the John Rylands University Library of Manchester), also designated Gr. P. 457, dates to the very beginning of the second century and may be the oldest surviving fragment of the Greek New Testament (though recently some have claimed that fragments of Matthew date to the first century itself). Papyrus 52 is a small fragment, containing John 18:31-33 (on the recto side), 37-38 (on the verso side).

$\mathfrak{p}^{66}$ Papyrus 66 (housed in the Bibliotheca Bodmeriana), also designated P. Bodmer II, dates to the second or third century. The Bodmer Papyri are very important. Papyrus 66 contains John 1:1–6:11; 6:35–14:26, 29-30; 15:2-26; 16:2-4, 6-7; 16:10–20:20, 22-23; 20:25–21:9, 12, 17.

$\mathfrak{p}^{75}$ Papyrus 75 (housed in the Bibliotheca Bodmeriana), also designated P. Bodmer XIV and XV, dates to the late second century. Besides portions of Luke, it contains John 1:1–11:45, 48-57, 12.3–13.1, 8-9, 14.8-29, 15:7-8.

$\mathfrak{p}^{80}$ Papyrus 80 (housed in the Fundación San Lucas Evangelista, Barcelona), also designated P. Barcelona 83, dates to the middle of the third century. All that survives is a single verse: John 3:34.

𝔭⁹⁰ Papyrus 90 (housed in the Ashmolean Museum in Oxford), also designated P.Oxy. 3523, dates to the middle or late second century. It contains John 18:36–19:7.

𝔭⁹⁵ Papyrus 95 (housed in the Biblioteca Medicea Laurenziana, Florence), also designated PL II/31, dates to the third century. It contains John 5:26-29, 36-38.

0162 Uncial 0162 (housed in the Metropolitan Museum of Art, New York), also designated P.Oxy. 847, is not a papyrus, but a single leaf of leather, or vellum. It dates to the late third or early fourth century and as such is an early example of the later uncial. It contains John 2:11-22.

Uncial refers to codices of the Bible written in the third to tenth centuries on parchment or vellum in large rounded capital letters. They are the next earliest copies of manuscripts after the papyri.

P.Oxy. = Oxyrhynchus Papyri, a trove of thousands of papyrus fragments found in Egypt at Oxyrhynchus, containing a variety of texts in six or more languages.

can no longer rest our faith on the faith of Peter or the faith of Paul."[7] On one level, he is right; I think I understand what he means. Christians must embrace what Jesus taught and what Jesus himself believed. Quite true. But on another level I think that Funk is seriously mistaken. Peter and Paul were foundational witnesses to the event that brought the church into existence: the resurrection of Jesus. Ignoring this witness runs the risk of abandoning authentic Christianity, Jesus and all.

The documents that the early Christian community gathered bore witness to this great event and struggled to interpret it and apply it in a variety of real-life situations. The books that make up the New Testament constitute a vital record of the early church's experience and witness. These witnesses and the records they left behind need to be taken seriously and studied carefully.[8] Failure to do so will almost certainly result in distorted portraits of Jesus and misguided understanding of what true Christian faith is all about.

2

CRAMPED STARTING POINTS AND
OVERLY STRICT CRITICAL METHODS

The Question of Authenticity

The Jesus Seminar gained a great deal of notoriety when it concluded in 1993 that only 18 percent of the sayings attributed to Jesus in the New Testament Gospels are actually something he said. The Seminar reached similar results with respect to the activities of Jesus.[1] Why was the percentage so low? Minimalist conclusions like these are arrived at through cramped starting points and overly strict critical methods.

CRAMPED STARTING POINTS

In recent years some scholars have come to some pretty surprising conclusions or at least have made some surprising assertions. We have been told that (1) Jesus was illiterate, (2) Jesus had no interest in Scripture, (3) Jesus had no interest in eschatology, and (4) Jesus certainly did not think of himself as Israel's Messiah or in any sense divine. In other words, some of these scholars think that almost everything of importance affirmed in the New Testament writings is wrong.

The problem is that some scholars, especially among the Jesus Seminar, use these conclusions as starting points. Accordingly, we hear comments from them to the effect: "Given that Jesus probably could not read . . . had no interest in Scripture . . . this saying does not go back to him." Given such cramped starting points, which often are little more than presuppositions and not documented and argued conclusions, it is no wonder that much of the material in the New Testament Gospels is regarded as inauthentic and unhistorical. All four of the assertions of the previous paragraph are misguided and almost certainly false. Let's review them one by one.

WAS JESUS ILLITERATE?

Recently a few scholars have suggested that Jesus was functionally illiterate. They allow that Jesus perhaps knew the alphabet and could make out a few words, perhaps even sign his own name, but probably could neither read nor write.[2] Other scholars think Jesus could read and perhaps write, but not at the level of proficiency expected of a professional scribe.[3] Scholars are divided on this question because the evidence is somewhat ambiguous.

Many Christians will immediately assert that, of course, Jesus was literate. He was the Son of God, after all, and could do anything. Christians in the second and third centuries, and later, began to assume this too. Some suggested that as a boy Jesus was a wonder student who made a fool out of his schoolteacher. But this is not consistent with Christian belief in the full humanity of Jesus. As a young child Jesus learned to speak, as a boy he learned to play, and as an older youth he learned the skills of the family trade. Indeed, according to Hebrews 5:8, Jesus "learned obedience through what he suffered." And an early Christian confession says that Jesus "emptied himself, taking the form of a servant" (Phil 2:7). This clearly implies limitations of some sort.

The question of the literacy of Jesus is therefore a legitimate question to raise. In a theological sense there was no need for Jesus to have been literate to have accomplished his ministry. So the question is not whether Jesus as Son of God should have been able to read (or do advanced math, astronomy, or any other subject). Rather, the question is, Could and did Jesus read? The evidence, viewed in the light of general, contextual considerations, favors literacy.

There are three types of evidence that must be explored to answer this question. The first type of evidence concerns specific passages. There are only a few. Luke 4:16-30 describes Jesus reading from the scroll of Isaiah and then preaching a homily. Most scholars hesitate to draw firm conclusions from this passage because it appears to be an expansion of Mark 6:1-6, which says nothing about reading Scripture. John 8:6 says Jesus stooped down and wrote in the dust with his finger. The problem here is that in all probability this passage (that is, Jn 7:53–8:11) is not part of the original version of the Gospel of John.[4] Even if the passage is accepted as preserving a genuine reminiscence of something Jesus did, it tells us nothing certain about Jesus' literacy. He may have been doing nothing more than doodling. John 7:15 speaks directly to the question of Jesus' literacy, though. Some in Jerusalem wonder: "How is it that this man has learning, when he has never studied?" Literally, they ask how he "knows letters, not having studied" (or "not having learned"). But the reference here is to a lack of formal, scribal training, not to having had no education whatsoever. Behind the question is the knowledge that Jesus has not sat at the feet of a trained, recognized rabbi or sage. Nevertheless, being recognized as one who possesses learning argues against illiteracy.

The evidence of these specific New Testament Gospel narratives favors literacy, or at the least the assumption in early Christianity that Jesus was in fact literate. However, the level of literacy is not made clear. Of course, some scholars discount the evidence of these Gospel narratives, claiming that they do not really reach back to the historical Jesus but only to assumptions about Jesus held by second- and third-generation Christians. In any event, these passages do not settle the question.

The second type of evidence is contextual, inquiring into general levels of literacy in the Roman Empire in the time of Jesus and into levels of literacy among the Jewish people as a distinctive group. Here again scholarly opinion varies widely, with some concluding that literacy was low (as low as 5 percent or less) and others concluding that literacy rates were somewhat higher, especially among Jewish men.[5]

The major problem with this type of contextual evidence is that whatever it says about the general public, it does not necessarily tell us anything about a specific individual, in this case Jesus of Nazareth. If the data that we have truly support the conclusion that literacy rates were indeed higher among Jewish men, then the case for the literacy of Jesus is strengthened. But again, the question is not settled.

The third type of evidence is also contextual, focusing on Jesus' activities and style of ministry, how he was perceived by his contemporaries—friend and foe alike—and what emerged from his ministry. The evidence here, I believe, decisively tips the balance in favor of concluding that Jesus was indeed functionally literate.

According to the commands of Old Testament Scripture, Jewish parents were to teach their children the law (see Deut 6:9; 11:20). Of course, this does not mean that all parents did this or that all parents necessarily interpreted this command as requiring literacy. Teaching the law, or summaries of key portions of it, could have been done and probably was done orally. Literacy was not necessarily required to comply with this particular command of Scripture. Nevertheless, such a command would encourage literacy, even if it did not require it.

According to various Jewish authors living about the time Jesus did, Jewish parents in fact did educate their children in the law and in literacy. For example, according to the unknown author of the *Testament of Levi*, a writing that probably dates to the first century B.C.: "Teach your children letters also, so that they might have understanding throughout all their lives as they ceaselessly read the Law of God" (13:2). Josephus, the first-century A.D. Jewish historian, states, "Above all we pride ourselves on the education of our children, and regard as the most essential task in life the observance of our laws and of the pious practices, based thereupon, which we have inherited" (*Against Apion* 1.60). He says later, "[The law] orders that [children] shall be taught to read, and shall learn both the laws and the deeds of their forefathers" (*Against Apion* 2.204).

These expressions, admittedly from priestly sources that probably do not reflect the social and educational realities and expectations of most Jewish adults, do underscore the great value placed on Scripture and literacy in the Jewish world, especially among Jews who take the law of Moses seriously. From everything that we can learn of him, this is just the sort of person Jesus was. He took Scripture seriously. He quoted it, he taught it, and he debated it with priests, scribes, and various religious persons and groups. This sort of evidence clearly argues in favor of Jesus' literacy.

Statistics and generalities are of some use. But it is the big picture of Jesus' ministry itself that makes us conclude that Jesus indeed could read. Jesus is frequently called "teacher" (sometimes with the Hebrew *rabbi* or the Aramaic *rabbouni*). Jesus refers to himself in this manner and is called such by supporters, opponents and nonpartisans. Jesus and others called his closest followers "disciples," which in Hebrew and Greek literally means "learners."[6] The terminology of *teacher* and *learner* creates a strong presumption in favor of Jesus' literacy. In the Jewish setting an *illiterate* rabbi who surrounds himself with disciples and debates Scripture and its interpretation with other rabbis and scribes is hardly credible.

On occasion Jesus himself refers to reading Scripture. He asks Pharisees who criticized his disciples for plucking grain on the sabbath: "Have you never read what David did, when he was in need and was hungry?" (Mk 2:25; see Mt 12:3). To this passage Matthew adds, "Or have you not read in the law how on the sabbath the priests in the temple profane the sabbath, and are guiltless?" (Mt 12:5; see Mt 19:4). In another polemical context Jesus asks the ruling priests and elders, "Have you not read this scripture?" (Mk 12:10). Later he asks the Sadducees, who had raised a question about resurrection, "And as for the dead being raised, have you not read in the book of Moses, in the passage about the bush, how God said to him, 'I am the God of Abraham, and the God of Isaac, and the God of Jacob'?" (Mk 12:26). In a discussion with a legal expert who has asked what one must do to inherit eternal life, Jesus asks in turn, "What is written in the law? How do you read?" (Lk 10:26). Jesus' rhetorical and pointed "have you not read?" seems to be distinctive of his style and surely would have little argumentative force if he himself could not read. It should be noted too that in the Gospel stories reviewed, Jesus' literacy is never an issue. There is no evidence of apologetic tendencies in which Jesus' literary skills are exaggerated. Jesus' ability to read appears to be a given, but not an issue. The upshot of all of this is that whatever the literacy rates were in late antiquity, it is more than likely that Jesus himself could read.

WAS JESUS INTERESTED IN SCRIPTURE?

Related to the question of Jesus' literacy is the question of his interest in Scripture. The Jesus Seminar maintains the curious position that Scripture was of interest to early Christians but not to Jesus. Therefore, when we encounter passages in the Gospels where Jesus quotes or alludes to Scripture, the Seminar thinks it is the early church that is speaking, not Jesus.

This view is very strange. Jesus was nothing if not a teacher. A teacher of what? Everything that Jesus taught—from the rule of God to the Golden Rule—is rooted in Scripture. His disciples—"learners"—learned and passed on his teaching. Is it really likely that Jesus' original teaching made little or no reference to Scripture and that this is what his disciples had to add to it? This makes little sense. A far better and simpler explanation is that the reason that certain passages of Scripture became important to the early church and understood in a certain way is because this is what Jesus taught and his disciples learned and passed on to other believers. The creative genius behind early Christian thought is Jesus himself, not several anonymous figures.

According to the Synoptic Gospels, Jesus quotes or alludes to twenty-three of the thirty-six books of the Hebrew Bible (counting the books of Samuel, Kings and Chronicles as three books, not six).[7] Jesus alludes to or quotes all five books of Moses, the three major prophets (Isaiah, Jeremiah and Ezekiel), eight of the twelve minor prophets, and five of the "writings."[8] In other words, Jesus quotes or alludes to *all* of the books of the Law, *most* of the Prophets and *some* of the Writings.

According to the Synoptic Gospels, Jesus quotes or alludes to Deuteronomy fifteen or sixteen times, Isaiah about forty times and the Psalms some thirteen times. These appear to be his favorite books, though Daniel and Zechariah seem to have been favorites also. Superficially, then, the "canon" of Jesus is pretty much what it was for most religiously observant Jews of his time,[9] including—and especially—the producers of the scrolls at Qumran.[10] Moreover, there is evidence that villages and synagogues in the time of Jesus possessed biblical scrolls (see 1 Maccabees 1:56-57; Josephus *Jewish Wars* 2.229 [in reference to Antiochus IV's efforts to find and destroy Torah scrolls]; *Life of Flavius Josephus* 134 [in reference to scrolls in Galilee during the early stages of the revolt against Rome]).

The data that we have surveyed are more easily explained in reference to a literate Jesus, a Jesus who could read Scripture, could paraphrase and interpret it in Aramaic (his native tongue) and could do so in a manner that indicated his familiarity with current interpretive tendencies in both popular circles (as in the synagogues) and in professional, even elite circles (as seen in debates with scribes, ruling priests and elders). Moreover, the movement that Jesus founded produced a legacy of literature, including four Gospels, a narrative of the early church (the book of Acts) and a number of letters. The sudden emergence of a prolific literary tradition from an illiterate founder is not impossible, but it is less difficult to explain if Jesus was in fact literate and frequently appealed to Scripture.

WAS JESUS INTERESTED IN ESCHATOLOGY?

Perhaps one of the most astonishing claims made by influential members of the Jesus Seminar is that Jesus was noneschatological. But before the Seminar's views can be evaluated, it is necessary to say a few things about eschatology.

The word *eschatology* refers to the study of final or last things. In Jewish and Christian theology it usually refers to God's final accomplishment of his purposes. Some day in the future, things will be very different.

Exactly how Jesus' announcement of the presence of the kingdom of God relates to eschatology has been a subject of debate since the days of Jesus. Long ago the disciples asked the risen Jesus: "Lord, will you at this time restore the kingdom to Israel?" (Acts 1:6). Speculations about end times have been a preoccupation with many people of faith down through the centuries. The disciples' question is still being asked.

Unfortunately, many Christians, including pastors and Bible teachers, do not understand either the meaning of the expression "kingdom of God" or the meaning of the biblical concept of eschatology. Some Christians think that by "kingdom of God" Jesus meant heaven or the millennium. Some even try to make a distinction between kingdom of *God* and kingdom of *heaven*. Worse, some think eschatology refers to the "end of the world." Oddly enough, it is to these popular misunderstandings that the Jesus Seminar has, by and large, responded. When the Seminar interprets Jesus in a "noneschatological" way, the Seminar is rejecting the idea that in proclaiming the kingdom of God, Jesus was proclaiming the end of the world. Unfortunately, in misunderstanding both eschatology and Jesus' proclamation of the kingdom of God, the Seminar rejects eschatology altogether and misinterprets what Jesus meant by "kingdom."[11] Here, I believe, we have an example of throwing the baby out with the bath water.

With eschatology removed as something imposed on the teaching of Jesus by fanatical followers who thought the world was about to end, the kingdom of God is variously misinterpreted among influential Seminar members as a "mystical perception of self" (so Marcus Borg) or as egalitarian community (so John Dominic Crossan).[12] In its red-letter edition of the Gospels, the Jesus Seminar chose to translate "kingdom of God" (Greek, *basileia tou theou*) "God's imperial rule." This curious rendering shows that the Seminar simply does not know what it is talking about.[13]

The expression "kingdom of God" is neither difficult nor complicated when we take into account the biblical data. A reading of the Psalms shows that God is understood as King—King of his people Israel as well as King of all the peoples of the earth. God is King now and forever. God is King in heaven, but he is also King on earth. In other words, the kingship of God entails temporal elements (God rules now, and he will rule in the future) and spatial elements (God rules in heaven, but he also rules here on earth). When the linguistic dimension of *kingdom* is taken into account, especially in reference to God, it is best to translate the word as "rule." Accordingly, when Jesus proclaims the kingdom of God, he is proclaiming the *rule of God*. He demonstrates that God's rule is truly making itself felt in his ministry through healing and especially through exorcism: "If it is by the finger of God that I cast out demons, then the kingdom [*or* rule] of God has come upon you" (Lk 11:20).

Eschatology needs to be understood in the light of the meaning of the rule of God. The "last things" entailed in Jesus' proclamation of the rule of God is that now *at last* God's rule is making itself felt on earth, as the prophets had promised. Jesus has not proclaimed the end of the world but the beginning of the world's renewal. He is calling on his people to repent and embrace God's rule. Repenting and embracing God's rule will transform lives.

It is in this light that the Lord's Prayer should be understood:

Father, let your name be made holy;
may your kingdom come.
Give us each day our daily bread.
And forgive us our sins, for we ourselves forgive every one who is indebted to us.
And lead us not into temptation. (Lk 11:2-4)

Interpreters think that Luke's shorter, simpler form of the prayer may be closer to the original prayer of Jesus. This could be true. But even the longer form of the prayer in Matthew probably correctly reflects Jesus' thinking. It reads as follows:

> Our Father, who is in heaven, let your name be made holy.
> May your kingdom come.
> May your will be done, on earth as it is in heaven.
> Give us this day our daily bread.
> And forgive us our debts, as we also have forgiven our debtors.
> And lead us not into temptation, but deliver us from evil. (Mt 6:9-13)

Lying at the core of Jesus' prayer is an old Aramaic Jewish prayer called the Qaddish (also spelled *Kaddish,* from the first word of the prayer, meaning "may be made holy"). This prayer reads:

> May his great name be glorified and made holy in the world that he created according to this will.
> May he establish his kingdom in your lifetime and during your days . . .

Although the form of the Qaddish that we now have has probably been expanded in the passage of time, the original two petitions—that God make his name holy, and that he establish his kingdom (or rule) soon—stand out and obviously parallel the first two petitions of Jesus' prayer. The implication of this is that Jesus taught his disciples a prayer similar to the prayer that all devout Jews prayed. Jesus' innovation is to link people's behavior to these two petitions. That is, we are to pray that God make his name holy and that God's rule come soon, and we are to pray that we live rightly and expectantly in the light of this prayerful hope.

Jesus has not taught his disciples to pray for the end of the world; he has enjoined his disciples to pray that God's rule come finally and fully, "on earth as it is in heaven," as the interpretive phrase correctly elaborates in the form of the Lord's Prayer that we have in Matthew's Gospel.

When Jesus' proclamation of the kingdom of God is correctly understood, and when we avoid distorted understandings of eschatology, we find that the message of Jesus was indeed profoundly eschatological. Jesus did not call his disciples to find their inner, mystical selves or to form an egalitarian community; he called on his disciples to repent and embrace the rule of God, a rule that transforms the individual and society and will eventually engulf the whole earth.

DID JESUS UNDERSTAND HIMSELF TO BE ISRAEL'S MESSIAH?

It was fashionable throughout much of the modern period of biblical scholarship (say, in the last two centuries or so) to doubt that Jesus thought of himself as Israel's Messiah. It was argued that the confession that Jesus was the Messiah arose among his Jewish following in the aftermath of the Easter proclamation that Jesus had been resurrected.

Doubts along these lines continued into and through most of the twentieth century, especially in German scholarship. At most, some scholars were willing to allow for an implicit messianic self-understanding on the part of Jesus, seen, for example, in Jesus' expressions of authority, either in word or deed. However, the picture has changed in recent years, thanks largely to a better understanding of Jewish messianism in the time of Jesus and to some important texts from the Dead Sea area finally published in the 1990s.

But before we go further in this discussion, it will be helpful to define *messianism*. The word *messiah* is Hebrew and means "anointed." In the Old Testament the word is used in reference to three offices: the anointed priest, the anointed king, and the anointed prophet. Normally, however, when we speak of messianism we are referring to ideas about the anointed king, who is usually understood to be a descendant of David. In the days of Jesus, messianism had to do with hopes of a coming anointed descendant of David who would restore Israel. The Dead Sea Scrolls have enriched our understanding of messianic ideas in late antiquity.

Perhaps the single most important scroll for Jesus' messianic self-understanding is 4Q521 (that is, document number 521, from cave 4 of Qumran). A portion of this text speaks of things that will take place when God's Messiah comes on the scene. The relevant portion reads:

> [For the *hea*]*vens and the earth* shall listen to his Messiah [and *all t*]*hat is in them* (Ps 146:6) shall not turn away from the commandments of the holy ones. Strengthen yourselves, O you who seek the Lord in his

service. Will you not find the Lord in this, all those who hope in their heart? For the Lord attends to the pious and calls the righteous by name. Over the humble *his spirit hovers* (Is 11:2), and he renews the faithful in his strength. For he will honor the pious upon the th[ro]ne of his eternal kingdom, *setting prisoners free* [Ps 146:7], *opening the eyes of the blind, raising up those who are bo[wed down]* (Ps 146:8). And for[ev]er I shall hold fast [to] those [who h]ope and in His faithfulness sh[all . . .] and the frui[t of] good [dee]ds shall not be delayed for anyone and the Lord shall do glorious things which have not been done, just as he said. For he shall heal the critically wounded; he *shall make alive the dead* (Is 26:19); he *shall send good news to the afflicted* (Is 61:1); he shall sati[sfy the poo]r (Ps 132:15); he shall guide the uprooted; he shall make the hungry rich (Ps 107:9). (4Q521 frag. 2, col. 2, lines 1-13)

[The italics indicate words and phrases quoted or paraphrased from the Old Testament, with references placed in parentheses. The words and letters placed in square brackets are restorations (that is, educated guesses).]

This fragment from 4Q521 consists of a number of phrases drawn from Psalms (especially Ps 146) and Isaiah. All of these phrases are viewed as prophecy, to be filled when "his" (that is, God's) "Messiah" makes his appearance. The author of this fragmentary scroll evidently held a rather exalted view of God's Messiah. Heaven and earth and all that is in them "shall listen to" or "obey" the Messiah. Prisoners will be set free, the eyes of the blind will be opened, the bowed down will be raised, the wounded will be healed (probably in reference to the aftermath of the anticipated great war between the "sons of light" and the "sons of darkness"), the dead will be made alive, and good news will be sent to the poor. All of these wonderful things are to happen when the Messiah, the Lord's anointed, makes his appearance.

What makes all of this interesting for understanding Jesus is that he says something similar when he replies to the imprisoned, discouraged John the Baptist. John asks Jesus, "Are you he who is to come, or shall we look for another?" (Mt 11:3). Jesus replies with his own selection of words and phrases from prophecy:

Go and tell John what you hear and see: the *blind receive their sight* and *the lame walk* [Is 35:5-6], lepers are cleansed and the *deaf hear* [Is 35:5], and *the dead are raised up* [Is 26:19], and *the poor have good news preached to them* [Is 61:1]. And blessed is he who takes no offense at me. (Mt 11:4-6, emphasis added)

What is interesting is that Jesus has appealed to some of the same passages and phrases that were employed by the author of 4Q521. Jesus tells John that the blind have regained their sight, the dead are raised up, and the poor (or afflicted) have heard good news. The implication is quite clear. In answering John's question in this way, Jesus has clearly implied that he is indeed Israel's Messiah, for the wonderful things that are supposed to happen when the Messiah appears are in fact happening in Jesus' ministry.

At other points too the Dead Sea Scrolls have helped us understand more accurately the messianic ideas of Jesus' time and even specific messianic ideas expressed in the New Testament. For example, in the angelic announcement of Jesus' birth, Mary is told that her son will be "called Son of the Most High" and "Son of God" (Lk 1:32, 35). At one time some critics argued that the idea that the Messiah would be called "Son of God" reflected Greco-Roman influence on early Christianity (in that the Roman emperor was called "son of God" and the like). But the expected saving figure of 4Q246, an Aramaic text that dates to the first century B.C., is called "Son of the Most High" and "Son of God." This idea was right at home in Palestine after all.

After his baptism, Jesus is told by the heavenly voice: "You are my beloved Son, in whom I well pleased" (Mk 1:11). The allusion to Psalm 2:7 is apparent: "You are my son, today I have begotten you." Although earlier in Psalm 2 it is clear that this remarkable utterance is made in reference to the Lord's Messiah (see v. 2), some scholars were not sure if this psalm was understood in a messianic sense in the time of Jesus. One of the Rule scrolls from Qumran suggests that it was. According to 1QSa, the Messiah will come, "when God will have begotten him" (2:11-12).

What all of this shows us is that at important places the messianism of Jesus was rooted in the messianic ideas current in his time. But more important, the remarkable parallels between 4Q521 and his reply to John the Baptist shows that Jesus clearly understood his ministry in messianic terms.

Regarding the question of what impact the Easter announcement would have had, there is no doubt that seeing him resurrected would have elevated Jesus in the thinking of Jesus' followers. But there was no ancient Jewish expectation that the Messiah would die and be raised up. Death and resurrection, therefore, do not constitute a messianic pattern. Had Jesus not encouraged his disciples to think of him in messianic terms, I doubt very much that the exciting discovery of the empty tomb and the resurrection appearances would have in themselves led the disciples to think of Jesus as Israel's Messiah. Had there been no messianic content in Jesus' teaching and activities prior to Easter, it is doubtful that there would have been any after Easter. The best explanation of the data is that Jesus was indeed understood as the Messiah prior to Easter and that Easter confirmed this understanding in the minds and faith of the disciples.

Finally, Jesus' frequent reference to himself as the "Son of Man" is another indication of his messianic self-understanding. It is true that there is no clear evidence that "Son of Man" in the time of Jesus was understood as a title of the Messiah. But by calling himself the "Son of Man," Jesus alludes to the mysterious son of man figure in Daniel 7.[14] This figure approaches God (the "Ancient of Days") and receives kingdom (or kingly) rule and authority. That Jesus understood himself as this figure supports the point that has been made—Jesus did indeed understand himself as Israel's Messiah. The messianic identity of Jesus is no post-Easter Christian invention.

THE CRITERIA OF AUTHENTICITY

Not only are the starting points of some scholars cramped and unjustified, their methods are often quite severe and skeptical. Some scholars seem to think that the more skeptical they are, the more critical they are. But adopting an excessive and unwarranted skeptical stance is no more critical than gullibly accepting whatever comes along. In my view, a lot of what passes for criticism is not critical at all; it is nothing more than skepticism masking itself as scholarship. This way of thinking is a major contributor to distorted portraits of Jesus and the Gospels in much of today's radical scholarship.

This overly skeptical thinking, for example, leads to the conclusion that much of what Jesus said in public or to his disciples in private was either forgotten or was irrelevant and that, therefore, what eventually came to be written in the Gospels was for the most part from later Christians, not from Jesus himself. Indeed, this is absurd. That is, if Jesus really said little of lasting significance and was unable to train his disciples to remember accurately what little he did say, then we must really wonder why the Christian movement emerged at all.

Some of this skepticism is due to improperly formulated criteria used in deciding what is authentic and what is not. These criteria are variously termed the "criteria of authenticity" or the "authenticity criteria." This may sound terribly technical and complicated, but it actually is an attempt to apply common sense in trying to determine whether ancient documents are trustworthy sources for learning what happened, and who said what.

No matter what perspective we bring to the New Testament Gospels (and to the extracanonical Gospels, for that matter), we need to have criteria. The word *criterion* (plural, *criteria*) is a Greek word that means "judgment" or "basis for passing judgment." We all have criteria for passing judgment with respect to many things in life. When someone says, "I think this story is true," and you respond, "Why do you think so?" you are asking the person to explain his or her criteria or basis for making the judgment.

Some conservative Christians will, of course, simply respond by saying, "Whatever the New Testament Gospels say Jesus said or did I accept as historical." That may work for those who already accept the inspiration and authority of the Bible. But what about those who would like to have sound, compelling reasons for accepting the Gospel narratives as reliable? Telling them that the Bible is inspired and therefore true without providing any criteria that historians would recognize will not satisfy them. After all, don't Mormons say the same thing with respect to the Book of Mormon? Don't Muslims affirm the inspiration of the Qur'an? One holy book after another could be appealed to in this manner. Is this the only defense that can be made?

Thoughtful people rightly apply criteria in evaluating claims (for example, "This is true," "This is valuable," "This really happened," and so forth). So also historians apply criteria for assessing the historical worth of documents. They ask questions such as, When was this document written? Who wrote this document? Do the details in this document cohere with other known and trusted sources? Was the author of this document in a position to know what really happened and what really was said? Are claims in this document supported by archaeological evidence and geographical realities?

Over the years, biblical scholars have developed historical and literary criteria for assessing biblical literature. Discussions of criteria for the study of the Gospels have been especially intense, with a great number of criteria proposed. I have seen hair-splitting studies that list as many as twenty-five criteria. Some of these criteria seem unnecessarily complex. Some criteria are questionable. But a few of the criteria are consistently invoked.[15] Here is a review of those criteria I think are the best. (I will also discuss one that I think is often misused and misapplied.)

Historical coherence. When the Gospels tell us things that cohere with what we know of Jesus' historical circumstances and principal features of his life and ministry, it is reasonable to believe that we are on solid ground. Jesus drew a following, attracted the attention of the authorities, was executed and yet was proclaimed Israel's Messiah and God's Son. Deeds and sayings attributed to him in the Gospels that cohere with these major elements and, indeed, help us understand these major elements should be judged authentic.

This criterion provides a basis for accepting the narrative of Jesus in the temple precincts, quarreling with and criticizing the ruling priests (as we see in Mk 11–12 and parallel passages in other Gospels). This criterion also encourages us to accept as authentic Jesus' affirmation that he is indeed Israel's Messiah and God's Son (Mk 14:61-63), for this makes sense of his crucifixion on the grounds of his claim that he is "king of the Jews" (Mk 15:26).

Multiple attestation. This criterion refers to sayings and actions attributed to Jesus that appear in two or more independent sources (such as Mark and Q, the sayings source used by Matthew and Luke). Sayings and actions of Jesus that appear in two or more independent sources suggest that they were circulated widely and early and were not invented by a single writer. The fact that there is a good amount of material that enjoys multiple attestation is itself a witness to the antiquity and richness of our sources.

Here are a few examples of sayings with multiple attestation: Jesus' saying on the lamp appears in Mark 4:21 and in the sayings source (Mt 5:15; Lk 11:33). This saying is followed by the saying on what is revealed, which appears in Mark 4:22 and in the sayings source (Mt 10:26; Lk 12:2). Jesus' saying on the evil generation that seeks a sign is found in Mark 8:12 and in the sayings source (Mt 12:39; Lk 11:29).

Embarrassment. This criterion is easily misunderstood. All it means is that material that potentially would have created awkwardness or embarrassment for the early church is not likely something that a Christian invented sometime after Easter. "Embarrassing" sayings and actions are those that are known to reach back to the ministry of Jesus, and therefore, like it or not, they cannot be deleted from the Jesus data bank.

Perhaps the classic example of "embarrassing" tradition is the baptism of Jesus (Mk 1:9-11 and parallels). What makes Jesus' baptism embarrassing? John's baptism called for repentance of sins and yet, according to Christian teaching, Jesus was sinless. So why would sinless Jesus go to John for baptism? Good question. No Christian would make up this story. Its preservation in the Gospels argues strongly that it is authentic material. The fact that it is preserved in the Gospels and not deleted also shows that the writers of the Gospels made every effort to tell the truth.

Another important example is seen in the narrative in which the imprisoned John sends messengers to Jesus, asking: "Are you he who is to come, or shall we look for another?" (Mt 11:2-6; Lk 7:18-23). Jesus answers John's question in an indirect, almost veiled way, "Go and tell John what you hear and see." As presented, this exchange is awkward, perhaps even embarrassing. Who would make up a story in which John—an ally of Jesus—expresses doubts about Jesus' identity and mission? And why would an invented reply by Jesus fail to make explicit his messianic identity and mission? Why not have Jesus affirm loudly and clearly, "Go and tell John that I am he who is to come"? The story as we have it preserved in Matthew and Luke gives historians confidence that it faithfully and accurately reports the exchange between John and Jesus and is not a later Christian fiction.

Dissimilarity. No criterion has been more discussed than the criterion of dissimilarity. Used properly, it can lend support to the conclusion that a given saying or deed is authentic. Applied improperly, it unnecessarily and unreasonably rules out of bounds a host of sayings and deeds. Improperly applied it requires sayings and deeds attributed to Jesus to be dissimilar to (or inconsistent with) the theology of the early church and tendencies and emphases within the Judaism of Jesus' day. If you find the logic of this elusive, don't feel bad; the logic is indeed a bit strained.

What this form of the criterion is trying to do is to rule out sayings and deeds that may have originated in Jewish circles, on the one hand, or in early Christian circles, on the other. So, if a saying is not dissimilar to both of these contexts (hence in this form it is called "double dissimilarity"), there is no guarantee that the saying (or deed) originated with Jesus. The problem with the criterion applied this way is that it rules out almost everything attributed to Jesus. After all, Jesus was Jewish and much of what he taught reflected themes and concepts current among religious teachers of his day (not to mention Israel's Scripture). So shouldn't we expect Jewish tendencies and emphases to be present in authentic teachings of Jesus? Of course. And the early church clung to Jesus' teaching as precious and formed its thinking and practices in conformity with it. So shouldn't we expect lines of continuity between Jesus and the movement that he founded?[16] Yes.

Nevertheless, the criterion does have its uses—when it is applied in a positive fashion. There is some material in the New Testament Gospels that the early church did not choose to develop as part of its theology and practice. Accordingly, it is hard to explain it as invented by the early church. The best explanation is that it derives from Jesus. In some cases the same may be true with respect to Jewish tendencies. Jesus' free and easy association with sinners was not the sort of thing that religious teachers in his day did (and even Christians could be a little reserved in this matter). So again, we may have an instance where Jesus' actions and teachings are somewhat at variance with the actions and teachings of his Jewish contemporaries.

Semitisms and Palestinian background. This criterion, which is sometimes subdivided into two or more criteria, suggests that sayings and deeds that reflect the Hebrew or Aramaic language (Semitisms), or reflect first-century Palestine (geography, topography, customs, commerce) are what we should expect of authentic material. Of course, material that enjoys the support of this criterion may derive from early Jewish Christians and not necessarily from Jesus. But this criterion, nevertheless, is important. After all, the Gospels were written in Greek and yet they purport to preserve the sayings of Jesus, who spoke Aramaic, and the deeds of Jesus, who ministered in first-century Palestine. If these Greek Gospels faithfully preserve the sayings and deeds of Jesus, then these Greek Gospels should show evidence of Semitism and Palestinian background; and this they do.

Coherence (or consistency). Finally, the criterion of coherence (or consistency) is also useful and functions in some ways as a catch-all. According to this criterion, material that is consistent with material judged authentic on the basis of the other criteria may also be regarded as authentic.

All of these criteria have their place and can make (and have made) useful contributions to the scholarly study of the historical Jesus. They enable historians to give good reasons for judging this saying or that deed attributed to Jesus as authentic. The problem is in assuming that everything that is attributed to Jesus that does not enjoy support from one or more of the criteria should be regarded as inauthentic. Lack of support from the authenticity criteria does not necessarily mean that the saying or deed in question cannot derive from Jesus.

Here is where I think many skeptical scholars, especially among the prominent members of the Jesus Seminar, go wrong. They not only misapply some of the criteria (such as dissimilarity) and ignore or misunderstand others (such as Semitisms and Palestinian background), they tend to assume that sayings and deeds not supported by the criteria must be judged as inauthentic. This severe, skeptical method leads to limited results, results that can be badly skewed, if the starting points themselves are off-base and wrong-headed.

The portrait of Jesus can be distorted badly through misapplication of the authenticity criteria to the New Testament Gospels. When the extracanonical Gospels and sources are thrown into the mix and treated as though they were as ancient and as reliable as the canonical Gospels, then the problem of distortion is taken to new levels. That is the concern addressed in chapters three and four.

QUESTIONABLE TEXTS—PART I

The Gospel of Thomas

 F or many people the most disturbing feature in contemporary reports concerning the Jesus of history is the attention given to texts outside of the New Testament, some of which are called "Gospels." These Gospels—which are also referred to as "extracanonical Gospels"—are purported to make important contributions to our knowledge of the historical Jesus. Sometimes it is even claimed that these texts give us more reliable information about Jesus than the New Testament Gospels themselves. Is this claim valid? Do the extracanonical Gospels provide us with reliable, historical information about Jesus? Should our understanding of Jesus be shaped by what these nonbiblical Gospels have to offer?

In this chapter and the next we will look closely at five extracanonical Gospels, the ones that get the most attention and are said to support portraits of Jesus different from what we find in the New Testament. Some scholars claim that these writings reach back to the first century, perhaps even to the middle of the first century, and contain information that is at least as historically reliable as the information contained in the New Testament Gospels. We will see—to the contrary—that none of these extracanonical writings originated earlier than the middle of the second century and in two cases probably did not originate before the end of the second century. Because of the late dates of these extracanonical Gospels, it is unlikely that they contain information that adds to our knowledge of Jesus. The whole edifice of the non-New Testament Jesus collapses when these extracanonical writings get the critical scrutiny they deserve but often do not receive.

There is nothing wrong in appealing to texts outside of the New Testa-

EXTRACANONICAL GOSPELS AND FRAGMENTS

The extracanonical Gospels and fragments that are frequently given serious consideration include the following:

Apocryphon of James (preserved in NHC 1)

Dialogue of the Savior (preserved in NHC 3)

Gospel of the Ebionites (preserved in quotations by Epiphanius)

Gospel of the Egyptians (preserved in quotations by Clement of Alexandria)

Gospel of the Hebrews (preserved in quotations by various church fathers)

Gospel of the Nazoreans (preserved in quotations by various church fathers)

Gospel of Peter (allegedly preserved in a large fragment from Akhmim and a small fragment P.Oxy. 2949 and possibly P.Oxy. 4009)

Gospel of Thomas (preserved in NHC 2 and P.Oxy. 1, 654, and 655)

Protevangelium of James (preserved in numerous Greek manuscripts)

Secret Gospel of Mark (preserved in a supposed letter of Clement of Alexandria)

P.Oxy. 840

P.Oxy. 1224

Papyrus Egerton 2 (+ Papyrus Köln 255), or the *Egerton Gospel*

Fayyum Fragment (= Papyrus Vindobonensis Greek 2325)

NHC = Nag Hammadi Codex
P.Oxy. = Papyri Oxyrhynchus

ment in the task of reconstructing the history of Jesus and the early church, or in the task of interpreting New Testament writings. That is an appropriate and necessary thing to do. For example, the Dead Sea Scrolls shed important light on various aspects of Jesus' teaching, on key elements in Paul's theology, and on teachings in James, Hebrews and other books in the New Testament. Other writings from the New Testament era also assist in the task of interpretation by fleshing out the historical and cultural context.[1] Thus,

DATES OF GOSPELS AND

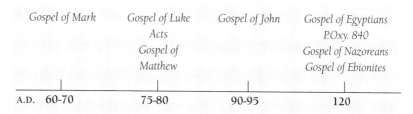

Gospel of Mark	Gospel of Luke Acts Gospel of Matthew	Gospel of John	Gospel of Egyptians P.Oxy. 840 Gospel of Nazoreans Gospel of Ebionites
A.D. 60-70	75-80	90-95	120

making use of extracanonical writings isn't the problem.

What is troubling is the ready, often uncritical acceptance of some of the extracanonical Gospels. Some of the same scholars who criticize the New Testament Gospels severely and push the dates of their composition toward the end of the first century are ready to treat the extracanonical sources generously and argue for dates of composition near the beginning of the second century, perhaps in the first century itself. The result is that all of the Gospels—inside and outside the New Testament—are treated as though they have been composed in the same generation.[2] We must not "privilege" the New Testament Gospels, we are told. After all, skeptics say, most of these writings, whether in or outside the canon, were composed at about the same time and therefore have about the same historical value. In the interests of objective scholarship we are to treat all of the sources as potentially useful. But it seems to me that some of these scholars are privileging the extracanonical texts, and to do this they obscure important aspects of when various texts were written.[3]

DATING THE GOSPELS

Before moving on, let's get some important dating clear. Jesus taught and ministered in the late 20s and early 30s of the first century. Paul wrote his letters in the late 40s to the early or mid-60s. Although its date of composition is debated, the Gospel of Mark was likely written in the mid to late 60s, and the Gospels of Matthew and Luke sometime after that (and some scholars in fact argue that Mark, Matthew, and Luke—also called the Synoptic

RELATED SOURCES COMPARED

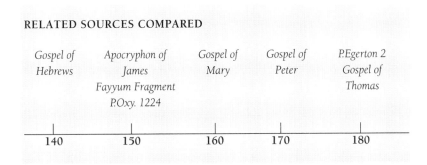

Gospel of Hebrews	*Apocryphon of James* *Fayyum Fragment* *P.Oxy. 1224*	*Gospel of Mary*	*Gospel of Peter*	*P.Egerton 2* *Gospel of Thomas*
140	150	160	170	180

Gospels—date to the 50s and 60s). The Gospel of John is usually dated sometime in the 90s. This means that most, perhaps even all of the New Testament writings date to the first century. It also means the Gospel of Mark was written within one generation of the death of Jesus, which in all probability means that some people who had known Jesus were still living when this Gospel was written and circulated. Some think that the sayings source (or Q), which Matthew and Luke used, dates to the 50s, perhaps even earlier. Accordingly, it is likely that the authors of documents that date to the middle of the first century (such as Q and Mark) had access to authentic sayings of Jesus and stories about him, and that their works would have been read (or heard) by living witnesses. It would not be easy for a Gospel that misrepresents the life and teaching of Jesus to have gained widespread acceptance when many of Jesus' followers were still living and in a position to challenge distortions.

Not only do the earliest New Testament Gospel sources date to the middle of the first century, Paul also refers to Jesus' teaching, to his words at the Last Supper, to his death and burial, and to his resurrection. This is important, for Paul, who was converted to the Christian faith in the 30s, knew some of the original disciples and apostles, such as Peter and James, the brother of Jesus. Consequently, the New Testament writings provide us with early information about Jesus. This is why writings believed to have originated in the first century, especially in the middle of the first century, are widely accepted as our best sources of information about the historical Jesus.

EXTRACTING HYPOTHETICAL SOURCES
FROM EXTANT TEXTS

Scholars sometimes are able to extract early sources from later extant texts. (A text that is *extant* is one that still exists, as opposed to one that is merely *thought* to have existed.) A clear example of this is seen in the Synoptic Gospels. Matthew and Luke share a large number of sayings that did not come from Mark. Scholars believe that Matthew and Luke had access to a source in addition to Mark. They have called this source of sayings Q (usually understood as an abbreviation of the German word *Quelle*, "source" or "spring"). Another helpful example is seen in two writings found in the Nag Hammadi Library. One writing is called *Eugnostos the Blessed* (Nag Hammadi Codex [NHC] 3.3; 5.1), a non-Christian religious/philosophical text, and the other is called *The Sophia of Jesus Christ* (NHC 3.4; Berlin Gnostic Codex 8502.3), a revelation discourse given by Jesus. *Eugnostos the Blessed* probably approximates the original form of the text, while *The Sophia of Jesus Christ* represents a later reworking of the text, with insertions in which Jesus is identified as the speaker.

In these examples we have plausible evidence of early texts embedded in later texts. Other examples could be cited, such as Jude and 2 Peter, where the former appears to be embedded in the latter. But in the cases of the *Gospel of Thomas* and the *Gospel of Peter,* to cite just two examples, we do not have such evidence. Both of these writings drip with indications of lateness, yet some scholars hope to date forms of these writings to the first century. They do this by attempting to extract early, hypothetic forms of the text from the actual texts that we have. But they do this without any evidence.

When were the Gnostic Gospels and other extracanonical sources written? All of the Gnostic Gospels and extracanonical sources were written in the second century or later. Typical dates range from A.D. 140 to 160. Some scholars argue for earlier dates, such as 120 to 140 (and some argue for later dates). Although it is theoretically possible that early, reliable information about Jesus not found in the New Testament writings could be preserved in some of these second-century writings, it is not likely. This is why biblical scholars in the past have rarely appealed to writings such as the *Gospel of Thomas,* the *Gospel of Peter* and the *Gospel of Mary* for additional information about Jesus. These writings are viewed as simply too late—written at least one hundred years after the death of Jesus, or fifty to eighty years after the New Testament Gospels were written.

In the scholarly and popular press the most frequently mentioned writings outside of the New Testament are the *Gospel of Thomas,* the *Gospel of Peter,* the Egerton Papyrus 2 (or *Egerton Gospel*), the *Secret Gospel of Mark,* and the *Gospel of Mary.* Most people had not heard of these writings until relatively recently, most often in connection with a book or television documentary making sensational claims. If these extracanonical Gospels were written long after the New Testament Gospels, why do some scholars appeal to them? This is where the discussion gets interesting.

Some scholars have argued that early editions of the *Gospel of Thomas* and the *Gospel of Peter* reach back to the middle of the first century, that the *Egerton Gospel* predates Mark and John—and may have been on the writing table of the evangelist Mark himself—and that the *Secret Gospel of Mark* may represent an earlier form of the canonical Gospel of Mark. It is no wonder then (if these early dates and hypothetical early forms of these writings are valid) that some scholars make use of these extracanonical sources in their reconstructions of the historical Jesus. Accordingly, the Jesus Seminar's assessment of the authentic words of Jesus came out under the title *The Five Gospels,* with the "fifth Gospel" being the *Gospel of Thomas.*[4] What are we to make of all this? Is there solid evidence that these writings date, at least in some form, to the first century and contain sayings from and stories about Jesus that are early, independent, and perhaps even superior to what is found in Matthew, Mark, Luke, and John?

Before continuing, I should mention that besides the extracanonical Gospels that contain unusual sayings, there are dozens of isolated, free-floating sayings attributed to Jesus that are found in a variety of sources. These isolated sayings are called the *agrapha* (from the Greek meaning "not written," that is, not written in the New Testament Gospels). Some of these sayings come into play in today's scholarly work. They will not be discussed in this chapter, but they are treated briefly in appendix one.

Two Recent and Very Different Assessments

In 1991 two engaging and competent studies of the life of Jesus appeared, one by John Dominic Crossan and the other by John P. Meier.[5] One of the most remarkable discrepancies between their works is the sharp divergence of opinion with respect to the value of the extracanonical Gospels for Jesus research. In Crossan's work, these writings play an important role; in Meier's, their role is negligible. A brief comparison of these two scholars' respective approaches and conclusions will illustrate this striking divergence, which in many ways is a characteristic of the current debate among New Testament specialists, and will serve as a point of departure for the evaluation of these writings.

In his reconstruction of the historical Jesus, Crossan relies heavily on the extracanonical materials, many of which he dates quite early. It is not surprising then that Crossan often concludes that traditions contained in the extracanonical Gospels—traditions that parallel those of the New Testament Gospels—are more primitive and historically superior. Often he thinks he finds the earliest, most original form of Jesus' teaching in the extracanonical Gospels. Sometimes Crossan will extract a hypothetical early version of one of these Gospels. For example, Crossan thinks he can identify two early versions of the *Gospel of Thomas.* The earliest version he dates in the 50s, while a somewhat later version he dates in the 60s or 70s. From the mid-second-century *Dialogue of the Savior* Crossan believes he can identify an early "dialogue collection," perhaps dating in the 70s. He dates an early version of the *Gospel of the Egyptians*—another second-century work—in the early 60s, and he extracts from the *Gospel of Peter* (late second century, perhaps even later) a hypothetical *Cross Gospel,* which he dates in the 50s. We will look at the *Gospel of Peter* again in chapter four.

Crossan's analysis of extracanonical sources contributes to his picture of the historical Jesus in significant ways. But many rightly wonder about the validity of this analysis, for it appears to be little more than subjective guesswork and special pleading. In any case, some of his assumptions will be put to the test in the following discussion.

Meier's conclusion, however, could hardly be more at odds with Crossan's. All the extracanonical writings, he concludes, contribute little to what can be known of the historical Jesus. Here is his assessment of these writings:

> Contrary to some scholars, I do not think that the . . . agrapha, the
> apocryphal gospels . . . (in particular the *Gospel of Thomas*) offer us re-

CROSSAN'S PROPOSED EARLY DATES
FOR EXTRACANONICAL WRITINGS

John Dominic Crossan has proposed early dates for the extracanonical writings, which most scholars do not accept. Moreover, he also proposes the existence of even earlier versions of some of these writings. Crossan dates and names the extracanonical writings as follows:

Gospel of Thomas (earliest edition: A.D. 50s)

Egerton Gospel (i.e., Papyrus Egerton 2: A.D. 50s)

Fayyum Fragment (A.D. 50s)

Papyrus Oxyrhynchus 1224 (A.D. 50s)

Gospel of the Hebrews (A.D. 50s)

Cross Gospel (= a pruned version of the *Gospel of Peter*, A.D. 50s)

Gospel of the Egyptians (earliest version, A.D. 60s)

Secret Gospel of Mark (early A.D. 70s)

Papyrus Oxyrhynchus 840 (A.D. 80s)

Gospel of Thomas (later draft, A.D. 60s or 70s)

Dialogue Collection (= a pruned version of the Coptic Gnostic tractate *Dialogue of the Savior*, late [?] A.D. 70s)

Apocryphon of James (dating from first half of second century , but containing tradition reaching back to the A.D. 50s)

Gospel of the Nazoreans (A.D.150s)

Gospel of the Ebionites (A.D. 150s)

Gospel of Peter (A.D. 150s)

Crossan claims that the *Gospel of Thomas*, the *Egerton Gospel*, Papyrus Vindobonensis Greek 2325, Papyrus Oxyrhynchus 1224, the *Gospel of the Hebrews* and the *Gospel of the Egyptians* are independent of the New Testament Gospels, with the *Dialogue of the Savior* and the *Apocryphon of James* containing independent traditions. He further concludes that the *Cross Gospel*, which is now embedded in the *Gospel of Peter*, preserves the Passion narrative on which all four of the New Testament Gospels are based. *Reader beware: These early dates and hypothetical sources are not widely accepted among scholars.*

See John Dominic Crossan, *The Historical Jesus: The Life of a Mediterranean Jewish Peasant* (San Francisco: HarperCollins, 1991), pp. 427-34. The dates noted in the parentheses refer not to the dates of the actual manuscripts but to Crossan's conjectured dates of the autographs (that is, originals). On the alleged *Cross Gospel*, see John Dominic Crossan, *The Cross That Spoke: The Origins of the Passion Narrative* (San Francisco: Harper & Row, 1988).

liable new information or authentic sayings that are independent of
the NT. What we see in these later documents is rather . . . imaginative
Christians reflecting popular piety and legend, and gnostic Christians
developing a mystic speculative system. . . . It is only natural for scholars—to say nothing of popularizers—to want more, to want other access roads to the historical Jesus. This understandable but not always
critical desire is, I think, what has recently led to the high evaluation,
in some quarters, of the apocryphal gospels . . . as sources for the
quest. It is a case of the wish being father to the thought, but the wish
is a pipe dream. For better or for worse, in our quest for the historical
Jesus, we are largely confined to the canonical Gospels; the genuine
"corpus" is infuriating in its restrictions. For the historian it is a galling
limitation. But to call upon the *Gospel of Peter* or the *Gospel of Thomas*
to supplement our Four Gospels is to broaden out our pool of sources
from the difficult to the incredible.[6]

Note Meier's contention that the "wish" is "father to the thought." It is the
desire to have alternative sources, rather than compelling historical evidence
for the legitimacy of those sources, that has led to the positive evaluation of
these extracanonical sources.

Meier suspects that far from representing independent and possibly
earlier tradition, the agrapha (that is, the independent sayings of Jesus "not
written" in the New Testament) and extracanonical Gospels ultimately derive from the New Testament Gospels. He offers the careful qualification
that this dependence is indirect. That is, the agrapha and extracanonical
Gospels reflect second- and thirdhand acquaintance with the traditions of
the New Testament Gospels. Rarely do their authors quote from the canonical Gospels in their written form. By and large, what the authors of the
extracanonical Gospels knew was oral tradition, but it was an oral tradition generated by the written Gospels of the New Testament, an oral tradition that was itself edited and adapted in its transmission. This is why,
Meier explains, the extracanonical writings often contain sayings and stories that appear to be combinations of elements from two or more of the
New Testament Gospels. The extracanonical Gospels, he says, should not

MORE WIDELY ACCEPTED DATES
FOR EXTRACANONICAL WRITINGS

Gospel of the Egyptians (A.D. 120)

Papyrus Oxyrhynchus 840
(A.D. 120)

Gospel of the Nazoreans (A.D. 120)

Gospel of the Ebionites (A.D. 120)

Gospel of the Hebrews (A.D. 140)

Apocryphon of James (A.D. 150)

Fayyum Fragment (A.D. 150)

Papyrus Oxyrhynchus 1224
(A.D. 150)

Gospel of Mary (A.D. 160)

Gospel of Peter (A.D. 170)

Egerton Gospel (A.D. 180)

Gospel of Thomas (A.D. 180)

Secret Gospel of Mark (A.D. 1960)

These dates are approximate and often are no more than educated guesses. The dates refer to the date of composition, not to the date of the fragment that has been found. No imaginary documents that can be dated to the first century are listed.

For further information, see J. K. Elliott, *The Apocryphal New Testament: A Collection of Apocryphal Christian Literature in an English Translation based on M. R. James* (Oxford: Clarendon Press, 1993); Wilhelm Schneemelcher, ed., *New Testament Apocrypha*, vol. 1, *Gospels and Related Writings*, rev. ed. (Cambridge: James Clarke; Louisville: Westminster/John Knox Press, 1991).

be dated earlier than the second century. Accordingly, these Gospels outside the New Testament are hardly capable of providing researchers with reliable, independent information that they can use to supplement or even correct the New Testament Gospels.

WHAT'S AT STAKE

The importance of this debate can hardly be exaggerated. What is at stake is a considerable body of material and the contribution it might make to Jesus research. If Crossan and other like-minded scholars are correct, then Jesus research cannot make genuine and meaningful progress apart from careful study of the extracanonical Gospels. If Meier is correct, then the agrapha and extracanonical Gospels offer little of value to Jesus research. Indeed, an overly positive assessment of their value may lead to a distorted picture of the historical Jesus, the scholar fabricating a Jesus of his or her own imagination. Are these writings, in the words of Helmut Koester, longtime professor of New Testament at Harvard, "just as important" as the New Testament writings for the study of early Christianity? Do they "contain many traditions which can be traced back to the time of the very origins of Christianity"?[7] With these questions in mind, let's take a close look at the most talked about extracanonical Gospels.

EXTRACANONICAL GOSPELS

A little historical perspective is helpful here. Until recently the extracanonical Gospels were not taken seriously as potential sources for Jesus research. Three quarters of a century ago Rudolf Bultmann—who was *not* a conservative biblical scholar—regarded these Gospels and related writings as nothing more than "legendary adaptations and expansions" of the canonical Gospel tradition. Almost no one in his generation disagreed. Today the picture has changed.

Of the thirty or so documents that have been identified as Gospels or Gospel-like writings, five of them receive most of the attention, and all of them have defenders who advocate their antiquity, independence and perhaps even superiority over against the New Testament Gospels. These writings are the *Gospel of Thomas,* the *Gospel of Peter,* Egerton Papyrus 2 (or the *Egerton Gospel*), the *Gospel of Mary* and the *Secret Gospel of Mark.* The *Gospel of Thomas* has influenced research on the historical Jesus far more than the other writings despite how egregious its misdating has been. The most recent document to gain popular attention is the newly published *Gospel of Judas,* for which I served as a consultant. (For my brief comments on the *Gospel of Judas,* see appendix two.)

THE *GOSPEL OF THOMAS*

Thirteen leather-bound books (or codices), written in the Coptic language, dating to about A.D. 350-380, were found in Egypt sometime near the end of 1945 (near a place called Nag Hammadi). One of these books contains a writing that begins, "These are the secret words that the living Jesus spoke and Judas, even Thomas, wrote," and ends with the words, "the Gospel ac-

GREEK AND COPTIC *GOSPEL OF THOMAS* COMPARED

P.Oxy. 654 = *Gospel of Thomas* prologue, sayings 1-7 and a portion of saying 30.

P.Oxy. 1 = *Gospel of Thomas* sayings 26-33.

P.Oxy. 655 = *Gospel of Thomas* sayings 24, 36-39, 77.

With one or two exceptions, most scholars have assumed that *Thomas* was originally composed in Greek and that the Oxyrhynchus Papyri stand closer to the original form of the tradition. I believe the evidence better supports the contention that *Thomas* was originally composed in Syriac and that both the Greek and the Coptic are later translations.

cording to Thomas." Third- and fourth-century church fathers mention a Gospel that went by the name of the apostle Thomas.[8] It seems, then, that the *Gospel of Thomas* mentioned by Christian theologians seventeen centuries ago had turned up in the dry sands of Egypt. This was a remarkable find by any reckoning. But there is more.

When the new discovery was read and translated (and was found to contain a prologue and 114 sayings, or logia, mostly attributed to Jesus), scholars realized that parts of the *Gospel of Thomas* had in fact been found a half century earlier, in the 1890s, in a place called Oxyrhynchus, also in Egypt. Three Greek papyrus fragments (called the Oxyrhynchus Papyri [hereafter abbreviated P.Oxy.]) published at the turn of the century, numbered 1, 654 and 655, contain about 20 percent of the *Gospel of Thomas*, at least as compared with the Coptic version. The Greek fragments range in date from A.D. 200 to 300.

The *Gospel of Thomas* is an esoteric writing, purporting to record the secret (or "hidden") teachings of Jesus, teachings reserved for those qualified to hear these teachings. The following is my translation of the prologue and the first seven sayings, according to the Greek version (that is, P.Oxy. 654), with restored letters and words placed in square brackets. (We are able to complete most of the missing Greek text thanks to the fully preserved Coptic translation.)

Prologue These are the [secret] words [that] the living Jesus [spo]ke a[nd Judas], even Thomas, [wrote].

1 And he said, ["Whoever finds the interpretat]ion of these words will not taste [death]."

2 [Jesus says], "Let him who se[eks] not cease [to seek until] he finds, and when he finds [he will be amazed; and when he is am]azed he will reign, an[d when he has reigned he will atta]in rest."

3 Jesus says, ["If] those who lead you [say to you, 'Behold,] the kingdom is in the sk[y, then] the birds of the sk[y will precede you. If they say th]at it is under the earth, then the fish of the se[a will enter it, preced]ing you. And the king[dom of God] is within you, [and it is outside of you. Whoever] knows [himself] will discover this. [And when you] know yourselves, [you will realize that] you are [sons] of the Father who l[ives. But if you will not] know yourselves, in [poverty you are] and you are pov[erty]."

4 [Jesus says,] "A ma[n full of day]s will not hesitate to ask a ch[ild of seven day]s concerning the place of [life, and you will li]ve. For many who are fi[rst] will be [last and] the last will be first, and they [will become one and the same]."

5 Jesus says, "K[now what is befo]re your sight, and [what is hidden] from you will be reveal[ed to you. For there is nothing] hidden which will not [become] reveal[ed], nor buried which [will not be raised]."

6 [His disciples] q[ue]stion him [and s]ay, "How [shall we] fast, [and how shall we pr]ay, and how [shall we give alms]? What [diet] shall [we] observe?" Jesus says, "[Do not lie and what you ha]te, do not do; [for all things are revealed in the presence] of truth. [For nothing] hid[den will not become manifest]."

7 "[. . . B]lessed is [the lion which man eats, and the li]on become[s man; and cursed is the man] whom [the lion eats . . .]."

The Jesus of the *Gospel of Thomas* is different from the Jesus of the New Testament Gospels. The private, esoteric orientation of the text is plainly evident. Unlike the canonical Gospels, these writings were for the spiritually elite, not for the common people. The opening line, "These are the secret words that the living Jesus spoke," should not be understood to imply that all of Jesus' teaching was secret (or hidden). Writings such as the *Gospel of Thomas* recognize and presuppose the public teachings of Jesus (as recorded, for example, in the New Testament Gospels). What the *Gospel of Thomas* claims to record are the secret or hidden words that Jesus spoke in private to Thomas and to his other disciples. Thomas, of course, is the favored disciple, who understands Jesus more deeply than the other disciples and who is the one who writes the words of Jesus. The Jesus of the *Gospel of Thomas* urges his followers not to cease seeking until they find. They must know themselves if what is hidden is to be revealed to them.

In contrast to the Jesus of the New Testament Gospels, who urges his followers to have faith, in saying 1 the Jesus of the *Gospel of Thomas* encourages his disciples to find "the interpretation of these words." If they do, they "will not taste death." The esoteric slant is also seen in sayings that have counterparts in the Synoptic Gospels. For example, in reference to the need for faith, the Synoptic Jesus encourages his disciples to ask, seek and knock. If they do so, they will receive good things from their Father in heaven (Mt 7:7-11). But the Jesus of the *Gospel of Thomas* promises his disciples that if they seek until they find, they will be amazed, they will reign, and they will find rest.

Another strange dimension appears in the *Gospel of Thomas*. Like other writings, *Thomas* places emphasis on knowledge and knowing. Scholars call this Gnosticism, from the Greek word *gnōsis,* which means "knowledge." Church fathers of the second, third and fourth centuries called those who claimed to possess secret or hidden knowledge "Gnostics" (that is, "Knowers"). We don't know if these people called themselves Gnostics.

Gnosticism took many forms and was condemned by leading theologians as heresy. At its simplest, Gnosticism might be described as an orientation that focused more on knowledge and the mystical, and less on faith. Gnosticism tended to hold the Old Testament and the Jewish people in low esteem, especially the more radical form of Gnosticism that believed that the world was created by an evil god, the god of the Jews. This more radical form of Gnosticism saw the physical world as hopelessly flawed and the human body as corrupt and as a prison, designed to hold the soul captive. The goal of salvation, then, is not pardon from sin but acquisition of knowledge whereby the physical body and the corrupt, fallen physical world can be escaped. Jesus came not to redeem as much as to reveal, to show his true disciples the way to escape this world of darkness and join him in the world of light above. There were, of course, many variations of these Gnostic and mystical ideas.

The main thing to see, however, is that Gnosticism was not a neutral variation of general Christian belief but indeed an essentially different and opposing religion that simply borrowed terminology from the New Testament Gospels and changed its meaning.

Although not an instance of this kind of full-blown Gnosticism, there is a strong Gnosticizing element in the *Gospel of Thomas*. We see it in a cluster of sayings preserved in P.Oxy. 1:

36 [Jesus says, "Do not be anxious fr]om morning un[til evening an]d from eve[ning until morn]ing, neither [about y]our [food], what you should eat, [nor] about your clo[thing, what you should we]ar. You a[re much bet]ter than the [lill]ies, whic[h do n]ot co[m]b or s[pi]n. (If) you have n[o garme]nt to put on, what [will you put] on? Who will add to your stature? (It is) h[e who will g]ive you your garment."

37 His disciples say to him, "When will you become revealed to us and when shall we see you?" He says, "When you disrobe and you are not ashamed . . . [nor are afrai]d."

38 [Jesus s]ays, ["Often,] there[fore, you have desired to hear the]se wo[rds of mine] an[d you have no o]n[e else to hear.] Da[ys will come when you will s]ee[k me and will not find me."]

39 [Jesus says, "The Pharisees and the scribes] to[ok the keys] of [knowledge. They h]id [them. They neither] enter[ed nor permit those who] would ent[er to enter.] But you be [wise] a[s serpents and in]noce[nt as dov]es."

77 "Li[f]t the ston[e] and there you will find me, split the wood and I am there."

Saying 36 exploits the Synoptic sayings regarding faith and anxiety (Mt

6:25-34; Lk 12:22-31) in order to advance the Gnostic idea of being properly attired and, paradoxically, of being ready to strip off one's clothing without shame (37).[9] The Gnosticizing orientation is also seen in saying 39. In contrast to the Synoptic Jesus, who pronounces a woe on the scribes and Pharisees because they "shut the kingdom of heaven against people" and do not "allow those who would enter to go in" (Mt 23:13), the Jesus of the *Gospel of Thomas* says that the Pharisees and the scribes have taken the keys of knowledge [Greek loan word *gnōsis*] and hidden them." The Jesus of *Thomas* defines the kingdom of heaven in terms of knowledge. And finally, saying 77 testifies to the mystical presence of Jesus, a theme that comes to fuller expression in other Gnostic texts. Sayings such as these strongly suggest that the *Gospel of Thomas* is indeed a Gnostic writing.

When Was the *Gospel of Thomas* Written?

Most of the codices that make up the Nag Hammadi Library have been dated to the second half of the fourth century, though of course many of the writings within these old books date to earlier periods. The codex that contains the *Gospel of Thomas* may date to the first half of the fourth century. In the case of the *Gospel of Thomas* itself we have the three Greek fragments from Oxyrhynchus that date to the beginning and middle of the third century. One of the fragments may date as early as A.D. 200. Although almost all scholars concede that *Thomas* could have been composed as early as the middle of the second century, the evidence strongly suggests that *Thomas* was not composed before A.D. 175 or 180.

A few scholars still argue that the *Gospel of Thomas* contains primitive, pre-Synoptic tradition.[10] This is possible theoretically, but it is difficult to cull from this collection of sayings (114 in the apparently complete Coptic edition) material that can confidently be judged primitive, independent of the New Testament Gospels, or even authentic.

Among the compelling evidence that leads to the conclusion that *Thomas* is a late writing, not an early one are the following: (1) *Thomas* knows many of the New Testament writings. (2) *Thomas* contains Gospel materials that scholars regard as late. (3) *Thomas* reflects later editing in the Gospels. (4) *Thomas* shows familiarity with traditions distinctive to Eastern, Syrian

Christianity, traditions that did not emerge before than the middle of the second century. Let's review these four types of evidence. Although some readers may find aspects of this discussion technical and complicated, it is important to understand why the *Gospel of Thomas* really should not be considered an ancient source for the historical Jesus.

1. Thomas *knows many New Testament writings.* Quoting or alluding to more than half of the writings of the New Testament (that is, Matthew, Mark, Luke, John, Acts, Romans, 1-2 Corinthians, Galatians, Ephesians, Colossians, 1 Thessalonians, 1 Timothy, Hebrews, 1 John, Revelation),[11] *Thomas* seems to be a collage of New Testament and apocryphal materials that have been interpreted, often allegorically, in such a way as to advance late-second-century Gnostic ideas. Moreover, the traditions contained in *Thomas* hardly reflect a setting that predates the writings of the New Testament, which is why Crossan and others attempt to extract hypothetical early versions of *Thomas* from the Coptic and Greek texts that we possess today. Attempts such as these strike me as special pleading—that is, because the evidence that actually exists undermines the theory, appeals are made to hypothetical evidence more accommodating to the theory.

The problem here is that we do not know if there ever was an edition of the *Gospel of Thomas* substantially different from the Greek fragments of Oxyrhynchus or the later Coptic version from Nag Hammadi. Proposing an early form of *Thomas*, stripped of the embarrassing late and secondary features, is a gratuitous move. The presence of so much New Testament material in *Thomas* argues for a date well into the second century, when Christians would have had access to more than just a few of the writings that eventually made up the New Testament. *Thomas's* familiarity with so much of the New Testament should give us pause before accepting theories of the antiquity and independence of this writing.

2. Thomas *contains late Gospel material.* Another problem with viewing the *Gospel of Thomas* as independent of the canonical Gospels is the presence of a significant amount of material that is distinctive to Matthew (M for short), Luke (L for short) and John. This is an important observation because scholars usually view Mark and Q (the material common to Matthew and Luke, and not derived from Mark)—not M, L and the Johannine tradi-

tion—as repositories of material most likely to be ancient. Yet *Thomas* parallels the later traditions often, as we see in the following lists:

PARALLELS BETWEEN "M" AND THE *GOSPEL OF THOMAS*

Matthew 5:10—*Gospel of Thomas* 69a
Matthew 5:14—*Gospel of Thomas* 32 (= P.Oxy. 1.7)
Matthew 6:2-4—*Gospel of Thomas* 6, 14 (= P.Oxy. 654.6)
Matthew 6:3—*Gospel of Thomas* 62
Matthew 7:6—*Gospel of Thomas* 93
Matthew 10:16—*Gospel of Thomas* 39
Matthew 11:30—*Gospel of Thomas* 90
Matthew 13:24-30—*Gospel of Thomas* 57
Matthew 13:44—*Gospel of Thomas* 109
Matthew 13:45-46—*Gospel of Thomas* 76
Matthew 13:47-50—*Gospel of Thomas* 8
Matthew 15:13—*Gospel of Thomas* 40
Matthew 18:20—*Gospel of Thomas* 30 (= P.Oxy. 1.5)
Matthew 23:13—*Gospel of Thomas* 39, 102 (= P.Oxy. 655.2)

PARALLELS BETWEEN "L" AND THE *GOSPEL OF THOMAS*

Luke 11:27-28 + 23:29—*Gospel of Thomas* 79
Luke 12:13-14—*Gospel of Thomas* 72
Luke 12:16-21—*Gospel of Thomas* 63
Luke 12:49—*Gospel of Thomas* 10
Luke 17:20-21—*Gospel of Thomas* 3 (= P.Oxy. 654.3), 113

PARALLELS BETWEEN JOHN AND THE *GOSPEL OF THOMAS*

John 1:9—*Gospel of Thomas* 24 (= P.Oxy. 655.24)
John 1:14—*Gospel of Thomas* 28 (= P.Oxy. 1.28)
John 4:13-15—*Gospel of Thomas* 13
John 7:32-36—*Gospel of Thomas* 38 (= P.Oxy. 655.38)
John 8:12; 9:5—*Gospel of Thomas* 77

If the *Gospel of Thomas* really does represent an early, independent collection of material, as its advocates argue, then how do we explain the presence of so much M, L and Johannine material? The presence of this material suggests that *Thomas* has been influenced by the New Testament Gospels, not early Jesus tradition that is earlier than the New Testament Gospels.

3. Thomas *reflects later editing in the Gospels.* A telling factor that should give us pause before assuming too quickly that the *Gospel of Thomas* offers early and independent tradition lies in the observation that features characteristic of editing (or "redaction") by Matthew and Luke are also found in *Thomas.* Two of the passages of the M list (Mt 15:13; 13:24-30) contain editing by Matthew. Other sayings in *Thomas* that parallel the triple tradition (that is, material common to Matthew, Mark and Luke) agree with Matthew's wording (for example, Mt 15:11 = *Gospel of Thomas* 34b; Mt 12:50 = *Gospel of Thomas* 99) rather than with Mark's wording. Matthew's unique combination of alms, prayer and fasting (Mt 6:1-18) appears to be echoed in *Gospel of Thomas* 6 (= P.Oxy. 654.6) and 14. In *Thomas* alms, prayer and fasting are discussed in a negative light, probably reflecting Gnostic antipathy toward Jewish piety, which surely argues for viewing *Thomas* as secondary to Matthew. All of this suggests that *Thomas* has drawn upon the Gospel of Matthew.

There is also evidence that the *Gospel of Thomas* was influenced by the Gospel of Luke. The Evangelist Luke alters Mark's somewhat awkward "For there is nothing hid, except to be made manifest" (Mk 4:22) to the much smoother "For nothing is hid that shall not be made manifest" (Lk 8:17). It is this edited version that is found in *Gospel of Thomas* 5-6, with the Greek parallel preserved in P.Oxy. 654.5 matching Luke's text exactly. If *Thomas* truly represents early, independent material, how is it that Luke's later editorial improvements appear in *Thomas*?

Elsewhere there are indications that *Thomas* has followed Luke (for example, *Gospel of Thomas* 10 influenced by Lk 12:49; *Gospel of Thomas* 14 influenced by Lk 10:8-9; *Gospel of Thomas* 16 influenced by Lk 12:51-53 as well as Mt 10:34-39; *Gospel of Thomas* 55 and 101 influenced by Lk 14:26-27 as well as Mt 10:37; *Gospel of Thomas* 73-75 influenced by Lk 10:2). Given the evidence, it is not surprising that a number of respected scholars have concluded that *Thomas* has drawn upon the canonical Gospels.[12]

Advocates of *Thomas's* independence of the canonical Gospels often point to the abbreviated form that many of the parables and sayings have in *Tho-*

mas. One of the best known examples is the parable of the wicked tenant farmers (Mt 21:33-41; Mk 12:1-9; Lk 20:9-16; *Gospel of Thomas* 65). In the opening verse of Mark's version approximately eleven words are drawn from Isaiah 5:1-7 to form the backdrop of the parable. Most of these words do not appear in *Thomas.* Crossan takes this as an indication that the older form of the parable has been preserved in *Thomas,* not in Mark, which supposedly preserves an expanded, secondary version.[13] However, in Luke's opening verse only two words from Isaiah 5 ("planted vineyard") remain. We have here a clear example of abbreviation of the tradition. Other scholars have concluded that the version in *Thomas* is an edited and abridged form of Luke's version of the parable.[14] The same possibly applies to the saying about the rejected stone (Mt 21:42; Mk 12:10-11; Lk 20:17; *Gospel of Thomas* 66). Mark's longer version quotes Psalm 118:22-23. But Luke only quotes Psalm 118:22. Once again Luke, who depends on Mark and is further removed from the original form of the tradition, has abbreviated the tradition. The shorter form also appears in *Thomas.* Thus, it is risky to draw firm conclusions relating to priority on the basis of which form of the tradition is the shortest and appears abbreviated. It is thus possible that *Gospel of Thomas* 65 and 66 are neither separate logia nor derived from pre-Synoptic tradition, but constitute an edited version of Luke's abbreviation of Mark's parable.

4. Thomas *shows familiarity with late traditions distinctive to Eastern, Syrian Christianity.* Not long after the publication of the *Gospel of Thomas* it was noticed that the new Gospel shared several affinities with Eastern, or Syrian, Christianity, especially as expressed in second-century traditions, including Tatian's harmony of the four New Testament Gospels, called the *Diatessaron.* This point is potentially quite significant, for the *Diatessaron* was the only form of New Testament Gospel tradition known to Syrian Christianity in the second century. We must carefully consider the implications of this evidence.

Proponents of the independence and first-century origin of the *Gospel of Thomas* are aware of at least some aspects of this writing's relationship to Syrian Christianity. Dominic Crossan and Stephen Patterson rightly call attention to Edessa, eastern Syria, as the original context of *Thomas.* They point out, among other things, that the name "Judas Thomas" is found in other works of Syrian origin and circulation, such as the *Book of Thomas the Con-*

tender (NHC 2.7), which begins in a manner reminiscent of the *Gospel of Thomas:* "The secret words that the Savior spoke to Judas Thomas, which I, even I Mathaias, wrote down" (138.1-3; see 142.7: "Judas—the one called Thomas"), and the *Acts of Thomas,* in which the apostle is called "Judas Thomas, who is also (called) Didymus" (1; see 11: "Judas who is also Thomas"). The longer form of the name in the *Acts of Thomas* agrees with the prologue of the *Gospel of Thomas,* where the apostle is identified as "Didymus Judas Thomas." In the Syriac version of John 14:22, "Judas (not Iscariot)" is identified as "Judas Thomas." This nomenclature continues on into later Syrian Christian traditions.[15]

Despite these parallels with Syrian tradition, whose distinctive characteristics, so far as we can trace them, emerged in the second century, Crossan and Patterson (and others) are confident that the *Gospel of Thomas* in fact originated quite early. Patterson thinks *Thomas* must have existed before the end of the first century (though he allows for later editing). Crossan believes that the first edition of Thomas emerged in the 50s and the later edition—essentially the extant (existing) text—emerged in the 60s or 70s. In other words, the *Gospel of Thomas* in its first edition is earlier than any of the New Testament Gospels. Indeed, Crossan supposes that even the later edition of *Thomas* may be earlier than the New Testament Gospels.[16]

In summary, scholars have weighed in on both sides of this question, with many arguing that the *Gospel of Thomas* dates to the second century and with almost as many (several of whom are numbered among the members of the Jesus Seminar) arguing that *Thomas* dates to the first century. The latter usually date *Thomas* to the end of the first century but believe they can identify independent tradition that in some cases should be preferred to its parallel forms in the Synoptic Gospels.

This important question cannot be settled by taking a poll. I think we need to take a hard look at the *Gospel of Thomas,* especially as it relates to Syrian tradition. In my view this text should not be dated before the middle of the second century. Indeed, the evidence suggests that *Thomas* was likely composed in the last quarter of the second century and nothing in *Thomas* can be independently traced back to the first century. Let's consider the evidence.

In print and in public lectures Crossan has defended the antiquity and independence of the *Gospel of Thomas* principally on two grounds: (1) He can find "no overall compositional design" in the Gospel, apart from a few clusters of sayings linked by catchwords, and (2) he finds several differences in the parallels with the New Testament Gospels that he believes cannot be explained in terms of editing on the part of the author of *Thomas*. Patterson's arguments are similar.[17] As it turns out, the Syrian evidence addresses both points.

Almost from the beginning, a few scholars with Syriac expertise recognized the Semitic, especially Syriac, style of the *Gospel of Thomas*. This was, of course, consistent with what has already been said about the form of the name of the apostle (that is, "Judas Thomas," not simply "Thomas"). These scholars also noticed that at points distinctive readings in *Thomas* agree with the Syriac version of the New Testament or with the earlier *Diatessaron* by Tatian.[18] Further, the scholars wondered if perhaps portions of *Thomas* originated in the Syriac language instead of the Greek language, as was widely assumed.

In a recent study Nicholas Perrin has put this question to the test. He has analyzed the entire text of *Thomas,* translating the Coptic version into Syriac and Greek. The results of his investigation are quite impressive. On the assumption that the *Gospel of Thomas* was not originally written in Greek or Coptic but in Syriac, which is not implausible given its Syrian provenance, more than five hundred catchwords can be identified linking almost all of the 114 sayings that make up this work. In fact, there were only three couplets (56 and 57, 88 and 89, and 104 and 105) for which Perrin could find no linking catchwords. These exceptions are hardly fatal to Perrin's analysis, for the original Syriac catchwords could easily have been lost in transmission or in translation into Coptic.[19]

Moreover, Perrin is not only able to explain the order of the whole of *Thomas* in reference to catchwords, he is able to show in places the Gospel's acquaintance with the order and arrangement of material in Tatian's *Diatessaron*. The mystery of the order of the sayings that make up the *Gospel of Thomas* appears to have been resolved. Perrin concludes that the *Gospel of Thomas* is indeed dependent on the New Testament Gospels, but not directly. *Thomas* depends on the New Testament Gospels as they existed in the *Diatessaron*, in Syriac.

In my view the principal argument that Crossan and others have advanced in support of the literary independence of the *Gospel of Thomas* from the New Testament Gospels has been dealt a crippling blow. It is no longer justified to say that there is no discernible framework or organizing principle lying behind the composition of *Thomas*. There clearly is, when this writing of acknowledged Syrian origin is studied in the light of the Syriac language.

Just as impressive is the number of specific contacts between the *Gospel of Thomas* and Syrian Gospel traditions and other Syrian religious traditions. What we see is that again and again, where *Thomas* differs from the New Testament Gospels, this is where *Thomas* agrees with Syrian tradition. This point has not been sufficiently appreciated by Crossan and others. There are many examples that could be examined, but space (and perhaps the patience of most readers) permit review of only two.

Jesus' paradoxical saying on peace and sword offers an instructive example. I will present the familiar forms of this saying found in English translations of the Greek New Testament followed by the parallel saying in the *Gospel of Thomas*, which is then followed by the English translation of the Syriac version of Matthew's form of the saying and the parallel in yet another Syriac text.

> Greek Matthew 10:34: "Do not think that I have come to bring peace to the earth; I have not come to bring peace, but a sword."

> Greek Luke 12:51: "Do you think that I have come to bring peace to the earth? No, I tell you, but rather division!"

> *Gospel of Thomas* 16a: "They do not know that it is division I have come to cast upon the earth: fire, sword, and war."

> Syriac Matthew 10:34b: "I came not to bring peace but division of minds and a sword." (Curetonian Syriac)

> Syriac *Recognitions* 2.26.6: "I have not come that I might cast peace on the earth but rather war."

The *Thomas* form of the saying appears to reflect elements from both Matthew and Luke. *Thomas*'s "division" derives from Luke, and *Thomas*'s "sword" derives from Matthew. Both of these elements appear in the Syriac version of

Matthew: "I came not to bring peace but division of minds and a sword." Moreover, *Thomas*'s "war" reflects a version of Jesus' saying in the Syriac *Recognitions*: "I have not come that I might cast peace on the earth but rather war."[20] The evidence strongly suggests that the form of the saying preserved in *Gospel of Thomas* 16a derives from a Syriac form of Matthew 10:34, with further embellishment from other Syrian sources, such as that reflected in the Syriac version of the *Clementine Recognitions*. There are many examples like this, where the form of a saying in *Thomas* agrees with either the form of the saying in Tatian's *Diatessaron* or in the later Syriac Gospels.

Our second example concerns Jesus' beatitude pronounced on the poor. Here again the English of Greek New Testament forms of the saying is presented, followed by the parallel saying in *Thomas*, which in turn is followed by the Syriac forms.

> Greek Matthew 5:3: "Blessed are the poor in spirit, for theirs is the kingdom of heaven."
>
> Greek Luke 6:20: "Blessed are you who are poor, for yours is the kingdom of God."
>
> *Gospel of Thomas* 54: "Blessed are the poor, for yours is the kingdom of heaven."
>
> Syriac Matthew 5:3: "Blessed are the poor in spirit, for yours is the kingdom of heaven"
>
> *Diatessaron*: "Blessed are the poor in spirit—"

Crossan views *Thomas* 54 as providing strong evidence of the independence of the tradition in *Thomas*. He notes that Matthew's apparent gloss "in spirit" is missing in *Thomas* and that the forms of the two clauses are mixed, with the first clause in the third person (as in Matthew) and the second clause in the second person (as in Luke). Crossan cannot imagine how the author/collector of *Thomas* could have done this: "One would have at least to argue that *Thomas* (a) took the third person 'the poor' from Matthew, then (b) the second person 'yours' from Luke, and (c) returned to Matthew for the final 'kingdom of heaven.' It might be simpler to suggest that *Thomas* was mentally unstable."[21] As it turns out, however, it is simpler to review the Syrian tradition.

Thomas 54 follows the Syriac form of Matthew (probably from the *Diatessaron,* the only form in which the New Testament Gospel tradition was available for Syriac speakers in the late second century). The omission of the qualifying prepositional phrase "in spirit" should hardly occasion surprise. Not only is it missing from Luke, its nonappearance in *Thomas* is consistent with the worldview of *Thomas.* That is, it's not too difficult to explain in light of *Thomas's* antimaterialistic perspective (see *Gospel of Thomas* 27, 63, 64, 65, 95, 110), a perspective consistent with the ascetic views of the Syrian church. No, *Thomas* declares, it is not the poor in spirit who are blessed, it is the (literal) poor. So, to return to Crossan's argument, all one needs to say is that *Thomas* (a) took the saying as it existed in Syriac (which accounts for the mix of third and second person as well as the presence of the phrase "kingdom of heaven"), and (b) deleted the unwanted qualifying phrase "in spirit."

Before concluding the discussion of the *Gospel of Thomas,* one other issue needs to be addressed. Stephen Patterson, James Robinson and others have argued that the literary form of the *Gospel of Thomas* supports an early date. Because *Thomas* is like Q, the sayings source on which Matthew and Luke drew, then *Thomas* in its earliest form may approximate the age of Q.[22] This argument is wholly specious, not only because it does not take into account the extensive coherence with late-second-century Syrian tradition or the lack of coherence with pre-70 Jewish Palestine, it fails to take into account of the fact that other sayings collections, some in Syria, emerged in the second and third centuries. Among these are the rabbinic collection that became known as the *Pirqe Avot* ("Chapters of the Fathers") and the *Sentences of Sextus.* The latter is particularly significant because it originated in Syria in the second century, the approximate time and place of the emergence of the *Gospel of Thomas.* The evidence suggests that the *Gospel of Thomas* is another second-century collection that emerged in Syria.

When all of the appropriate evidence is taken into consideration, I find it hard to avoid the conclusion that the *Gospel of Thomas* originated in the late second century, not in the middle of the first century. Let me make this emphatically clear: This is where all of the evidence takes us: (1) the association of the *Gospel of Thomas* with "Judas Thomas," (2) the arrangement and order of the sayings explained by hundreds of Syriac catchwords that link the sayings, and (3) the coherence of the readings in *Thomas,* which differ from the Greek New Testament Gospels, with the readings either in the *Diatessaron* or other Christian Syriac works from this period compellingly argue for a late-second-century Syrian origin of the *Gospel of Thomas.* In short, it is this flood of factors that point to the Eastern, Syriac-speaking church, a church that knows the New Testament Gospels primarily—perhaps exclusively—through Tatian's *Diatessaron,* a work not composed before A.D. 170, that persuades me that the *Gospel of Thomas* does not offer students of the Gospels early, independent material that can be used for critical research into the life and teaching of Jesus. Reliance on this writing can only lead to a distorted portrait of the historical Jesus.

4

QUESTIONABLE TEXTS—PART II

The Gospel of Peter, the Egerton Gospel,
the Gospel of Mary and the Secret Gospel of Mark

Having looked closely at the *Gospel of Thomas* in chapter three, we will move a little more quickly in this chapter in surveying four other extracanonical Gospels.

THE *GOSPEL OF PETER*

Church historian Eusebius of Caesarea (c. A.D. 260-340) states that 1 Peter is accepted and has been used by the ancient elders, but other writings attributed to the apostle are rejected (*Ecclesiastical History* 3.3.1-4). The rejected writings that are attributed to Peter include the second letter (presumably 2 Peter), the apocalypse (that is, the *Apocalypse of Peter*), the Gospel (that is, the *Gospel of Peter*), and the preaching (that is, the *Preaching of Peter*). Later in his history Eusebius refers to the "writings that are put forward by heretics under the name of the apostles containing Gospels such as those of Peter, and Thomas, and Matthias, and some others besides" (*Ecclesiastical History* 3.25.6). Still later Eusebius once again mentions the Gospel attributed to Peter, this time in reference to Serapion, bishop of Antioch (in office A.D. 199-211). Eusebius quotes a portion of the bishop's letter, titled "Concerning What Is Known as the Gospel of Peter." Serapion states:

> For our part, brothers, we receive both Peter and the other apostles as Christ, but the writings that falsely bear their names we reject, as men of experience, knowing that such were not handed down to us. For I myself, when I came among you, imagined that all of you clung to the

true faith; and, without going through the Gospel put forward by them in the name of Peter, I said: "If this is the only thing that seemingly causes a mean spirit among you, let it be read." But since I have now learned, from what has been told me, that their mind was lurking in some hole of heresy, I shall give diligence to come again to you. Therefore, brothers, expect me quickly. But we, brothers, gathering to what kind of heresy Marcianus belonged (who used to contradict himself, not knowing what he was saying, as you will learn from what has been written to you), were enabled by others who studied this very Gospel, that is, by the successors of those who began it, whom we called Docetists (for most of the ideas belong to their teaching)—using [the material supplied] by them, were enabled to go through it and discover that the most part was indeed in accordance with the true teaching of the Savior, but that some things were added, which also we place below for your benefit. (*Ecclesiastical History* 6.12.3-6)

The testimony of Serapion confirms the existence of a work known as the *Gospel of Peter,* a work that emerged sometime in the second century. For us, however, the value of his statement is limited, for almost nothing is said of the contents of the *Gospel of Peter* and no part of it is actually quoted. To the best of our knowledge, no other church father quotes any part of this Gospel. This lack of specific information will have a bearing on the question of the identity of the various manuscript finds that are thought to relate to this writing.

In the winter of 1886-1887, during excavations at Akhmîm in Egypt, a codex was found in the coffin of a Christian monk. The manuscript comprises a fragment of a Gospel, fragments of Greek *Enoch,* the *Apocalypse of Peter,* and, written on the inside of the back cover of the codex, an account of the martyrdom of St. Julian. The Gospel fragment bears no name or hint of a title, for neither the beginning nor the conclusion of the work has survived. Because the apostle Peter appears in the text, narrating in the first person ("But I, Simon Peter" [v. 60]), because it seemed to have a docetic orientation (that is, where the physical reality of Jesus is discounted), and because the Gospel fragment was in the company of the *Apocalypse of Peter,* it was widely assumed that the fragment belonged to the *Gospel of Peter* mentioned by Eusebius.[1]

Critical assessments of the then newly published Gospel fragment diverged widely, with some scholars, such as Percival Gardner-Smith claiming that the fragment was independent of the New Testament Gospels and others such as Henry Barclay Swete claiming that the fragment is dependent on the New Testament Gospels.[2] Throughout this debate no one asked if the Akhmîm fragment really was part of the second-century *Gospel of Peter.* It was simply assumed that it was.

Then, in the 1970s and 1980s, two more Greek fragments from Egypt were published, P.Oxy. 2949 and P.Oxy. 4009, which with varying degrees of confidence were identified as belonging to the *Gospel of Peter.* Indeed, one of the fragments was thought to overlap with part of the Akhmîm fragment. The publication of these fragments renewed interest in the Gospel, because it was felt that the identity of the Akhmîm fragment as the second-century *Gospel of Peter,* initially accepted and later rejected by Serapion, was confirmed. Indeed, it has also been suggested that the Fayyum Fragment (P.Vindob. G 2325) is yet another early fragment of the *Gospel of Peter.*[3]

In recent years Helmut Koester and a circle of colleagues and students have given new life to Gardner-Smith's position. According to Koester the *Gospel of Peter's* "basis must be an older text under the authority of Peter which was independent of the canonical Gospels." Koester's student Ron Cameron agrees, concluding that this Gospel is independent of the canonical Gospels, may even predate them, and "may have served as a source for their respective authors."[4] This position has been worked out in detail by John Dominic Crossan, who accepts the identification of the Akhmîm fragment with Serapion's *Gospel of Peter.* In a lengthy study that appeared in 1985 Crossan argued that the *Gospel of Peter,* though admittedly in its final stages influenced by the New Testament Gospel tradition, preserves an old tradition, on which all four of the Passion accounts in the canonical Gospels are based.[5] This old tradition is identified as the *Cross Gospel.*

Crossan's provocative conclusion calls for evaluation. I will translate a selection from the Akhmîm Gospel fragment that Crossan thinks reflects the earlier *Cross Gospel.*[6]

VII

(25) Then the Jews and the elders and the priests, knowing what sort of harm they had done to themselves, began to lament and say: "Woe (to us) for our sins; the judgment and the end of Jerusalem have drawn near."

VIII

(28) But the scribes and the Pharisees and the elders, having gathered together, heard that all the people were grumbling and murmuring and beating their breasts, saying: "If at his death these great signs have happened, behold how righteous he must have been!"

(29) They were afraid and went to Pilate entreating him and saying:

(30) "Give us soldiers, that we might guard his tomb for three d[ays], lest his disciples come and steal him and the people suppose that he had been raised from the dead, and do us harm."

(31) And Pilate gave them Petronius the centurion, with soldiers, to guard the tomb. And elders and scribes went with them to the tomb.

(32) And having rolled a large stone, all who were there, with the centurion and the soldiers, place (it) at the door of the tomb

(33) and put on it seven seals, and after pitching a tent they kept guard.

IX

(34) Early in the morning of the sabbath a crowd from Jerusalem and the surrounding countryside came in order to see the sealed tomb.

(35) Now in the night in which the Lord's Day dawned, while the soldiers kept guard in pairs in every watch, a loud voice rang out in heaven,

(36) and they saw the heavens opened and two men descending from there in great brightness and drawing near to the tomb.

(37) But that stone which had been placed at the door rolled by itself and withdrew to one side. The tomb opened and both of the young men entered.

X

(38) Then those soldiers, observing these things, awakened the centurion and the elders (for they themselves were there on guard).

(39) And while they were relating what they had seen, again they see three men coming out of the tomb—two of them supporting the one, and a cross following them—

(40) and the head(s) of the two reached to heaven, but (the head) of the one being led by the hand extended above the heavens.

(41) And they heard a voice from heaven, saying: "Did you preach to those who sleep?"

(42) And an answer was heard from the cross: "Yes."

XI

(45) Having seen these things, those about the centurion hurried (that) night to Pilate, abandoning the tomb which they had been guarding, and reported everything that they had seen, being greatly disturbed and saying: "Truly he was the Son of God."

(46) Pilate answered and said: "I am clean of the blood of the Son of God. To you this seemed (right)."

(47) Then all came and were beseeching him and urging him to command the centurion and the soldiers to relate to no one what they had seen.

(48) "For it is better," they said, "for us to be guilty of the greatest sin before God than to fall into the hands of the people of the Jews and be stoned."

(49) Pilate therefore commanded the centurion and the soldiers to say nothing.

Crossan's hypothetical *Cross Gospel* contains elements that suggest that the Akhmîm fragment (or *Gospel of Peter*) was written after, not prior, to the Synoptic Gospels, particularly the Gospels of Matthew and Mark. The confession of the Jewish authorities' guilt (7.25; 11.48), which in itself lacks historical realism, could owe its inspiration in part to Jesus' woe and lament for Jerusalem (Lk 21:20-24; see Lk 23:48) and perhaps to Caiaphas's ominous counsel (Jn 11:49-50). Does it really seem likely that the Akhmîm fragment's tradition that the "Jews and elders" expressed grief by acknowledging their sins and the imminence of "judgment and the end of Jerusalem" is early, independent and pre-Synoptic? Don't such statements reflect the relationship between "Jews" and "Christians" after A.D. 70, when the various groups and subgroups of Jews were reduced largely to two principal movements (followers of Hillel [and Shammai] and Jesus), and the destruction of Jerusalem in 70 is viewed as the result of the Jews' failure to recognize Jesus as "Messiah"? Is such a statement as "it is better to be guilty of the greatest sin before God than to fall into the hands of the people" earlier than what we find in the Synoptic tradition? Such a statement bears the stamp of enthusiastic Christian exaggeration unrestrained by realistic knowledge of Jewish piety and sentiment. It has, moreover, an anti-Jewish ring to it as well.

Similarly, the statement of the people in the Akhmîm fragment at 8.28 ("all the people were grumbling and murmuring and beating their breasts, saying: 'If at his death these great signs have happened, behold how righteous *[dikaios]* he must have been!' ") surely represents an embellishment of Luke 23:47-48: "Now when the centurion saw what had taken place, he praised God, and said: 'Certainly this man was righteous *[dikaios]* ' And all the multitudes who assembled to see the sight, when they saw what had taken place, returned home beating their breasts."

The author of the Akhmîm Gospel fragment apparently possessed little accurate knowledge of Jewish customs and sensitivities. According to 8.31 and 10.38 the Jewish elders and scribes camp out in the cemetery, as part of the guard keeping watch over the tomb of Jesus. Given Jewish views of corpse impurity, not to mention fear of cemeteries at night, the author of our fragment is unbelievably ignorant. Who could write such a story only twenty years after the death of Jesus? And if someone did at such an early time, can we really believe that the Evangelist Matthew, who was surely Jewish, would make use of such a poorly informed writing? One can scarcely credit this scenario.

There are worse problems. The Jewish leaders' fear of harm at the hands of the Jewish people (Akhmîm fragment 8.30) smacks of embellishment, if not Christian apologetic. The "seven seals" (8.33) and the "crowd from Jerusalem and the surrounding countryside" that "came in order to see the sealed tomb" (9.34) serve an apologetic interest: The resurrection story is well attested. These details are probably secondary to the canonical versions of the story. The appearance of the expression "the Lord's Day" (9.35), of course, is another indication of lateness (see Rev 1:10; Ignatius's *Epistle to the Magnesians* 9:1), not antiquity. The centurion's confession (Akhmîm fragment 11.45) appears to reflect Matthew (Mt 27:54; see Mk 15:39; Lk 23:47).[7]

Finally, can it be seriously maintained that the Akhmîm fragment's resurrection account, complete with a talking cross and angels whose heads reach heaven, constitutes the most primitive account? Is this the account that the canonical Evangelists had before them? Or isn't it more prudent to conclude what we have here is still more evidence of the secondary, fanciful nature of this apocryphal writing?[8] Doesn't the evidence suggest that the Akhmîm Gospel fragment is little more than a blend of details from the four canonical Gospels, especially from Matthew, that has been embellished with pious imagination, apologetic concerns and a touch of anti-Semitism?

It is difficult to conclude that this material, no matter how deftly pruned and reconstructed (and don't we have here again an example of special pleading?) could possibly constitute the earliest layer of tradition on which the Passion narratives of the New Testament Gospels are dependent. Scholars a generation or two ago found no independent traditions in the Akhmîm Gospel fragment. Recently, other scholars have reached similar conclusions. John P. Meier describes the fragment as a second-century "pastiche of traditions from the canonical Gospels, recycled through the memory and lively imagination of Christians who have heard the Gospels read and preached upon many a time." Moody Smith's rhetorical question only underscores the problematical dimension of Crossan's hypothesis: "Is it thinkable that the tradition began with the legendary, the mythological, the anti-Jewish, and indeed the fantastic, and moved in the direction of the historically restrained and sober?"[9] Indeed, Crossan's case appears to be another example of special pleading, of wish becoming father to the thought.

The evidence strongly suggests that the Akhmîm Gospel fragment is a late work, not an early work, even if we attempt to find an earlier substratum, gratuitously shorn of imagined late additions. But more pressing is the question that asks if the existing ninth-century Akhmîm Gospel fragment really is a fragment of the second-century *Gospel of Peter* condemned by Bishop Serapion in the early third century. The extant Akhmîm fragment does not identify itself, nor do we have a patristic quotation of the *Gospel of Peter* to compare it to and possibly settle the questions. Nor is the Akhmîm Gospel fragment docetic, as many asserted shortly after its publication. If the fragment is not docetic, then the proposed identification of the fragment with the *Gospel of Peter* is weakened still further. After all, the one thing that Serapion emphasized was that the *Gospel of Peter* was used by docetists to advance their doctrines.[10] And finally, as Paul Foster has shown, the connection between the Akhmîm Gospel fragment and the small papyrus fragments that may date as early as 200-250 is quite tenuous.[11] Thus we have no solid evidence that allows us with any confidence to link the extant Akhmîm Gospel fragment with a second-century text, whether the *Gospel of Peter* mentioned by Bishop Serapion or some other writing from the late second century. Given its fantastic features and coherence with late traditions, it is not advisable to make use of this Gospel fragment for Jesus research.

THE *EGERTON GOSPEL*

Papyrus Egerton 2 was found somewhere in Egypt and fell into the hands of scholars in 1934. It consists of four fragments. The fourth fragment yields nothing more than one illegible letter. The third fragment yields little more than a few scattered words. The first and second fragments offer four (or perhaps five) stories that parallel stories found in John and the Synoptic Gospels. Papyrus Köln 255, discovered sometime later, is a related fragment of the text. Its lines will be inserted in italics where appropriate in the following translation of the *Egerton Gospel*. (Note: *recto* refers to the side of the papyrus in which the fibers run horizontally, while *verso* refers to the other side of the papyrus, where the fibers run vertically.)[12]

PAPYRUS EGERTON 2

Fragment 1 verso

(1a) [2][And Jesus said] to the lawyer[s: "[3]Punish e]veryone who acts con[trary to [4]the l]aw, but not me. Fo[r [5]he knows not] what he does (or) how he does it." [But [6]t]urn[ing] to [the] rulers of the people [7]he sa[id t]his word: "Sea[rch [8]t]he scriptures, in which you thi[nk] [9]you have life. Those [10]ar[e what tes]tify about me. Do not [11]s[uppose th]at I came to accu[s]e [12][you] before my Father. [13]Moses is [the one who ac]cuses you, (the one) in whom [14]you have hoped." And when th[e]y [15]s[ai]d: "We know [full] well that [16]God spo[ke] to Moses, but we do not know [17][whence you are]," answering, Jesus sa[id [18]to the]m: "Now accuses (you) [19][your un]belie[f] *in the things [20]written by him. For if you had [21]believed in Moses], you would have believed [22a][in me]; for concerning me that one [23a][wrote] to your fa[th]ers."*

Fragment 1 recto

(1b) [22][. . . that they] should draw together, c[arrying] [23]stones, that they might sto[ne [24]h]im. And the [rul]ers laid [25]han[ds] upon him, [26][th]at they should arrest (him) and hand (him) [27][over] to the crowd; and they were not [able] to [28]arrest him because [29]his hour of delivera[nce] (into their hands) had not yet c[ome]. [30]But the Lord himself, going [out from their ha]nds, [31]escaped from th[em].

(2) [32]And [be]hold a leper draw[ing] near to him [33]says: "Teacher Jesus, wandering with lep[ers] [34]and eatin[g with them] [35]in the inn, I also con[tracted leprosy]. [36]If then [you will it], [37]I shall be cleansed." Immediately the Lord [said to him]: [38]"[I] will it; be cleansed." [and immediately] [39]the lep[rosy de]parted from him. [40]*But [said] Jesus to him, "Go, show [41]yourself to th[e priests.] [42a]and offer for [43a][pur]ifica-tion, as Moses com[manded, and] [44a]sin no longer."*

Fragment 2 recto

(3) [42][. . . com]ing [43]to him to examine [44]him they began testing him, say[ing]: [44a]"Teacher Jesus, we know that [from God] [46]you have come,

for what you are doing tes[tifies] [47]beyond all the prophets. [Therefore, tell] [48]us: Is it proper to [give [49]payment] to the kings that which pertains to their rule? Should [we pay th]em [50]or n[ot]?" But Jesus knowing th[eir [51]th]inking, becoming ang[ry], [52]said to th[em]: "Why do you call me [53]'[Te]acher' [with y]our mouth, n[ot he]aring [54]what I [s]ay? Well did Is[aiah pr]ophesy [concerning [55]y]ou, saying: 'Th[is people] [56]with the[ir li]ps [honor] [57]me, [but their hea]rt is [far] [58]from m[e. In v]ain [they worship me.] [59]Command[ments of men . . .'"]

Fragment 2 verso

(4) [60][. . .] in the place, having shut [61][. . .] it had been laid beneath [62][. . .] its wealth uncertain [63][. . .] But while those ones were perplexed [64]at this strange question, [65]Jesus then walked and stood [66]at the bank of the Jordan [67]River. And stretching out [68]his right hand [. . .] filled [69][. . .] and sowed (it) upon the [70][rive]r (?). And then [. . .] [71]the water having produced [. . .] the [72][. . .] and [. . .] before [73]their eyes brought forth fruit [74][. . .] much [. . .] to (their) joy (?) [75][. . .]

Fragment 3 verso

(5) [76][. . .] [77][. . .] if [78][. . .] his [79][. . .] [80][. . .] knowing [81][. . .]

Fragment 3 recto

(6) [82]"We are one [. . .] [83]I abide w[ith" . . . st]ones [84]to [. . . that they] [85]should kill [him . . .] [86]he says: "The one [. . .] [87][. . .]

At many points these fragments parallel the New Testament Gospels. The first story is filled with allusions to the Gospel of John. Jesus' assertion in lines 7-10 could well be drawn from John 5:39, 45. The lawyers' reply in lines 15-17 appears to be taken from John 9:29, while Jesus' rejoinder in lines 20-23a reflects John 5:46.[13] The attempt to stone Jesus in lines 22-24 parallels John 10:31, while the declaration in lines 25-30 that they were unable to do so because his "hour had not yet come" echoes John 7:30; 8:20. Reference to Jesus in line 30 as "the Lord" has a secondary ring. The second story is mostly Synoptic. The opening sentence in line 32, "and behold a leper drawing near to him says," agrees with Matthew 8:2a (but not the parallel Mk 1:40a) nearly verbatim. The leper's petition in line 36 employs the same vocabulary, though not the forms, of that of the leper's request in Mark 1:40b (and parallel). Jesus' response in line 38 agrees with the Synoptic story exactly (Mk 1:41b and parallel). The statement in lines 38-43a that "immediately the leprosy departed from him" agrees almost exactly with Mark 1:42 (and with Lk 5:13, but for the word order). The Egerton Papyrus has no equivalent of the command of secrecy found in Mark (Mk 1:43-44), which could argue for Egerton's independence, if not priority. But then most of this material has been omitted by Matthew also (Mt 8:4). Its absence in the Egerton Papyrus may suggest nothing more than that the author had no more interest in the Gospel of Mark's secrecy theme than had Matthew and Luke, who often chose to abbreviate this theme or remove it altogether. Jesus' order that the man show himself to the "priests" parallels Mark 1:44. But the plural betrays a lack of acquaintance with Jewish law and custom. The plural may have been inspired by the final part of Jesus' saying "as a witness to them," which is found in all three Synoptic Gospels but not paralleled in the Egerton Papyrus. The final part of the admonition (line 44a) parallels John 5:14.

The third story again combines elements from John and the Synoptic Gospels. The opening statement in lines 45-47, "Teacher Jesus, we know that [from God] you have come, for what you are doing tes[tifies] beyond all the prophets," is based on John 3:2 and John 9:29 (see also Jn 1:45; Acts 3:18). Egerton's use of "teacher" (*didaskale*) is secondary to John's transliteration *rabbi,* and may be due to its appearance in Mark 12:14a ("Teacher, we know that you are true"). The question put to Jesus in lines 48-50 is taken from Mark 12:14b (and parallel) but appears to have missed the original point. Jesus' emotion in line 51 recalls Mark 1:43, while his question in lines 52-54 recalls a form of the question found in Luke 6:46. The remainder of Jesus' saying, which is a paraphrase of Isaiah 29:13, echoes Mark 7:6-7 and parallel.

Crossan concludes from these fragments that Papyrus Egerton 2 represents a tradition that predates the canonical Gospels. He thinks that "Mark is dependent on it directly" and that it gives evidence of "a stage before the distinction of Johannine and Synoptic traditions was operative." Helmut Koester agrees with Crossan's second point, saying that in Papyrus Egerton

2 we find "pre-Johannine and pre-synoptic characteristics of language [which] still existed side by side." He thinks it unlikely, against other scholars, that the author of this papyrus could have been acquainted with the canonical Gospels and "would have deliberately composed [it] by selecting sentences" from them.[14]

Serious questions concerning Crossan's and Koester's assessment, however, must be raised. First, several times editorial improvements introduced by Matthew and Luke appear in Egerton (for example, compare Egerton line 32 with Mk 1:40; Mt 8:2; Lk 5:12; or Egerton lines 39-41 with Mk 1:44; Mt 8:4; Lk 17:14). There are other indications that the Egerton Papyrus is later than the canonical Gospels. The plural "kings" is probably secondary to the singular "Caesar" that is found in the Synoptics (and in *Gospel of Thomas* 100). The flattery, "what you do bears witness beyond all the prophets," may reflect John 1:34, 45 and is again reminiscent of later pious Christian embellishment that tended to exaggerate the respect that Jesus' contemporaries showed him (see the examples in *Gospel of the Hebrews* 2 and Josephus *Antiquities of the Jews* 18.64).

A second question arises in response to Koester's statement about the improbability that the author of the Egerton Papyrus "would have deliberately composed [it] by selecting sentences" from the canonical Gospels. Isn't this the very thing that Justin Martyr and his disciple Tatian did? Sometime in the 150s Justin Martyr composed a harmony of the Synoptic Gospels and some years later Tatian composed a harmony (that is, the *Diatessaron*) of all four New Testament Gospels. If Justin Martyr and Tatian, writing in the second century, can compose their respective harmonies through the selection of sentences and phrases from this Gospel and that Gospel, why couldn't the author of the Egerton Papyrus do the same thing? Indeed, it is likely that this is the very thing that he did.

A third question arises out of Koester's suggestion that the mixture of John-like and Synoptic elements is primitive, while their separation into the existing canonical forms is secondary. If Koester's suggestion is correct, then the *Egerton Gospel* does indeed derive from the middle of the first century, as Crossan in fact argues. It would have to be this early if it were to be used by the Synoptic Evangelists. If this is the case, then we must wonder why we have no other fragment or any other evidence of the existence of this extraordinarily primitive Gospel. Why don't we have other papyri, extracanonical Gospels or patristic quotations attesting this primitive pre-Synoptic, pre-Johannine unified tradition?

Several examples of passages made up of mixed and confused texts can be found in Justin Martyr's quotations, which sometimes combine materials from two or more Gospels. Here is an instructive example:

> For not those who make profession, but those who do the works, shall be saved, according to his word: "Not every one who says to me, 'Lord, Lord,' shall enter the kingdom of heaven, but the one who does the will of my Father who is in heaven [see Mt 7:21]. For whoever hears me, and does my sayings [see Mt 7:24 = Lk 6:47], hears him who sent me [see Lk 10:16 (Codex D); Jn 5:23-24; 13:20; 12:44-45; 14:24; see also Justin's *Apologia* 1.63.5]. And many will say to me, 'Lord, Lord, have we not eaten and drunk in your name, and done wonders?' And then I will say to them, 'Depart from me, you workers of lawlessness [see Lk 13:26-27].' Then shall there be wailing and gnashing of teeth, when the righteous shall shine as the sun, and the wicked are sent into eternal fire [see Mt 13:42-43]. For many shall come in my name [see Mt 24:5 and parallel], clothed outwardly in sheep's clothing, but inwardly they are devouring wolves [see Mt 7:15]. By their works you will know them [see Mt 7:16, 20]. And every tree that does not bring forth good fruit is cut down and cast into the fire [see Mt 7:19]." (*Apologia* 1.16.9-13)

Justin has assembled, either from memory or by picking and choosing from written texts, a "word" of Jesus that is in reality a blending of Synoptic materials, which at one point may also reflect the influence of the Gospel of John. Although drawn from a variety of contexts, there is nevertheless a general thematic unity that holds these materials together. With respect to composition, the sayings in Egerton Papyrus 2.1, 3 are quite similar to Justin's "word" of Jesus.

Another feature that tells against the antiquity and priority of the Egerton Papyrus is the story related in the badly preserved verso of fragment

2. The story is reminiscent of the kind of stories we find in the late and fanciful apocryphal Gospels. For example, in the *Infancy Gospel of Thomas* we are told of the boy Jesus, who sowed a handful of seed that yielded a remarkable harvest:

> Now when it was seed-time, Joseph went forth to sow corn, and Jesus followed after him. And when Joseph began to sow, Jesus put forth his hand and took of the corn so much as he could hold in his hand, and scattered it. Joseph therefore came at the time of the harvest to reap his harvest. And Jesus also came and gathered the ears which he had sown, and they made an hundred measures of good corn: and he called the poor and the widows and fatherless and gave them the corn which he had gained, save that Joseph took a little thereof unto his house for a blessing. (*Infancy Gospel of Thomas* 10:1-2 [Latin]; see *Infancy Gospel of Thomas* 12:1-2 [Greek MS A]; *Gospel of Pseudo-Matthew* 34)[15]

The relevant part of Papyrus Egerton 2 reads:

> But while those ones were perplexed at this strange question, Jesus then walked and stood at the bank of the Jordan River. And stretching out his right hand [. . .] filled [. . .] and sowed (it) upon the [rive]r (?). And then [. . .] the water having produced [. . .] the [. . .] and [. . .] before their eyes brought forth fruit [. . .] much [. . .] to (their) joy. (Lines 63-74)

Although we cannot be certain, given the condition of the text, it is likely that these lines tell a story in which, by way of illustration, Jesus took a handful of seed and sowed it on the river, with the result that the water—to the astonishment of those present—produced an abundance of fruit. The reference to joy suggests that the people benefited from the miracle, much as the "poor and the widows and the fatherless" did in the lighthearted tale in the *Infancy Gospel of Thomas*. Whether or not these two stories derive from a common source is not important. What is important is to appreciate the presence of what appears to be a quite fanciful tale among the passages preserved by the Egerton Papyrus. The appearance of this tale, which is like those that are all too common among the later extracanonical Gospels, significantly increases the burden of proof for those who wish to argue that the Egerton traditions are primitive, even pre-Synoptic.

Admittedly, while the hypothesis of Crossan, Koester and others remains a theoretical possibility, the evidence available at this time favors the likelihood that Papyrus Egerton 2 (or the *Egerton Gospel*) represents a second-century combination of elements from the Synoptic Gospels and the Gospel of John rather than primitive first-century material on which the canonical Gospels depended.

THE *GOSPEL OF MARY*

The *Gospel of Mary* narrates a story in which Mary Magdalene relates to the disciples the revelations that Jesus gave her. Andrew and Peter express doubts that Mary is telling the truth because the teaching is at variance with what they themselves had been taught. Mary weeps, saddened that they would think that she would misrepresent the words of the Savior. Levi rebukes Peter, defending Mary and exhorting the disciples to preach the gospel, "neither setting boundaries nor laying down laws, as the Savior said." The disciples then go forth and the *Gospel of Mary* comes to an end.

Three overlapping fragments of the *Gospel of Mary* have been found. At most, we have half of the original text.[16] The following is a translation of the Greek papyrus fragments:

"[N]or have I established law, as the lawgiver." . . . having said these things, he departed. But they were grieved, shedding many tears and saying, "How shall we go to the nations, preaching the gospel of the kingdom of the Son of Man? For if they neither spared that One, how will they spare us?"

Then Mary stood up and greeting them she kissed them all and says, "Brothers, weep not; do not be grieved nor distressed, for his grace shall be with you, sheltering you. Rather, let us give thanks for his greatness, because he has joined us together and made us human beings."

Having spoken these things Mary turned their minds to the good and they began to ask about the utterances of the Savior. Peter says [to?] Mary, "Sister, we know that you were much loved by the Savior, as no other woman. Therefore tell us what words of the Savior you know, what we have not heard."

Mary answered, saying, "What escapes you and I remember I shall report to you." And she began (to speak) to them these words. "One time while seeing the Lord in a vision, I said, 'Lord, I saw you today.' He answered, saying, 'You are blessed . . .'" (4:10–7:2 = P.Oxy. 3525)

" '. . . the remainder of the course of the season of the age (I shall have) rest in silence.'" Having said these things Mary became silent, since it was to this point that the Savior had spoken.

Andrew says, "Brothers, what does it seem to you concerning the things that have been said? For I do not believe that the Savior has said these things, for it seems different from his thought."

Thinking about these matters (Peter says), "Was the Savior speaking to a woman in secret and (not) openly, in order that we all might hear? He was not wishing to indicate that she is more worthy than we are, was he?"

[Then Mary wept . . .] "[Do you think I have told lies] about the Savior?"

Levi says to Peter, "Peter, anger always lies within you; and now thus you question the woman as opposing her. If the Savior regarded her worthy, who are you to despise her? For that one, having known her, loved her always and assuredly. Rather, we should be ashamed and having put on perfect humanity, let us do that which was commanded us. Let us preach the gospel, neither setting boundaries nor laying down laws, as the Savior said."

Having said these things Levi, going out, began to preach the gospel. [The Gospel according to Mary] (9:29–10:14 = Papyrus Rylands 463)

The purpose of the *Gospel of Mary* was to challenge those who "set boundaries" and "lay down laws." Because Peter and Andrew reject Mary's teaching, we probably should infer that those who lay down laws appeal to the better-known apostles whose teachings are preserved in the better-known, more-widely circulated documents of the Christian communities.

The group behind the *Gospel of Mary* is attempting to defend its teachings and, perhaps, the right of women to be teachers, perhaps in opposition to a growing institutionalization of Christianity and an increasing restrictiveness of the role of women (as perhaps seen in the Pastoral Letters). This tension is also attested in the *Gospel of Thomas,* where Peter demands, "Make Mary leave us, for females are not worthy of (eternal) life" (114). Jesus rebukes Peter, declaring that he will be able to transform Mary into a male so that she and all other women thus transformed will gain entry into the kingdom of heaven.[17]

In some recent writings, including Dan Brown's popular novel *The Da Vinci Code,* it has been speculated that Jesus and Mary were lovers, perhaps married. Those who hold this view appeal to the *Gospel of Mary,* where it says: "Sister, we know that you were much loved by the Savior, as no other woman." The *Gospel of Philip* is also appealed to: "And the companion of the [Savior is] Mary Magdalene. [But Christ loved] her more than [all] the disciples [and used to] kiss her [often] on her [. . .]" (NHC 2.3.63.32-36). Some translations restore the text to read, "he used to kiss her often on her mouth," but that is pure conjecture. The author of this text may have imagined that Jesus kissed Mary often on the hand, forehead or cheek. We don't know what the original text said, and in any case there is no warrant for assuming from these passages in the *Gospel of Mary* and the *Gospel of Philip* that Jesus and Mary were lovers. The texts do *not* say this. There is no evidence from antiquity that anyone thought this.

The *Gospel of Mary* may well reflect struggles over church polity, the role of women, the issue of legalism in one form or another, and the limits of apostolic authority. But this writing, however it is to be understood, reflects a setting no earlier than the middle of the second century. We find in it nothing that with any confidence can be traced to the first century or traced back to the life and ministry of the historical Jesus and the historical Mary Magdalene.[18]

THE *SECRET GOSPEL OF MARK*

At the annual Society of Biblical Literature meeting in New York in 1960 Morton Smith announced that during his sabbatical leave in 1958, at the

Mar Saba Monastery in the Judean wilderness, he found the first part of a letter of Clement of Alexandria (c. A.D. 150-215) penned in Greek, in what was said to be an eighteenth-century hand, in the back of a seventeenth-century edition of the letters of Ignatius. In 1973 Smith published two editions of his find, one learned and one popular. From the start, scholars suspected that the text was a forgery and that Smith was himself the forger. Many scholars—including several members of the Jesus Seminar—defended Smith and the authenticity of the Clementine letter.

What made the alleged find so controversial were two quotations of a mystical or secret version of the Gospel of Mark, quotations of passages not found in the canonical Gospel of Mark. In the first, longer passage, Jesus raises a dead man and then later, in the nude, instructs the young man in the mysteries of the kingdom of God. The homoerotic orientation of the story is hard to miss. This mystical version of Mark has since become known as the *Secret Gospel of Mark.*

Despite the facts that no one besides Smith has actually studied the physical document and that the paper and ink have never been subjected to the kinds of tests normally undertaken, many scholars have accepted the Clementine letter as genuine and its testimony as valid that there really was in circulation, in the second century, a secret version of the Gospel of Mark. Indeed, some scholars have suggested that *Secret Mark* may help us better understand how the Gospels of Matthew, Mark and Luke relate to one another (that is, the Synoptic Problem), and of course some scholars have suggested that *Secret Mark* is older and more original than public Mark. Learned studies continue to appear, including two recent major monograph-length studies.[19]

The sad thing is that all of this labor has been misspent; the Clementine letter and the quotations of *Secret Mark* embedded within it are a modern hoax, and Morton Smith almost certainly is the perpetrator. Several scholars have for years suspected this to be the case, but the clear, recently published color photographs of the document have given experts in the science of the detection of forgeries the opportunity to analyze the handwriting of the document and compare it with samples of the handwriting of the late Professor Smith.[20] The evidence is compelling and conclusive: Smith wrote the text.

The following is some of the evidence that Stephen Carlson has compiled and analyzed:

1. Magnification of the handwritten text reveals the telltale presence of what handwriting experts call the "forger's tremor." That is, the handwriting in question is not really written; it is drawn, in the forger's attempt to imitate a style of writing not his own. These telltale signs are everywhere present in the alleged Clementine letter.

2. Comparison of the style of the Greek of the handwritten text with Morton Smith's style of writing Greek (as seen in his papers and marginal notes in his books) has shown that Smith is the person who wrote (or "drew") the Clementine letter. For example, Smith had an unusual way of writing the Greek letters tau, theta and lambda. These unusual forms occasionally intrude in what otherwise is a well-executed imitation of eighteenth-century style of Greek handwriting in the document in question.

3. Some of the distinctive themes in the document are in evidence in some of Smith's work published before the alleged find in 1958.

4. The discolored blotch that is plainly visible in the lower left-hand corner of the final page of the printed text of the volume and in the lower left-hand corner of the second page of the handwritten text prove that the handwritten pages were originally part of the printed edition of the letters of Ignatius. These corresponding blotches, as well as many of the other blotches and discolorations that can be seen in the color photographs, are mildew. The presence of this mildew strongly suggests that the book in question was not originally a part of the library of Mar Saba, whose dry climate does not produce mold and mildew in books. The mildew in the printed edition of the letters of Ignatius suggests that the book in which the alleged Clementine letter was discovered spent most of its existence in Europe. We may speculate that in Europe, or perhaps in North America, the book was purchased and the Clementine letter was drawn onto the blank end papers. The book was then taken to the Mar Saba Monastery, where it was subsequently "found" in the library.

5. One of the Mar Saba documents cataloged by Smith is written in the same hand as the alleged Clementine letter. This document Smith dated to the twentieth century (not to the eighteenth century, as in the case of the

Clementine letter). Moreover, the document Smith dates to the twentieth century is signed "M. Madiotes." This name is a pseudo-Greek name, whose root means "sphere" or "globe," or, in reference to a person, "baldy." Carlson plausibly suggests that here Smith, who was quite bald, is facetiously alluding to himself (that is, "M[orton] the baldhead").

6. The entire story—finding a long-lost document in the Mar Saba Monastery that is potentially embarrassing to Christianity—is foreshadowed by James Hunter's *The Mystery of Mar Saba* (New York: Evangelical Publishers, 1940). Indeed, one of the heroes of the story, who helps to unmask the perpetrators and expose the fraud, is Scotland Yard Inspector Lord Moreton. The parallels between Morton Smith's alleged Mar Saba discovery and Hunter's Mar Saba mystery are fascinating. It should be added that Smith says in the preface to his publication of the Clementine letter that his invitation to visit Mar Saba came in 1941 (the year after the publication of Hunter's novel).

7. Carlson plausibly identifies the motives behind Smith's playful deception. We need not go into these details in this context. They possess a great deal of explanatory power.

The upshot of the whole matter is that Smith's Mar Saba Clementine is almost certainly a hoax and Smith the hoaxer. No research into the Gospels and the historical Jesus should take Smith's document seriously. Yet some scholars have made bold claims about the origins, dates and meaning of the New Testament Gospels on the basis of this spurious writing.[21]

CONCLUSION

Many scholarly portraits and reconstructions of the historical Jesus are badly distorted through the use of documents that are late and of dubious historical value. The irony is that in trying to "go behind" the New Testament Gospels to find truth buried under layers of tradition and theology, some scholars depend on documents that were composed sixty to one hundred years after the New Testament Gospels. This is a strange way to proceed.

Three of the five extracanonical Gospels reviewed in chapters three and four originated in the second half of the second century. These are the *Gospel of Thomas,* the Egerton Papyrus, and the *Gospel of Mary.* A fourth writing, the

Akhmîm Gospel fragment, also cannot date earlier than the middle of the second century, if indeed it is the *Gospel of Peter* mentioned by Bishop Serapion at the beginning of the third century. But there are grave doubts that this document is the *Gospel of Peter* in the first place. The Akhmîm Gospel fragment may be part of an unknown writing from an even later period of time. In any case, scholars are in no position to extract from the Akhmîm fragment a hypothetical mid-first-century Passion and resurrection narrative on which the first century New Testament Gospels relied. Such a theory completely lacks a critical basis.

The remaining document—the quotations of the *Secret Gospel of Mark,* embedded in a long-lost letter by Clement of Alexandria—is a modern hoax and therefore has nothing to offer critical scholarship concerned with Christian origins and the emergence of the Jesus and Gospel tradition. Yet this writing, along with the other texts, has been used in historical Jesus research.

The scholarly track record with respect to the use of these extracanonical Gospels is, frankly, embarrassing. In marked contrast to the hypercritical approach many scholars take to the canonical Gospels, several scholars are surprisingly uncritical in their approach to the extracanonical Gospels. Apart from the all-too-common human desire to challenge authority, it is hard to explain why scholars give such credence to documents that reflect settings that are entirely foreign to pre-A.D. 70 Jewish Palestine and at the same time reflect traditions and tendencies found in documents known to have emerged in later times and in places outside of Palestine.

Some of these scholars have even suggested reopening the New Testament canon to make room for works like the *Gospel of Thomas.* Professor Philip Jenkins, who is a historian and an "outsider" to historical Jesus research, remarks:

> Reviewing suggestions for a potentially revised New Testament canon, we are repeatedly struck by just how weak are the claims of most of the candidates. . . . Contrary to recent claims, the more access we have to ancient "alternative gospels," the more we must respect the choices made by the early church in forming its canon.[22]

Indeed. When students ask me why certain Gospels were omitted from the canon of the New Testament and whether some of them ought to be included, I tell them to read these Gospels. They do, and that answers their questions.

In this and the previous chapter we have reviewed the extracanonical Gospels that are most often appealed to as potentially important sources for understanding the historical Jesus, sources that supposedly supplement and sometimes even correct the Gospels of the New Testament. We have found that these extracanonical Gospels do not offer early, reliable tradition, independent of what we possess in the New Testament Gospels. The extracanonical Gospels are late and almost always reflect a context far removed in time and place from first-century Palestine. The scholarly predilection for settings foreign to first-century Palestine is the subject of chapter five.

5

ALIEN CONTEXTS

The Case Against Jesus as Cynic

Various scholars in the twentieth century have portrayed Jesus as a Pharisee, an Essene, a prophet, a great moral teacher, a philosopher, a charismatic holy man or a magician. These portraits, like Renaissance religious art in which Jesus and his disciples are depicted in sixteenth-century Venetian or Parisian dress, often tell us more about the scholars' biases than they do about Jesus in Nazareth or Jerusalem of the first century. Few are as misleading and distorted as the idea that Jesus was a Mediterranean Cynic.

Jesus grew up and ministered in Galilee in the first three decades of the first century A.D. His environment was thoroughly Jewish. His home village was Nazareth. Although the village was small (somewhere between two hundred and four hundred inhabitants), it had a synagogue. There were no pagan temples or schools in Nazareth. In all likelihood not a single non-Jew lived in Nazareth at this time.

Recent excavations in and around Nazareth suggest that the village in the time of Jesus may not have been a sleepy, isolated place (as many have imagined it). There is evidence of vineyards and grape presses, terrace farming, olive presses and the manufacture of olive oil, and even stone masonry. The old, quaint notion that the inhabitants of Nazareth had to look for work in nearby villages and cities is now obsolete. The economy of Nazareth was more than sufficiently active to keep its inhabitants fully occupied.

Of course, Nazareth was not isolated from the rest of Galilee. This is another popular myth still held by some. Nazareth is only a few miles from Sepphoris, a major city, and Nazareth is near a major highway that connects Caesarea Maritima (on the Mediterranean, to the southwest) to Tiberias (on

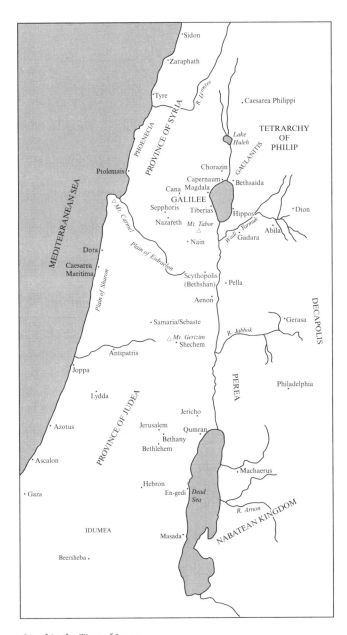

Israel in the Time of Jesus

the Sea of Galilee, to the northeast). Sepphoris, Caesarea Maritima and Tiberias were the three largest and most influential cities in Galilee, and Jesus grew up near one of them and near the highway that linked the other two.

But the Jewish reality of Jesus' upbringing and later ministry is not always appreciated in some of the books that have been published in recent years. Most writers, of course, acknowledge that Jesus was Jewish, but they propose strange contexts and settings in which they think Jesus should be interpreted. Some of these proposed contexts and settings simply did not exist in the Galilee of Jesus' day. This tendency, however, is not just a modern one; it is ancient as well. Pagans, Jews and Gnostics in the first two or three centuries A.D. expressed a variety of opinions of who Jesus was and what he was like.

ANCIENT INTERPRETATIONS OF JESUS

Non-Christians viewed the Christian movement with grave suspicions. Christians were regarded as lawless because they either did not obey the law of Moses or did not worship Caesar and the gods of the Romans. Christians were even accused of cannibalism, which was probably a gross misunderstanding of the Eucharist or Lord's Supper. Christians sometimes suffered terrible persecution, such as what took place at the hands of Nero, the mentally imbalanced megalomaniac who was emperor from A.D. 54 to 68.

The Romans tended to view Jesus as little more than a troublemaker. The great historian Tacitus, writing in the early second century A.D., described Jesus (called "Christus") as the founder of a "pernicious superstition," an evil that originated in Judea and eventually took hold in Rome itself, "where all things horrible and shameful collect and are practiced." Less extravagantly, his contemporary, Suetonius, viewed Jesus (whom he called "Chrestus") as an instigator of unrest, which may have been related in some way to the decision by Emperor Claudius in the middle of the first century to expel the Jews from Rome. Pliny the Younger, governor of Bithynia in the early second century, wrote to Emperor Trajan stating that Christians recited "a hymn antiphonally to Christus as to a god." He goes on to say that they "bound themselves with an oath not to commit any crime, but to abstain from theft, robbery, adultery, breach of faith, and embezzlement of property entrusted to them." Pliny's description suggests that the Christians he interrogated were slaves.

Greek writers held similar views. Celsus acknowledged Jesus' Jewish origins but said he apprenticed in Egypt as a magician. Evidently Jesus was successful. On "account of those powers [Jesus] gave himself the title of God." Lucian of Samosata says Christians worship Jesus, "the man who was crucified in Palestine," as a god. Far more generously, Mara bar Serapion, a Syrian in a letter to his son, regards Jesus as the "wise king" of the Jews, comparable to philosophers like Pythagoras and Socrates.

The opinions of the Jewish rabbis from about the same time are more uniform and negative. Jesus is viewed as a false prophet who practiced magic and led Israel astray. Accordingly, he was hanged on the eve of Passover. Moreover, his resurrection is linked in some way to incantations. Indeed, healing in the name of Jesus—no matter how effective—is not permitted. It might also be mentioned here that Josephus, who was not a rabbi but lived in the first century and became a historian and apologist, described Jesus as a "doer of amazing deeds, a teacher of persons who receive truth with pleasure." More will be said about Josephus in chapter eight.

The Gnostics (that is, "Knowers"), who absorbed some trappings of Christian teaching, viewed Jesus primarily as a revealer—not as the Messiah. They also described him in a variety of ways. According to them, Jesus appeared to his disciples as a child, or alternatively as an old man. His disciples were not always sure what to make of him, comparing him to an angel or even to a wise philosopher. Jesus' teaching was viewed as mysterious. In fact, it was so powerful, not even his own disciples could stand before Jesus and look him in the eyes.[1]

A MODERN INTERPRETATION: JESUS THE CYNIC?

Modern portraits have also run the gamut. Over the last century or so Jesus has been presented as a Pharisee (of one stripe or another), an Essene, a prophet or a great moral teacher. In more recent times Jesus has been interpreted as a philosopher, a rabbi, a sage, a charismatic holy man and a magician. Indeed, some of these portraits combine two or more of these categories.[2] The teachings of Jesus have also been compared to those of the Buddha.[3]

Perhaps one of the strangest proposals to come from qualified scholars in recent years is that Jesus was a Cynic. This line of interpretation has been em-

GRECO-ROMAN WRITERS ON JESUS

Cornelius Tacitus (c. A.D. 56-c. 118) was proconsul of Asia (A.D. 112-113), friend of Pliny the Younger and author of *Annals* and the *Histories*. Only portions of these works are extant. In *Annals* 15.44 he provides a passing reference to Jesus:

> Therefore, to squelch the rumor [that the burning of Rome had taken place by order], Nero supplied (as culprits) and punished in the most extraordinary fashion those hated for their vice, whom the crowd called "Christians." Christus, the author of their name, had suffered the death penalty during the reign of Tiberius, by sentence of the procurator *[sic]* Pontius Pilate. The pernicious superstition was checked for a time, only to break out once more, not merely in Judea, the origin of the evil, but in the capital itself, where all things horrible and shameful collect and are practiced.

In his fifth volume of *De Vita Caesarum* (c. A.D. 120) the Roman historian Suetonius refers to the expulsion of the Jews from Rome in A.D. 49 during the reign of Claudius (*Divus Claudius* 25.4; see Acts 18:2). In his description he refers to one "Chrestus":

> [Claudius] expelled the Jews from Rome who, instigated by Chrestus *[sic],* continuously caused unrest.

Pliny the Younger (or Gaius Plinius Caecilius Secundus, c. 61-c. 113), who in A.D. 111-113 was the governor of Bithynia in Asia Minor, wrote to Emperor Trajan for advice in how to deal with Christians. The passage that is of interest is found in his *Epistles* book 10, letter 96:

> They [the Christians] assured me that the sum total of their error consisted in the fact that they regularly assembled on a certain day before daybreak. They recited a hymn antiphonally to Christus as to a god and bound themselves with an oath not to commit any crime, but to abstain from theft, robbery, adultery, breach of faith, and embezzlement of property entrusted to them. After this it was their custom to separate, and then to come together again to partake of a meal, but an ordinary and innocent one.

According to Celsus (second century A.D.), a critic of early Christianity (as quoted by Origen):

> Jesus kept all the Jewish customs, and even took part in their sacrifices. (*Contra Celsum* 2.6)

He was brought up in secret and hired himself out as a workman in Egypt, and having tried his hand at certain magical powers he returned from there, and on account of those powers gave himself the title of God." (*Contra Celsum* 1.38)

Lucian of Samosata (c. A.D. 115-c. 200) refers to Jesus. According to *Passing of Peregrinus* 11:

Christians . . . revered him as a god, used him as a lawgiver, and set him down as a protector—to be sure, after that other whom they still worship, the man who was crucified in Palestine because he introduced this new cult into the world.

Some years after Rome conquered Comagena and its capital Samosata in A.D. 72, Mara bar Serapion, while in prison, wrote a letter to his son Serapion in which he said:

For what advantage did the Athenians gain by the murder of Socrates, the recompense of which they received in famine and pestilence? Or the people of Samos by the burning of Pythagoras, because in one hour their country was entirely covered in sand? Or the Jews by the death of their wise king, because from that same time their kingdom was taken away? God justly avenged these three wise men: the Athenians died of hunger; the Samians were overwhelmed by the sea; the Jews, ruined and driven from their land, live in complete dispersion. But Socrates did not die for good; he lived on in the teaching of Plato. Pythagoras did not die for good; he lived on in the statue of Hera. Nor did the wise king die for good; he lived on in the teaching, which he had given.

braced by some of the members of the Jesus Seminar. In his popular book on the historical Jesus, John Dominic Crossan argues that Jesus was a "peasant Jewish Cynic" and that Jesus and his followers were "hippies in a world of Augustan yuppies."[4] Although in places Crossan's work is helpful and occasionally insightful, the Cynic proposal is misguided and misleading. Given the popularity of Crossan's book and the support the Cynic hypothesis has found among a few other scholars, we will look at the evidence rather closely.

Who were the ancient Cynics, what did they believe, and how did they

ANCIENT JEWISH WRITERS ON JESUS

On the ministry of Jesus:

> Jesus had five disciples: Matthai, Nakai, Nezer, Buni, and Todah. (*b. Sanhedrin* 107b)

> Jesus practiced magic and led Israel astray. (*b. Sanhedrin* 43a)

On the teaching of Jesus:

> He [a judge] said to them, "I looked at the end of the book, in which it is written, '*I am not come to take away the Law of Moses and I am not come to add to the Law of Moses*' [see Mt 5:17], and it is written, 'where there is a son, a daughter does not inherit.'"

> She said to him, "*Let your light shine forth as a lamp*" [see Mt 5:16]. R. Gamaliel said to her, "The ass came and kicked the lamp over." (*b. Shabbat* 116b)

On the crucifixion of Jesus:

> On the eve of Passover they hanged Jesus the Nazarene. And a herald went out, in front of him, for forty days saying: "He is going to be stoned, because he practiced sorcery and enticed and led Israel astray. Let anyone who knows anything in his favor come and plead on his behalf." But, not having found anything in his favor, they hanged him on the eve of Passover. (*b. Sanhedrin* 43a)

On the resurrection of Jesus:

> He then went and raised Jesus by incantation. (*b. Gittin* 57a, ms. M)

On healing in the name of Jesus:

> It once happened that ben Dama, the son of R. Ishmael's sister, was bitten by a serpent; and Jacob [James?], a native of Kefar Sekaniah, came to him in the name of Jesus ben Pantera. But R. Ishmael did not permit him. (*t. Hullin* 2.22)

t. = Tosefta
b. = Babylonian Talmud

---

live? Cynicism was founded by Diogenes (c. 412-321 B.C.). The nickname *Cynic* comes from the Greek word meaning "doggish" or "doglike." Cynics earned this dubious sobriquet because of their ragged, unkempt appearance. Attractive apparel and grooming meant nothing to them. And, like dogs, Cynics would urinate and defecate in public. Yes, they could be quite gross.

The Cynic typically carried a cloak, a beggar's purse and a staff, and usually went barefoot. In a letter to his father, Diogenes says, "Do not be upset, Father, that I am called a dog and put on a double, coarse cloak, carry a purse over my shoulders, and have a staff in my hand."

This dress code has encouraged a few scholars to see significant parallels between Jesus and Cynics. After all, so goes the argument, Jesus gave his disciples similar instructions:

- He charged them to take nothing for their journey except a staff; they should take no bread, no bag, no money in their belts but to wear sandals and not put on two tunics. (Mk 6:8-9)

- "Take no gold, nor silver, nor copper in your belts, no bag for your journey, nor two tunics, nor sandals, nor a staff; for the laborer deserves his food." (Mt 10:9-10)

- "Take nothing for your journey, no staff, nor bag, nor bread, nor money; and do not have two tunics." (Lk 9:3)

- "Carry no purse, no bag, no sandals; and salute no one on the road." (Lk 10:4)

Are Jesus' instructions in step with the Cynic dress code? Clearly not. Jesus' instructions in fact do not agree with Cynic dress and conduct; they contradict them. The very things Jesus tells his disciples not to take with them (no bag, no tunic and no staff either, if we follow the version in Matthew and Luke) are the characteristic markers of the true Cynic, as one observer from late antiquity put it: "What makes a Cynic is his purse and his staff and his big mouth."[5] There is nothing Cynic-like in Jesus' instructions to his disciples.

The only parallel with Jesus is simply in giving instructions with regard to what to wear and what to take on one's journey. The only specific agreement is taking a staff (if we follow Mark; if we do not, then there is no agreement at all). The staff, however, is hardly distinctive to Cynics. On the contrary, in the Jewish context the staff has a long and distinguished association with the patriarchs, such as Jacob and Judah (Gen 32:10; 38:18), and the great lawgiver Moses and his brother Aaron (Ex 4:4; 7:9). Moreover, the staff is also a symbol

GNOSTIC WRITERS ON JESUS

On the manifestations of Jesus:

> Jesus took them all by stealth, for he did not reveal himself in the manner [in which] he was, but it was in the manner in which [they would] be able to see him that he revealed himself. He revealed himself to [them all. He revealed himself] to the great as great. He [revealed himself] to the small as small. He [revealed himself to the] angels as an angel, and to men as a man. (*Gospel of Philip* 57.28–58.2 [NHC 2.3])

> [And I was afraid, and behold I] saw in the light [a youth who stood] by me. While I looked [at him he became] like an old man. And he [changed his] form (again), becoming like a servant. (*Secret Book of John* 2.1-5 [NHC 2.1])

> Often he did not appear to his disciples as himself, but he was found among them as a child. (*Gospel of Judas* 33.19-21)

> Jesus said to his disciples: "Compare me to someone and tell me whom I am like." Simon Peter said to him, "You are like a righteous angel." Matthew said to him, "You are like a wise philosopher." Thomas said to him, "Master, my mouth is wholly incapable of saying whom you are like." (*Gospel of Thomas* 13, 34.30-35.4 [NHC 2.2])

On the power of Jesus' secret teaching:

> And he took (Thomas) and withdrew and told him three things. When Thomas returned to his companions, they asked him, "What did Jesus say to you?" Thomas said to them, "If I tell you one of the things that he told me, you will pick up stones and throw them at me; [and] a fire will come out of the stones and burn you up." (*Gospel of Thomas* 13, 35.7-14 [NHC 2.2])

> The spirits of (the disciples) did not dare to stand before [him], except for Judas Iscariot. He was able to stand before him, but he could not look him in the eyes, and he turned his face away. (*Gospel of Judas* 35.7-13)

Translations: James M. Robinson (ed.), *The Nag Hammadi Library* (Leiden: Brill, 1977); Rodolphe Kasser, Marvin Meyer, and Gregor Wurst, *The Gospel of Judas* (Washington, D.C.: National Geographic Society, 2006).

of royal authority, figuring in texts that in later interpretation take on messianic and eschatological significance (for example, Gen 49:10; Is 11:4; Ezek 19:14).

Besides the question of dress, some scholars suggest that Jesus' worldview is Cynic. Instead of being caught up with materialism and vanity, the Cynic lives a life of simplicity and integrity before God. According to one ancient writer, the "end and aim of the Cynic philosophy . . . is happiness, but happiness that consists in living according to nature."[6] Living according to nature also means treating fellow human beings as equals. A few scholars apparently think that this is more or less what Jesus taught. Was it? Here are teachings that are sometimes cited to make this point:

> And why are you anxious about clothing? Consider the lilies of the field, how they grow; they neither toil nor spin; yet I tell you, even Solomon in all his glory was not arrayed like one of these. But if God so clothes the grass of the field, which today is alive and tomorrow is thrown into the oven, will he not much more clothe you, O men of little faith? Therefore do not be anxious, saying, "What shall we eat?" or "What shall we drink?" or "What shall we wear?" For the Gentiles seek all these things; and your heavenly Father knows that you need them all. But seek first his kingdom and his righteousness, and all these things shall be yours as well. (Mt 6:28-33)

> You shall love your neighbor as yourself. (Mk 12:31; see Lev 19:18)

> For if you forgive people their trespasses, your heavenly Father also will forgive you; but if you do not forgive people their trespasses, neither will your Father forgive your trespasses. (Mt 6:14-15)

Superficially, Jesus' teaching is at points comparable to Cynic teaching. But Jesus' teaching is different at other significant points. For example, Jesus did not teach his disciples to pursue happiness and to live according to nature. What he taught was that nature reveals important things about God, namely, that he is loving, good and generous. Jesus urges his disciples to have faith and live in the light of God's goodness and care. But in the end the disciple is to seek God's kingdom (or rule) and righteousness. Then all the rest will fall into place. When the core values are understood, the profound differences between Jesus and the Cynics cannot be missed.

Cynics were also known for flouting social custom and etiquette, such as urinating, defecating and engaging in sexual intercourse in public.[7] Cynics

A "CYNIC" JESUS?

Jesus to his disciples:

> "Take no gold, nor silver, nor copper in your belts, no purse for your journey, nor two tunics, nor sandals, nor a staff." (Mt 10:9-10)

Crates to his students:

> Cynic philosophy is Diogenean, the Cynic is one who toils according to this philosophy, and to be a Cynic is to take a short cut in doing philosophy. Consequently, do not fear the name [Cynic], nor for this reason shun the cloak and purse, which are the weapons of the gods. For they are quickly displayed by those who are honored for their character. (*Cynic Epistles* 16)

Diogenes to Hicetas:

> Do not be upset, Father, that I am called a dog [that is, "Cynic"] and put on a double, coarse cloak, carry a purse over my shoulders, and have a staff in my hand. (*Cynic Epistles* 7)

Diogenes to Antipater:

> I hear that you say I am doing nothing unusual in wearing a double, ragged cloak and carrying a purse. (*Cynic Epistles* 15)

Diogenes to Anaxilaus:

> For a scepter I have my staff and for a mantle the double, ragged cloak, and by way of exchange, my leather purse is a shield. (*Cynic Epistles* 19)

For full texts of these epistles, see Abraham J. Malherbe, *The Cynic Epistles,* SBLSBS 12 (Missoula, Mont.: Scholars Press, 1977).

could be coarse and rude. In fact, one was remembered to have retorted, "What difference does it make to me, from which end the noise comes?"[8] There simply is no parallel to this kind of thinking or behavior in the teaching and lifestyle of Jesus and his disciples.

Jesus did indeed criticize some of his contemporaries for their religiosity, hypocrisy and mean-spiritedness toward the poor and marginalized:

Thus, when you give alms, sound no trumpet before you, as the hypocrites do in the synagogues and in the streets, that they may be praised by people. (Mt 6:2)

And when you pray, you must not be like the hypocrites; for they love to stand and pray in the synagogues and at the street corners, that they may be seen by people. (Mt 6:5)

And when you fast, do not look dismal, like the hypocrites, for they disfigure their faces that their fasting may be seen by people. (Mt 6:16)

Woe to you, scribes and Pharisees, hypocrites! For you tithe mint and dill and cummin, and have neglected the weightier matters of the law, justice and mercy and faith; these you ought to have done, without neglecting the others. (Mt 23:23)

Woe to you, scribes and Pharisees, hypocrites! For you build the tombs of the prophets and adorn the monuments of the righteous, saying, "If we had lived in the days of our fathers, we would not have taken part with them in shedding the blood of the prophets." (Mt 23:29-30)

You leave the commandment of God, and hold fast the tradition of people. (Mk 7:8)

Admittedly, all of this criticism could have been uttered by a Cynic. But this represents only one aspect of Jesus' teaching. Jesus criticized some of his critics, but he was not crude, nor did he suggest that religious faith was pointless. Herein lies a telling difference between the worldview of Jesus and that of Cynics. Whereas the latter railed against religion because the gods, they thought, were indifferent, Jesus urged his followers to believe in God, because he does take notice and cares deeply. Indeed, some of Jesus' statements we have looked at go on to assure that "your Father who sees in secret will reward you" (Mt 6:6, 18). Accordingly, Jesus urges his disciples to pray, "for your Father knows what you need before you ask him" (Mt 6:8). This is not the teaching of the Cynics.

Furthermore, Jesus proclaimed God's rule and urged his disciples to look to God for deliverance. Jesus longed for the redemption of his people and

JEWISH CUSTOMS AND SENSITIVITIES

Life in the Greco-Roman world in the time of Jesus was not easy for Jewish people who were committed to living according to Jewish law and customs. It is understandable that many, especially those living outside the land of Israel, compromised and accommodated themselves to non-Jewish customs. But many Jews did not.

For Jews who wished to maintain their ethnic and religious identity, it was important to observe laws and customs pertaining to food, to the sabbath and other holy days, and to aspects concerning personal purity. This meant avoiding pork and other meat not properly prepared, refraining from work on the sabbath, and avoiding activities and places that were morally and ritually suspect. Devout Jews avoided public baths, brothels, arenas, pagan shrines and temples, and the prostitutes that sometimes were part of these facilities. Jewish cities typically did not construct such buildings and did not permit such activities. Of course, the smaller the percentage of the Jewish population and the less the Jewish influence, the more likely some or all of these buildings would be present in a given city.

In the land of Israel itself these sensitivities were even greater. Not only would Jewish cities and villages not accommodate these buildings and activities, there were attempts to avoid or at least limit the trappings of paganism, including the circulation of coins with images of Caesar and legends describing Caesar as "god" or "son of god," and the placement of statues and idols of Greco-Roman deities. Not only did devout Jews wish to avoid personal impurity, they were concerned with the purity of the land itself. The presence of such pagan items would defile the land.

Of course, within the land of Israel and just east of the Jordan River there were several non-Jewish cities (such as Gerasa and Scythopolis, part of an area called the Decapolis), where Jewish customs were not observed.

---

believed deeply that the God of Israel would fulfill the prophecies and promises of old. These hopes and beliefs are not consistent with Cynic ideology.

Thus, I remain completely unpersuaded by the Cynic thesis. And I am not alone; most scholars concerned with the historical Jesus also find the thesis unlikely.[9] This should not be surprising, given the evidence I have cited. So why do some scholars compare Jesus with the Cynics? Good question.

THE ARCHAEOLOGICAL EVIDENCE

Comparison with Cynic thought was encouraged in part by a number of parallels, most of which are general and reflect the wisdom and social criticism of the eastern Mediterranean world of late antiquity.[10] But a major impetus for the exploration of the Cynic model came, I believe, from archaeological discoveries in the 1970s and 1980s. Boiled down, these discoveries comprise two things: First, archaeology shows how widespread the Greek language was in the time and place of Jesus. Second, it shows how urbanized, in Greco-Roman fashion, some parts of Galilee were in the time of Jesus. As it turns out, Galilee was far more integrated into the larger Roman Empire than at one time imagined. Galilee, Samaria and Judea were no backwater.

From these two discoveries some scholars infer the presence of Greco-Roman philosophy in Galilee. The logic goes something like this: Where there were Greco-Roman-style urban centers, and where Greek was spoken, it follows that there were Greco-Roman philosophers and philosophies. And that means, of course, the presence of Cynics. And then, when Sepphoris, some four miles north of Nazareth, was excavated and found to have possessed a paved main street and several large buildings in Greco-Roman style, it was further concluded that Cynics must have been present in this city as well. And if Cynics were present in Sepphoris, then surely Jewish youths—like Jesus—living in nearby villages like Nazareth would have come under the influence of these itinerant philosophers. This all seems to make sense, doesn't it? But is something missing? Alas, I am afraid it is—the rest of the evidence.

Why shouldn't we think Cynics were wandering about Sepphoris? The impressive discoveries in Galilee in general and in Sepphoris in particular have forced New Testament interpreters to reevaluate several things. For one, it is no longer tenable to think of Jesus as having grown up in rustic isolation—as was fashionable to think for so long. Jesus grew up in a village within reasonable walking distance from a large urban center, part of which was perched atop a hill and would have been visible to the inhabitants of Nazareth. "A city set on a hill cannot be hid," as Jesus himself once said (Mt 5:14).

Furthermore, the great number of Greek inscriptions as well as Greek literary finds in the Dead Sea region has led many scholars to conclude that Greek was spoken by many Jews living in Galilee. This does not mean that Greek was their first language; Aramaic was. But it does mean that Greek was spoken in the time and place of Jesus. (And a few scholars think that Jesus himself spoke some Greek.)

But the fact that many Jewish Galileans spoke Greek and that there were urban centers in Galilee, such as Sepphoris near Nazareth and Tiberias on the Sea of Galilee just a few miles southwest of Capernaum, does not mean that the Jewish people were soft on their historic faith and ready to absorb Greek philosophy, whether Cynicism or something else. Recent Jewish history suggests just the opposite.

We should remember that a century and a half before Jesus was born, the Jewish people, led by the Hasmonean family (that is, Judas Maccabeus and his brothers), fought a bitter war against Antiochus IV and the Greeks in order to preserve Jewish faith and life. Galilean Jews in the time of Jesus were no doubt influenced by Greek thought and customs to some extent, but not to the extent of embracing ideologies that seriously conflicted with Jewish faith.

And this is just what the archaeological evidence shows. So how Greek was Sepphoris, the city near the village of Nazareth, in the time of Jesus? This is an important question. Much of the archaeological work in the 1970s and 1980s revealed the extent of building. Besides paved, colonnaded streets and large buildings, a public theater was also excavated. Although it is disputed, it is likely that the first phase of the theater was built in the 20s and later expansion and renovation took place later in the century. But it was the further archaeological work in the 1990s, which included the discovery of the city dump, that led to the conclusion that Sepphoris was a thoroughly *Jewish* city in the days of Jesus.

Archaeologists are usually able to date the various layers of ancient cities. We might think of an ancient city as a layered cake. The top layer is the most recent; the bottom layer is the most ancient. Therefore, the deeper archaeologists dig, the older the material they find.

Archaeologists and scholars usually assume that most things that existed prior to A.D. 70 probably have relevance for understanding the world of

THE JEWISH STRUGGLE TO PRESERVE THE FAITH

For a variety of reasons, Antiochus IV, the Greek ruler of the empire that controlled Israel in the second century B.C., tried to outlaw the Jewish religion. He forbade circumcision, possession and production of copies of the law of Moses, and insisted that Jews eat pork and honor the Greek gods. Antiochus even called himself "Epiphanes," which implied that he was a physical manifestation of a god.

Jews who resisted the decree of Antiochus suffered grievously. One of the books of the Old Testament Apocrypha—2 Maccabees—provides a graphic account of the torture inflicted on Eleazar, a devout Jewish elder, and on a Jewish mother and her seven sons.

> Eleazar, one of the scribes in high position, a man now advanced in age and of noble presence, was being forced to open his mouth to eat swine's flesh. But he, welcoming death with honor rather than life with pollution, went up to the rack of his own accord, spitting out the flesh, as men ought to go who have the courage to refuse things that it is not right to taste, even for the natural love of life. (2 Macc 6:18-20)

> It happened also that seven brothers and their mother were arrested and were being compelled by the king, under torture with whips and cords, to partake of unlawful swine's flesh. One of them, acting as their spokesman, said, "What do you intend to ask and learn from us? For we are ready to die rather than transgress the laws of our fathers." (2 Macc 7:1-2)

In the time of Jesus and his disciples, these people, sometimes referred to as the Maccabean martyrs, were regarded as heroes of the faith. They set the example that all devout Jews should be willing to follow.

Jesus, while most things that came into existence after A.D. 70 probably do not have relevance. Accordingly, it is important to date the remains of Sepphoris that existed prior to A.D. 70 before we draw conclusions about what this city may tell us about Jesus and his world.

Archaeologists of the land of Israel usually can find the A.D. 70 layer in the excavation cake because of the devastation that resulted in the Jewish revolt from Rome (A.D. 66-70). Many cities and villages were badly damaged if not destroyed altogether. Damaged and destroyed buildings often became the fill and foundations on which the new structures were built.

Archaeologists of Sepphoris have found the A.D. 70 layer and the city dump. The dump is a great find because garbage reveals a lot about the people who lived at that time, especially when we are interested in knowing whether Jews lived in the city and whether they lived according to Jewish laws and customs. What archaeologists discovered is revealing.

Among the animal remains that date before A.D. 70 archaeologists have found virtually no pig bones, which is hard to explain if we are to imagine the presence of a significant non-Jewish population in Sepphoris.[11] In stark contrast to this finding, after A.D. 70 (that is, after the destruction of Jerusalem by the Roman army and the beginning of rebuilding throughout Israel) and after a sizeable growth in the non-Jewish population, pig bones come to represent 30 percent of the animal remains. This suggests that prior to the Jewish revolt, the population of Sepphoris was Jewish and observed the Jewish laws and customs. It was only after the revolt that support for Jewish law began to erode. This means that in the time of Jesus (a generation or more before the revolt), there was little and possibly no non-Jewish presence in Sepphoris. And this means there were no Cynics either.

But there is more evidence that supports this conclusion. Over one hundred fragments of stone vessels have been unearthed thus far, dating from before A.D. 70, again pointing to a Jewish population at Sepphoris concerned with ritual purity (that is because stone vessels—unlike ceramic vessels—cannot easily be made unclean [see Jn 2:6]). Non-Jews usually did not bother with expensive, heavy and hard to move stone vessels. For non-Jews ceramic vessels for drinking and cooking were quite acceptable. The large number of stone vessels found at Sepphoris is consistent with the absence of pork bones. That is, the people who lived in Sepphoris prior to A.D. 70 were Jewish and observed Jewish laws and customs. Consistent with concern over personal purity is the presence in Sepphoris of many *mikvoth,* or ritual bathing pools. Furthermore, a Hebrew pottery fragment and several lamp fragments bearing the image of the menorah (the seven-branched candelabra) have also been found, dating from the early period.

But there is still more. Coins minted at Sepphoris during the pre-A.D. 70 period do not depict the image of the Roman emperor or pagan deities (as was

THE CONTRAST IN THE FINDINGS AT SEPPHORIS

Before A.D. 70

What was found	*What was not found*
immersion pools (*mikvoth*)	pig bones
menorah	coins with image of Caesar
fragments of stone vessels	pagan idols and images
	pagan buildings (for example,
	odeum, nymphaeum, gymnasium,
	shrines)

After A.D. 70
What was found
pig bones
coins with image of Caesar
pagan idols and images
mosaics with pagan themes

commonly found on the coins of this time). In contrast, in the second century A.D. (long after the Jewish revolt had ended and the population had begun to change) coins were minted at Sepphoris bearing the images of the emperors Trajan (A.D. 98-117) and Antoninus Pius (A.D. 138-161), and the deities Tyche and the Capitoline triad. Indeed, in the reign of Antoninus Pius the city adopted the name Diocaesarea, in honor of Zeus (Dio) and the Roman emperor (Caesar).

What has not been found in pre-A.D. 70 Sepphoris is just as important as what has been found. Excavations have not uncovered any structures typically present in a Greco-Roman city (such as pagan temples, gymnasium, odeum, nymphaeum or shrines and statues, all of which were offensive to Jewish sensibilities). One way of looking at it is that devout Jews were not advocates of multiculturalism. It is only in the post-A.D. 70 period that pagan art and architecture begin to make their appearance (such as the beautiful mosaic, found in a mansion, depicting pagan themes). All this evidence leads to the firm conclusion that Sepphoris in Jesus' day was a thoroughly Jewish city.[12] There is absolutely no reason whatsoever to think there may have been Cynics loitering in the streets of Sepphoris, on the lookout for Jewish youths from nearby Nazareth village.

Commitment to the Jewish laws and customs is seen throughout Galilee; it is not limited to Sepphoris. Throughout Galilee the distribution of Jewish and non-Jewish pottery supports this conclusion. Whereas non-Jews purchased Jewish pottery, the Jews of Galilee did not purchase and make use of pottery manufactured by non-Jews. This is because non-Jews had no purity issues in the use of ceramic and pottery; they were happy to buy ceramic from any source—Jewish or non-Jewish. But not so in the case of Jews. From the Jewish perspective, ceramic was susceptible to impurity. Jews therefore pur-

WERE THERE CYNICS IN GALILEE IN THE TIME OF JESUS?

There is no evidence, neither literary nor archaeological, of the presence of a single Cynic in Galilee in the time of Jesus. There was one man, born in Galilee, who after leaving Galilee later embraced Cynicism, but he was not a Cynic when he lived in Galilee. So even this person does not count as a Cynic resident in Galilee in the time of Jesus. Cynicism flourished in an earlier period and, so far as we know, was never an influential presence in Israel.

We have few sources that go back to actual Cynics. What we mostly have are secondhand, idealized portraits of Cynic teaching and behavior. These portraits have been handed down, for the most part, by later Stoics, such as Epictetus. These Stoics admired aspects of Cynic teaching, though they were unwilling to embrace its coarse, difficult lifestyle.

Because most of our information about the Cynics comes from these second- and thirdhand idealized portraits, we really are not in a position to make careful, precise comparison with the teaching of Jesus of Nazareth. Regrettably, some scholars pick and choose from among alleged parallels (which in many cases probably reflect Stoic thought, not Cynic thought), exaggerating the similarities and ignoring the profound differences.

chased pottery only from Jews, never from non-Jews. Accordingly, Jewish pottery that dates prior to A.D. 70 is found in Jewish and non-Jewish sectors in and around Galilee, while non-Jewish pottery is found only in the non-Jewish sectors. These patterns of distribution strongly suggest that the Jewish people of Galilee were scrupulous in their observance of Jewish purity laws.

Furthermore, the actions of the Jewish people in this region also do not bear out the Cynic or Hellenistic interpretation. The revolts that took place after the death of Herod the Great (4 B.C.), the removal of Archelaus and the Roman census (A.D. 6), and the riot in Jerusalem that instigated the great revolt (A.D. 66-70) point to deep-seated Jewish resentment of the pagan presence in Israel as a whole, but also including Galilee.[13] Some of the prominent leaders in these various Jewish rebellions were from Galilee. Thus the evidence—archaeological, literary and historical—shows that despite a Greco-Roman presence in places, Galilean Jews consciously and at times violently attempted to maintain their religious identity and boundaries. Moreover, there is also no archaeological or literary evidence of a Cynic presence in Galilee in the early part of the first century A.D. No evidence whatsoever.

The actions undertaken by certain Jewish figures indicate the degree of commitment to Israel's biblical heritage and future redemption. This is seen in the activity of John the Baptist (c. A.D. 28), who urged fellow Jews to be baptized "in the Jordan" river (Mk 1:2-8). This action as well as reference to "these stones" (Mt 3:9; Lk 3:8) may have been part of a Joshua theme that envisioned a reconquest of the Promised Land (see Josh 4:3, 20-21). Similarly, we later hear of Theudas (c. A.D. 45), who summoned the poor to take up their possessions and join him at the Jordan, whose waters would be divided at the command of the prophet (Josephus *Antiquities of the Jews* 20.97-98; Acts 5:36), and the unnamed Jewish man from Egypt who summoned the faithful to the Mount of Olives that they may might watch the walls of Jerusalem collapse (Josephus, *Antiquities of the Jews* 20.169-70; Acts 21:38). Writings produced after the Romans gained control of Palestine, such as the intertestamental work *Psalms of Solomon* (esp. chaps. 17-18), longed for the expulsion of Gentiles from the land of Israel and for the purification of the land. These biblical ideas and patterns, accompanied by calls for renewal, testify to the strong desire on the part of many Jews to cleanse and restore their sacred land. It was within this thoroughly Jewish environment that Jesus developed and later conducted his ministry.

Given the evidence that Galilee in Jesus' time was populated with a Jewish people committed to their biblical heritage, and given the complete absence of evidence of any kind of Cynic presence in nearby Sepphoris or anywhere else in Galilee for that matter, the idea that Jesus was an itinerant Cynic is ludicrous. Jesus' teaching was much more like that of the rabbis and the Qumran community.

JESUS AND THE LAW OF MOSES

Jesus' respect for the law of Moses is seen in his summary of the greatest commandment (Deut 6:4-5) and the one like it (Lev 19:18):

> Jesus answered, "The first is, 'Hear, O Israel: The Lord our God, the Lord is one; and you shall love the Lord your God with all your heart, and with all your soul, and with all your mind, and with all your strength.' The second is this, 'You shall love your neighbor as yourself.' There is no other commandment greater than these." (Mk 12:29-31)

Jesus justifies his views of the sabbath by appeal to "what David did" (Mk 2:23-28; see 1 Sam 21:1-6). His pronouncement, "The sabbath was made for humans, not humans for the sabbath" (Mk 2:27), finds a close parallel in early rabbinic interpretation:

> "And you shall keep the Sabbath, for it is holy to you" [Ex 31:14]: This means: to you the Sabbath is given over; you are not given over to the Sabbath." (*Mekilta* on Ex 31:12-17 [*Shabbat* 1])[14]

Jesus also held to a high view of the temple and the altar. He teaches his disciples:

> So if you are offering your gift at the altar, and there remember that your brother has something against you, leave your gift there before the altar and go; first be reconciled to your brother, and then come and offer your gift. (Mt 5:23-24)

Jesus' teaching here is completely in step with the perspective of Israel's great prophets (for example, Jer 7:21-26; Hos 6:6; Amos 5:21-24; Mic 6:6-8). His older Jewish contemporary Philo also said something similar: "For, if the worshipper is without kindly feeling or justice, the sacrifices are no sacrifices, the consecrated oblation is desecrated . . . But, if he is pure of heart and just, the sacrifice stands firm." (*On the Life of Moses* 2.107-108). The second-century B.C. Jewish sage Yeshua ben Sira gave similar advice: "Do not offer [God] a bribe, for he will not accept it; and do not trust to an unrighteous sacrifice; for the Lord is the judge, and with him is no partiality" (Sirach 35:12).

What we see here is that at crucial junctures Jesus' teaching presupposes the validity of the law of Moses and in fact agrees with the best opinions on the law offered by Jewish teachers. Jesus values the law, appeals to Scripture to support his views and has high regard for the temple itself, which is why he severely criticizes the ruling priests (Mk 11:15-18).

Just as impressive are the meaningful parallels with the Dead Sea Scrolls, whose collectors and authors were the Essenes, a group that zealously contended for Jewish faith and life. Jesus' strict view on marriage and divorce closely parallels the views of the Essenes. His appeal to words and phrases from Isaiah in his reply to the imprisoned and questioning John the Baptist (Mt 11:2-6; Lk 7:18-23) parallels in a remarkable way a messianic scroll from Qumran (that is, 4Q521). Jesus' string of beatitudes finds a formal parallel in one of the scrolls (that is, 4Q525). Jesus' use of Isaiah's song of the vineyard (Is 5:1-7) in his parable of the wicked vineyard tenants (Mk 12:1-12) coheres with yet another scroll (that is, 4Q500). Indeed, some of the teaching that Jesus opposed is attested in the scrolls (for example, the belief that the condition of the poor, lame and sick is due to sin or is a sign of divine judgment, or that sinners are to be shunned).

We also may have grim allusions to the Maccabean martyrs, who gave their lives for the faith of Israel. In warning his disciples to avoid giving offense and causing brothers and sisters to stumble, Jesus paints gruesome examples:

> And if your hand causes you to sin, cut it off; it is better for you to enter life maimed than with two hands to go to hell, to the unquenchable fire. And if your foot causes you to sin, cut it off; it is better for you to enter life lame than with two feet to be thrown into hell. And if your eye causes you to sin, pluck it out; it is better for you to enter the kingdom of God with one eye than with two eyes to be thrown into hell. (Mk 9:43-47)

Commentators suspect that Jesus has alluded to the frightful injuries inflicted on the Maccabean martyrs, who refused to eat pork and violate the law of Moses (for example, the officer of the king "commanded that the tongue of their spokesman be cut out and that they scalp him and cut off his hands and feet" [2 Maccabees 7:4]; "even if you gouge out my eyes" [4 Maccabees 5:30]). Jesus' charge to his disciples that for one to be his disciple he or she must "take up his cross" (Mk 8:34) represents Jesus' own version of the frightful consequences the faithful will face, updated in the light of Roman practices in his time.

Thus the evidence is impressive, even overwhelming, that Jesus was at home in a Jewish world that took seriously the teaching and stories of Scripture (what we usually call the Old Testament). There is nothing that compels us to view the teaching of Jesus in Cynic terms. There was no Cynic presence in Galilee in the early first century A.D. Jesus grew up in Nazareth, a village in which there was a small synagogue. It was in the context of the synagogue of Nazareth and in the context of his family and the elders of the village that Jesus' understanding of life and faith was nurtured, not in the context of an imagined Cynic teacher in nearby Sepphoris.

Getting the context right is vitally important for understanding Jesus. Putting him in the wrong context will inevitably lead to a distorted portrait. Some scholars, however, prefer no context at all. We turn to this problem in chapter six.

6

SKELETAL SAYINGS

Maxims Without a Context

Another odd procedure of some scholars—and again, it is necessary to mention prominent members of the Jesus Seminar—is the tendency to take the sayings of Jesus out of the narrative contexts supplied by the New Testament Gospel writers. The contexts found in the Gospels themselves, we are told, reflect early Christian beliefs and interests, not the actual contexts of the historical Jesus. What does this mean?

In assessing the question of authenticity (that is, did Jesus really say this, or did someone else?), scholars often distinguish the words of the pre-Easter Jesus from sayings and teachings that arose among his followers *after* Easter. Accordingly, scholars speak of sayings of Jesus, on the one hand, and of Christian sayings or formulations, on the other. (And here scholars usually speak of Christians as existing only after Easter and Pentecost, not before.)

Some scholars assume that if there is continuity between something attributed to Jesus and what the early church came to believe and emphasize, then Jesus' saying may not have originated with him but with the early church. Lying behind this thinking is the so-called criterion of dissimilarity. This kind of thinking often lies behind the tendency to strip sayings of their narrative frameworks and contexts in the New Testament Gospels. In chapter two I challenged the misuse of the criterion of dissimilarity. In this chapter I will challenge one of its unfortunate results—the tendency to discount the historical and interpretive contexts of the sayings of Jesus as found in the New Testament Gospels.

THE GENERAL PROBLEM

The problem with this approach is that Jesus becomes, as it were, a talking head—a "laconic sage" who uses terse, almost unfeeling language. Jesus begins to sound like a philosopher whose utterances are truisms and maxims. We are told that the contexts of Jesus' sayings supplied by the Evangelists are artificial, secondary and misleading. We really don't know what the original contexts were. At best, so goes the argument, we can only make educated guesses.

And skeptical scholars are quick to make educated guesses. Although almost two millennia removed, these scholars somehow think they are able to locate the original, non-Gospel contexts, and sometimes they just happen to be different from the contexts of the Gospels—and accommodating to the portrait of Jesus these scholars present to the public.[1] The net result is that Jesus' sayings lose what ancient context they have and become, in effect, skeletal sayings, sayings on which scholars may hang any likeness of Jesus they wish to fabricate. Without a context the free-floating sayings can mean virtually anything the interpreter wants to make of them.[2]

It must be acknowledged that many, if not most, of the sayings attributed to Jesus in the New Testament Gospels are without a *specific* context; that is, we are not told precisely where Jesus was or at what stage in his ministry something was said or done. Some sayings, moreover, appear in more than one context. For example, the parable of the lost sheep appears in Matthew 18:12-14 and Luke 15:3-7. The respective versions of the parable are not identical, and the respective contexts are not identical. But the forms and contexts are not all that different either. In the context of Matthew the parable clarifies Jesus' teaching on the importance of every individual, even those that go astray. In the context of Luke the parable teaches essentially the same thing. Only in Luke the parable is directed to scribes and Pharisees, while in Matthew the parable is directed to the twelve disciples. But the point in both Gospels is basically the same: God desires the recovery of the lost.

Diversity of context is seen in the respective Gospel locations of the Lord's Prayer (Mt 6:9-13; Lk 11:2-4). In Matthew the prayer appears in the middle of the Sermon on the Mount (Mt 5–7), whereas in Luke the prayer does not appear in the Sermon (Lk 6:20-49) but near the beginning of Luke's central section (Lk 10–18). The content of the prayer is not identical either, with a somewhat fuller form found in Matthew. Yet, in both forms and contexts, the prayer is for the disciples and teaches the same truths about God and his will.

Luke's central section itself is quite instructive. When we follow this section passage by passage, from chapter 10 to chapter 18, we notice that events parallel with Matthew (which are numerous) and events parallel with Mark (which are rare) occur in a different order within the narrative. What this illustrates is that the Evangelists Matthew and Luke (and probably Mark too) placed in context and in sequence the stories and teachings of Jesus that they inherited. But this fact does not mean that they did this contextualizing in false and misleading ways. I am inclined to think that those whom Jesus taught, who in turn taught others, had a better sense of the original context and meaning of Jesus' sayings than many scholars do today. Even if many sayings lack specific contexts, all sayings are found in a *general* context and within the flow of the narrative. And again, this is an important dimension that some scholars do not seem to appreciate sufficiently.

In his important and influential book on the historical Jesus, E. P. Sanders rightly criticized scholars for focusing on the sayings of Jesus with little regard for the basic *facts* and the *results* of his life and ministry. Sanders begins his book by identifying the "almost indisputable facts" as follows:

1. Jesus was baptized by John the Baptist.
2. Jesus was a Galilean who preached and healed.
3. Jesus called disciples and spoke of there being twelve.
4. Jesus confined his activity to Israel.
5. Jesus engaged in a controversy about the temple.
6. Jesus was crucified outside Jerusalem by the Roman authorities.
7. After his death Jesus' followers continued as an identifiable movement.
8. At least some Jews persecuted at least parts of the new movement (Gal 1:13, 23; Phil 3:6), and it appears that this persecution endured at least to a time near the end of Paul's career (2 Cor 11:24; Gal 5:11; 6:12; see Mt 23:34; 10:17).[3]

To these facts we could add a few more details to round out the picture.

I think that it is highly likely that Jesus was viewed by the public as a prophet (Mk 6:4; Lk 7:16, 39), that he spoke often of the kingdom of God (Mk 1:15; Lk 6:20), that his temple controversy involved criticism of the ruling priests (Mk 11:15–12:12), and that the Romans crucified him as "king of the Jews" (Mk 15:26).

We find that many of the sayings of Jesus cohere with these historical elements, oftentimes either explaining them or being explained by them. These facts provide a general—but important—context, in the light of which Jesus' teachings should be interpreted. Jesus doesn't only talk; he acts and things happen. Sayings interpreted without reference to these important contextualizing facts may be misinterpreted. Indeed, some of the strange interpretations that a few scholars impose on the sayings require that these facts and the Gospel contexts be ignored.

Not only do some scholars cut the sayings of Jesus out of their Gospel contexts, some contend that the sayings have not been accurately remembered. This idea sometimes grows out of the questionable assumption that what eventually is written down in the Gospels is at great variance with what Jesus taught and what was then passed on orally from disciple to disciple and groups of believers to groups of believers before finally being committed to writing, rather like in a modern game of "Telephone."

But where is the evidence for this? Other researchers in the history of Jewish teaching and learning in the time of Jesus have come to the opposite conclusion. Birger Gerhardsson, a distinguished Swedish scholar of Jesus and the Gospels, has shown how early rabbinic teachers expected their students to memorize and pass on faithfully what is taught. He has concluded that this applies to Jesus and his disciples: Jesus taught his disciples, and his disciples taught those who came after them. What was taught could be adapted, even expanded, but not distorted. Accordingly, Gerhardsson believes that there is significant continuity between the original, oral teaching of Jesus and the later, written Gospels.

Shemaryahu Talmon, a scholar of Jewish antiquity, has reached the same conclusion with regard to the founding teacher of the Qumran sect and the later written records of his teachings (that is, the Dead Sea Scrolls). Talmon has found that the "Qumran evidence does not support the contention of contemporary [New Testament] theorists of orality that the spoken and the written word are 'contradictory and mutually exclusive.'"[4] Talmon's findings are consistent with what is known of Jewish teachers and teaching methods.

A SPECIFIC EXAMPLE

But some sayings do have specific contexts, and these contexts are important for understanding the meaning of the sayings. Perhaps the classic example is the parable of the wicked vineyard tenants. Some scholars simply refuse to take this parable in its Gospel context. They love to pare it down, put it into different, hypothetical contexts, and then guess at what the original meaning might have been. The wildly divergent interpretations are almost comical.

The parable of the wicked vineyard tenants is important because it speaks of a son who is rejected and murdered. Was Jesus speaking of himself? And if so, what does this imply about Jesus' self-understanding? Was he implying that he is the son of the vineyard owner, that is, the Son of God? Accordingly, this parable potentially makes a major contribution to Christology.

If the parable is taken in its Gospel context, then these questions will be answered affirmatively. Yes, Jesus did imply that he is the son of the vineyard owner, rejected and murdered by the tenant farmers. Given the symbolism of the parable—that Israel is the vineyard, God is the owner of the vineyard, and the ruling priests are the tenant farmers who refuse to comply with the owner's will—Jesus has implied that he is not simply one more messenger sent by God to Israel, but he is God's Son, whom Israel's religious leaders intend to kill.

Let's examine this parable and then review the various proposals some scholars have made, trying to interpret the parable without reference to its Gospel context. We will see that these attempts are as unsuccessful as they are unnecessary. In contrast, the weight of the evidence strongly supports interpreting the parable in the context that the New Testament Gospels have given it.

The parable of the wicked vineyard tenants reads as follows:

[1]And he began to speak to them in parables: "A man planted a vineyard; and he put a fence around it, and hewed out a winepress, and built a tower [Is 5:1-2], and leased it out to tenant farmers, and de-

parted. [2]And he sent to the tenant farmers in due course a servant, that he might receive from the farmers a portion of the fruit of the vineyard. [3]But taking him, they beat him and sent him away empty-handed. [4]And again he sent to them another servant; but they struck that one on the head, and treated him dishonorably. [5]So he sent another; and they killed that one, and many others, beating some and killing others. [6]He had yet one, a beloved son. He sent him last to them, thinking, 'They will respect my son.' [7]But those tenants said to themselves, 'This is the heir; come, let us kill him, and the inheritance will be ours.' [8]And taking him they killed him, and cast him out of the vineyard. [9]What [therefore] will the owner of the vineyard do? He will come and destroy the tenants, and give the vineyard to others. [10]Have you not even read this scripture:

> 'A stone that the builders rejected,
>   This has become the head of the corner;
> [11]This came about from the Lord,
>   and it is marvelous in our eyes' [Ps 118:22-23]?"

[12]And they were seeking to arrest him, but they feared the crowd, for they knew that he had spoken the parable to them. And leaving him, they departed. (Mk 12:1-12, my translation)

For those scholars who reject the Gospel context, the concluding quotation of Psalm 118:22-23 and the opening words and phrases taken from Isaiah 5:1-2, the original meaning of the parable of the wicked vineyard tenants proves elusive. The range of suggestions made by these scholars is amazing.

I begin with the suggestions offered by Charles Carlston's learned treatment of the parables in Matthew, Mark and Luke. Carlston doubts that the parable of the wicked vineyard tenants actually derives from Jesus himself, and he does not believe that the context of the parable in Mark is true to the original intent and meaning of the parable (whoever crafted it). Having rejected the parable's authenticity and having rejected the context it has in the New Testament Gospels, Carlston is not sure what the parable originally meant. He makes three suggestions.[5] All of them are little more than guesses.

His first suggested interpretation is: "It could mean that God will turn from the Jews who killed his Son and heir . . . to others who are more worthy of God's vineyard, i.e., to those who believe the gospel." But does this interpretation work? If this is the meaning of the parable, then what would the parable's "vineyard" mean to the early church? Is it the people of Israel? Is it the land of Israel? Our scholar speaks of God turning away "from the Jews who killed his Son and heir." But the Jews (or Israel) themselves constitute the "vineyard." So how can God turn away from the Jews and then give the Jews to others who are more worthy? If we interpret the parable in its Gospel context, this question is easily answered. Those who murder the son are the caretakers of the vineyard. That is, the religious leaders of Israel are the villains. God will take the vineyard (Israel) away from them and give it to others (such as Jesus' disciples and the righteous of Israel).

Let's look at Carlston's second suggested interpretation: "The parable could also imply that Jesus foresaw God's turning from the Jews to the Gentiles." But this interpretation has problems too. How did the Gentiles (that is, non-Jewish peoples) get into the picture? The wicked tenants will be destroyed and the vineyard will be given to other tenants, that is, to other Jewish religious leaders. Again, the best explanation of the parable emerges from its Gospel context. Jesus threatens the aristocratic priests. They are in danger of being removed and replaced with other (Jewish) religious leaders who will care for the vineyard (Israel) the way they should.

Here is Carlston's third suggested interpretation: "Finally, the parable could be understood to reflect a regular principle in the divine economy: just as God has turned from the Jews to the Gentiles, so he will always turn from those who do not produce 'fruit' to those who do." This third proposal is only slightly more convincing than the first two. The second half of the interpretation is correct: God will turn away from those who do not produce "fruit." According to the New Testament Gospel context of the parable, God turns away from the "builders," that is from the Jewish religious authorities. In their place he will appoint "other" (Jewish religious) authorities to care for the vineyard. But the first part of the third interpretation suffers the same fate as the first two interpretations. God has not turned away from *the vineyard,* but from *those who care for it.*

A major problem with all three suggested interpretations is in the assumption that while early Christians were skillful in creating the parable, they were clumsy in making its meaning clear. If the early church was skilled enough in understanding Scripture to choose the appropriate prophetic testimony (that is, Is 5:1-7) to identify the "vineyard," and to create an allegory that sums up the history of God's saving work in Israel's history—a history that involves Israel's habit of rejecting the prophets and finally rejecting God's Son—then is it plausible to think the early church forgot what the vineyard stood for? One cannot have it both ways. It really is not plausible that early Christians invented a parable that attempts to clarify the church's place in God's divine plan (as though to suggest that because of persistent rejection of the prophets and God's Son, God has rejected Israel), but then misrepresent the parable in such a way that it seems to be talking about who cares for the vineyard.

All attempts to interpret the parable as a creation not of Jesus but of the church suffer shipwreck on the rock of the parable's basic story line: the focus is not on the identity of the vineyard—it is Israel, and that is presupposed and remains constant—the focus is on the conflict between those who care for the vineyard and the owner of the vineyard, whom the tenant farmers do not respect and will not obey. This is the only plausible interpretation of the parable, and it is the meaning that is consistent with its context in the New Testament Gospels.

Fortunately, most interpreters today accept the parable as authentic. But some of them still reject the context given the parable in the New Testament Gospels, including the allusions to Isaiah 5:1-7 and the concluding quotation of Psalm 118:22-23. But these interpreters run into the same interpretive difficulties that plague Carlston's interpretive proposals. Let's briefly survey some of these attempts.

Bernard Brandon Scott opines, "Since the parable provides no ready identification models, no clear metaphorical referencing, an audience is left in a precarious position: *In the plot the kingdom fails and the inheritance is in doubt.*"[6] This proposal is extraordinary, for it contradicts both context and content. Scott says there are "no ready identification models." But of course there are: the biblical tradition in general (that is, the history of Israel's suffering prophets, of Israel's stubborn sinfulness, etc.) and the allusions to Isaiah 5:1-7 in particular (where God is the vineyard's owner and the vineyard is Israel). Scott believes the parable leaves the hearer in a precarious position because the "kingdom fails and the inheritance is in doubt." There is no doubt whatsoever about the kingdom and the inheritance if the quotation of Psalm 118:22-23 ("The stone that the builders rejected . . .") is allowed to stand as a scriptural quotation; it is an intrinsic part of the meaning of the parable.

Still other interpreters have expressed misgivings about the parable's context in the New Testament Gospels. In a commentary focused on social issues in the time of Jesus, Bruce Malina and Richard Rohrbaugh wonder if the parable originally had been "a warning to landowners expropriating and exporting the produce of the land."[7] What such a parable could possibly have meant in the context of Jesus' ministry is not clear, nor do these interpreters venture an opinion. Such an interpretation clarifies nothing.

Robert Funk and Roy Hoover, editors of the Jesus Seminar's *The Five Gospels,* the color-coded translation and commentary on the Gospels, think the parable of the wicked vineyard tenants is preserved in an earlier, more reliable form and context in the *Gospel of Thomas*. Accordingly, they think "Jesus' version was a disturbing and tragic tale, but it was told without specific application."[8] Really? "Without specific application"? On the contrary, the application is quite clear when the parable is read in its New Testament Gospel context. The parable loses its application only when it is removed from its context in the New Testament Gospels. Besides, the *Gospel of Thomas* was probably not composed prior to A.D. 175. It is unlikely to have an early, more original form of the parable. The Jesus Seminar's interpretation is a sorry case of special pleading.

The Jesus Seminar's recommendation also bears the stamp of John Dominic Crossan's earlier work. Crossan tells us that the parable "is a deliberately shocking story of successful murder."[9] But to what end? Crossan isn't sure. In other studies he offers other interpretations. Having taken the parable of the wicked vineyard tenants out of its New Testament Gospel context, Crossan, the Jesus Seminar and other interpreters really have no idea what the parable originally meant.

Despite seemingly tireless and ultimately fruitless efforts to find significant meaning in the parable of the wicked vineyard tenants, shorn of its New Testament Gospel context or when authenticity is denied, all that is left is banality. Either we have a clumsy attempt at Christian salvation history, or we have a warning against exporting the land's produce, or a tragedy, or maybe even a shocking story of successful murder. These decontextualized approaches leave us with a parable that there is no real reason to tell or to preserve.

We are better off by far to take more seriously the earliest context we have—that found in the New Testament Gospels—than the doubtful contexts found in later sources or in the imaginations and speculations of modern scholars.

There is one other feature mentioned earlier but not pursued in detail. This has to do with the question of whether Jesus really created the parable. Some scholars have found the parable of the wicked vineyard tenants so extreme they doubt its authenticity. They complain of the irrational behavior of the characters in the parable. The owner of the vineyard seems particularly inept. Why on earth would he repeatedly send servants? Why send his "beloved son" to face such danger? One interpreter exclaims that the owner of the vineyard acts throughout like a "total idiot." But it is obvious that the behavior of the tenant farmers themselves is hardly saner. Did they really think they could violate the terms of the lease, commit assault and murder, and then inherit the vineyard?

Because of these improbabilities, some think the parable is an invention after the time of Jesus, or that Jesus (or someone else) told a parable that originally was simpler and more realistic, and was later embellished. What had once made a simple, single point now has become a complicated allegory that no longer realistically reflects living conditions in first-century Palestine. It reflects, instead, the Christian concept of "the 'blessed idiocy' of grace," as Carlston has put it.[10] But objections such as these fail to understand the nature of Jewish parables, which often portray characters behaving in absurd ways and doing things normal people would never do.

The parable of the vineyard tenants immediately calls to mind several parables crafted by rabbis from the first centuries of the Christian era. Some rabbinic parables specifically liken Israel to a vineyard, sometimes actually appealing to Isaiah's Song of the Vineyard (Is 5:1-7), the passage of Scripture on which Jesus based his parable of the wicked vineyard tenants. Note how one of the rabbinic parables mixes metaphors by introducing "shepherds." Jesus likewise appends a proof text about "builders" (that is, Ps 118:22-23),

RABBINIC PARABLES ABOUT THE VINEYARD

Absentee Owners
To what may this be compared? To one man living in Galilee and owning a vineyard in Judea, and another man living in Judea and owning a vineyard in Galilee. (*Midrash Tanhuma* B, *Qedoshin* 6, attributed to Rabbi Simeon ben Halafta)

Tended Like a Vineyard
Rabbi Simeon ben Yohai said: "Why was Israel likened to a vineyard? In the case of a vineyard, in the beginning one must hoe it, then weed it, and then erect supports when he sees the clusters [forming]. Then he must return to pluck the grapes and press them in order to extract the wine from them. So also Israel—each and every shepherd who oversees them must tend them [as he would tend a vineyard]. Where [in Scripture] is Israel called a vineyard? In the verse, 'For the vineyard of the Lord of Hosts is the House of Israel, and the seedling he lovingly tended are the men of Judah' [Is 5:7]." (*Midrash Mishle*, on Prov 19:21)

Vineyard Vandals
They were like robbers who had broken into the king's vineyard and destroyed the vines. When the king discovered that his vineyard had been destroyed, he was filled with wrath, and descending upon the robbers, without help from anything or anyone, he cut them down and uprooted them as they had done to his vineyard. (*Exodus Rabbah* 30.17 [on Ex 21:18])

Translations
"Absentee Owners." My translation
"Tended Like a Vineyard." Based on Burton L. Visotzky, *The Midrash on Proverbs*, YJS 27 (New Haven: Yale University Press, 1992), p. 89.
"Vineyard Vandals." Based on Simon M. Lehrman, "Exodus," in *Midrash Rabbah,* ed. Harry Freedman and Maurice Simon (New York: Soncino, 1983), 3:367.

thus mixing the metaphors of farmers and builders. Other parables speak of absentee owners of vineyards, as does Jesus' parable. Another parable tells of an angry king who takes vengeance on men who had violated his vineyard, as is implied by the conclusion of Jesus' parable.

The rabbinic parable of the unworthy tenants makes use of the image of unruly, rebellious tenants. These unworthy tenants steal from the vineyard and later are evicted when the owner of the vineyard has a son. In this parable, as in the other parables, the owner of the vineyard is God. Perhaps the most amazing rabbinic parable—the parable of the foolish king attributed to Yose the Galilean (second century A.D.)—describes a remarkably foolish and incautious king who entrusts his son to a villain. Several details of this parable have significance for Jesus' parable, especially in view of the questions raised about its authenticity. In Yose's parable we have a man who appears to lack common sense. Against the advice of friends and counselors he entrusts his son to a man known to be a "wicked guardian." But the actions of the guardian are just as difficult to comprehend. We are not told that he stole anything or profited in any way by his actions. He destroys the king's city, burns down his house and murders his son. What could he possibly have hoped to gain? Did he imagine that he could get away with these crimes? Wouldn't every hearer of this parable suppose that the king would send troops after the guardian and have him executed?

These are the same kinds of questions critics have raised against the logic,

THE PARABLE OF THE UNWORTHY TENANTS

A parable: A king had a field which he leased to tenants. When the tenants began to steal from it, he took it away from them and leased it to their children. When the children began to act worse than their fathers, he took it away from them and gave it to the grandchildren. When these too became worse than their predecessors, a son was born to him. He then said to the grandchildren, "Leave my property. You may not remain in it. Give me back my portion, so that I may repossess it." (*Sipre Deuteronomy* 312 [on Deut 32:9])

Translation based on R. Hammer, *Sifre: A Tannaitic Commentary on the Book of Deuteronomy*, YJS 24 (New Haven, Conn.: Yale University Press, 1986), p. 318.

if not authenticity, of the parable of the vineyard tenants in Mark 12 and parallels.[11] How could the owner of the vineyard be so foolish and so reckless with the lives of his servants and especially the life of his son? What could the tenants realistically have hoped to gain? Didn't they know that the owner had the power to come and destroy them? Did they really imagine that they could inherit the vineyard?

Questions such as these do not constitute valid objections against the authenticity of parables, whether those of Jesus or those of the rabbis. The incomprehensible folly of the king in Yose's parable should not cast doubt on the question of its authenticity (note too that Yose applies the parable to God's trusting Nebuchadnezzar!). Nor should the folly of the vineyard owner and the vineyard tenants cast doubt on the authenticity of Jesus' parable. These parables do indeed provoke these kinds of questions—for ancient hearers as well as modern. But the shocking details and the questions they raise are supposed to lead the hearers to grasp and apply the intended lesson. Furthermore, all of the rabbinic parables that have been mentioned are to some extent allegorical, with the "king" or "owner" of the field or vineyard often representing God, the field or vineyard representing either the people or land of Israel, and tenants representing Gentiles or other unworthy people, and the king's or owner's "son" representing the people of Israel or the patriarchs Abraham, Isaac, Jacob, and the like. These are stock images, drawn from a common Jewish treasury of words and themes.

Accordingly, the contents and plot of the parable of the wicked vineyard tenants are true to the typical styles, themes and formats of parables found in Judaism of late antiquity. There is nothing in Jesus' parable that requires us to see at work the hand of later Christian allegorizers trying to give it a new look and meaning. On the contrary, there are elements present in this parable that tell against its origin in the church. For example, if the early church rather than Jesus himself was responsible for this parable, then why is there such a concern over who possesses or governs the vineyard? Furthermore, if an early Christian composed this parable, then why isn't the resurrection of Jesus mentioned? The parable ends with the murder of the vineyard owner's son and the threat of retaliation. Even the quotation of Psalm 118:22-23 after the conclusion of the parable doesn't really speak to resur-

THE PARABLE OF THE FOOLISH KING

The parable, as told by Rabbi Yose the Galilean, concerned a mortal king who had set out for a city far across the sea. As he was about to entrust his son to the care of a wicked guardian, his friends and servants said to him: "My lord king, do not entrust your son to this wicked guardian." Nevertheless the king, ignoring the counsel of his friends and servants, entrusted his son to the wicked guardian. What did the guardian do? He proceeded to destroy the king's city, have his house consumed by fire, and slay his son with the sword. After a while the king returned. When he saw his city destroyed and desolate, his house consumed by fire, his son slain with the sword, he pulled out the hair of his head and his beard and broke out into wild weeping, saying: "Woe is me! How <foolish> I have been, how senselessly I acted in this kingdom of mine in entrusting my son to a wicked guardian!" (from *Seder Elijah Rabbah* 28)

The parable of the foolish king tries to explain why God (the foolish king) would entrust his son (Israel), city (Jerusalem) and house (temple) to a wicked guardian (Nebuchadnezzar, king of Babylon, who destroyed Jerusalem, burned the temple, and killed many Israelites).

Translation based on William G. Braude and Israel Kapstein, *Tanna Debe Eliyyahu: The Lore of the School of Elijah* (Philadelphia: Jewish Publication Society, 1981), p. 369.

rection. It implies that Jesus will be vindicated (probably in the sense of becoming Israel's king) but says nothing about resurrection specifically.

There is something else about the parable of the wicked vineyard tenants: parts of it are not as unreal as they may seem to us moderns. The parable actually parallels real events, as seen in historical reports and in old letters and business papers from among the papyri recovered a century ago from the sands of Egypt. The business arrangement that the owner of the vineyard makes with the tenant farmers coheres with lease agreements from antiquity that have been found. Some papyri tell of failed attempts to collect debts, with the result that the collectors—in some cases servants of important people—are thrown out of town.

Roman statesman Cicero's account of collecting a debt from the leading citizens of Salamis offers a dramatic historical event (c. 50 B.C.) in which troops had to be employed and people died: "Appius had given him some

AN ANCIENT LEASE AGREEMENT

For the first year for a rent of two-thirds of all the fruits and produce that grow in this vineyard; viz., when all fruits have been turned into wine and deductions made for the apomoira due to the Treasury, wages for the treaders, hire of winepress and a contribution (in the month of the vintage?) of a half kados to the agricultural guild, the must remaining shall be divided into three portions, of which Nicomachus shall take two and Apollonius one. Each shall provide jars for himself and as required for the apomoira according to the proportions of his lease, and each shall carry down the jars for himself to the winepress. (P.Rylands 582 [c. 42 B.C.])

squadrons to put pressure on the people of Salamis. . . . I ordered the people . . . to pay the money. . . . I threatened to compel them" (*Ad Atticum* 5.21). These squadrons, Atticus is told in Cicero's next letter, "beset the Senate at Salamis in their own chamber, so that five members of the house died of starvation" (*Ad Atticum* 6.1). The troops were sent not against the peasants and rabble of Salamis but against the rulers of the city!

These actual episodes show how Jesus' parable of the wicked tenants is potentially true to life. But parables do not have to portray life as it actually is. Parables often indulge in exaggeration and portray characters (even when they represent God himself!) behaving in remarkably trusting and incautious ways. So it is in the case of the parable of the wicked vineyard tenants.

MISTREATED DEBT COLLECTORS

I have received your letter, to which you added a copy of the letter written by Zenon to Jeddous saying that unless he gave the money to Straton, Zenon's man, we were to hand over his pledge to him [Straton]. I happened to be unwell as a result of taking some medicine, so I sent a young man, a servant of mine, to Straton, and wrote a letter to Jeddous. When they returned they said that he had taken no notice of my letter, but had attacked them and thrown them out of the village. So I am writing to you. (P.CairoZenon 59.018 [258 B.C.])

Every detail is possible, but the story as a whole is highly unlikely. The intention of the exaggeration is to accent the crimes of the tenants and to heighten the sense of outrage in the hearers of the parable—to get the point across loud and clear.

There are many other details that could be explored. The use of Isaiah 5 at the beginning of the parable reflects acquaintance with the way Isaiah was understood in Aramaic and in the synagogue in the time of Jesus. The same is true of Psalm 118, part of which is quoted at the end of the parable, and other parts are quoted when Jesus enters the city of Jerusalem (Mk 11:1-11). Some scholars have rightly recognized interpretive sophistication at work here. It is far more plausible that this Aramaic-based sophisticated interpretation is the work of Jesus, not the work of the later church. When understood properly and in full context, everything about the parable of the wicked vineyard tenants—including its context in the New Testament Gospels—argues that it originated with Jesus, not with the early church.

I have treated one particular parable at length not only because it may be the most important parable that Jesus uttered, but because its historical context is probably the clearest of all the parables, and because some scholars—for whatever reasons—want to take this parable out of context and then with imagination and speculation find new meanings for it. This is no way to proceed. Scholars and nonexperts alike are better advised to read the parables and sayings of Jesus in their New Testament Gospel contexts, contexts that date to within one generation (if not earlier) of Jesus himself and his original disciples.

Chapter seven treats another important contextual issue—the mighty deeds of Jesus. If these deeds are not taken seriously and in the context of Jesus' public ministry, the message of Jesus cannot be understood properly.

DIMINISHED DEEDS

A Fresh Look at Healings and Miracles

One of the curious features in scholarly study of the historical Jesus has been the neglect of Jesus' works of power, though happily enough that seems to be changing in more recent years. For how can we really hope to understand who Jesus was and what his ministry was all about if one of the most distinguishing features about him—his miracles—are not taken into account?

Today, scholars are more open to talking about the miracles of Jesus because they rightly recognize that the task of the historian is to describe what people reported and recorded. It isn't the historian's task to engage in science and metaphysics. In other words, it is enough that historians acknowledge that Jesus' contemporaries observed what they believed were miracles; historians should not try to explain exactly what Jesus did or how he did it. This shift in thinking in recent years is welcome.[1]

Nevertheless, this important dimension of Jesus' public ministry is not sufficiently appreciated and—especially in work emanating from the Jesus Seminar—is not properly linked to Jesus' teaching and preaching. In the Seminar's work Jesus is too much of a philosopher and laconic sage, not enough a man of mighty deeds.[2]

E. P. Sanders has rightly suggested that crowds followed Jesus not so much because he was a great teacher but because of his reputation as a powerful healer.[3] The crowds grew because this reputation seemed to be well founded. An ineffective healer would have had difficulty sustaining an enthusiastic following.

Some of the criteria used for supporting the authenticity of Jesus' sayings apply in the case of his mighty deeds:

- *Multiple attestation.* The mighty deeds of Jesus are found in all of the New Testament Gospels, including Q (the sayings source used by Matthew and Luke). The attestation of miracles in Q is significant, for miracles do not play a significant role in this source. Not only does Q preserve a miracle story (Mt 8:5-13 = Lk 7:1-10; see Jn 4:46-54), it contains sayings, judged by most scholars to be authentic, that presuppose Jesus' miracles.[4] Some of these sayings in one form or another appear in Mark as well (for example, Mt 12:27 = Lk 11:19; see Mk 3:23) and so represent true examples of multiple attestation.

- *Dissimilarity.* There are aspects of Jesus' mighty deeds that are dissimilar to those attributed to various contemporary exorcists and healers, both among the Jewish people of Jesus' time and among Christians and non-Jews a generation or two later. In other words, if the New Testament Gospel stories reflected invented tales, we should expect them to reflect what people usually experienced.[5] But this is not the case. For example, unlike a few well-known exorcists and healers in the approximate time of Jesus, Jesus does not pray and ask for healing or make use of paraphernalia to cast out unclean spirits.

- *Embarrassment.* The criterion of embarrassment refers to sayings or deeds that are not easily explained as inauthentic creations of the early church, simply because there are aspects about them that would have been potentially embarrassing. One such event in the life of Jesus was his baptism by John. John summoned Israel to repent and be baptized. In what sense did Jesus need to repent? According to Christian theology, Jesus was sinless, so he did not need to repent. Hence, the story of Jesus' baptism is potentially awkward or embarrassing. Surely, the early church would not invent a story like this if it had no basis in historical fact. Therefore, even the most severe critics concede that the story of Jesus' baptism is authentic. So goes the argument in the case of some of the miracle stories. In one, we are told that Jesus' family attempted to restrain him because of negative reactions to the exorcisms (Mk 3:20-35). In another, we are told that Jesus was dismayed by the lack of faith on the part of the people of Nazareth and therefore he "could do no mighty work there" (Mk 6:5). In one story, a non-Jewish woman seems to win the argument (Mk 7:24-30). In yet another, it seems that Jesus has to make two attempts at healing (Mk 8:22-26). These stories are not the stuff of pious imagination. They are, rather, frank recollections of the give and take and the ups and downs of Jesus' ministry, a ministry marked by spontaneity and opportunity, not contrivance and artificiality.[6]

There are several important points that need to be made about Jesus' mighty deeds. First, his healings and exorcisms were an intrinsic part of his proclamation of the kingdom (or rule) of God. The mighty deeds and the proclamation must go together; neither can be understood without the other. Second, the miracles were viewed by Jesus and others as fulfillment of prophetic Scripture. His miracles were in step with what was expected of God's Messiah. Third, the mighty deeds of Jesus were revelatory; they revealed things about Jesus and his mission. Again, to discount the mighty deeds is to lose sight of important aspects of Jesus and his work. Fourth, Jesus' mighty deeds were different from and more impressive than those of his near contemporaries. That is, Jesus' healings were not simply the kind of healings associated with certain professional exorcists and Jewish holy men. Fifth, Jesus' reputation as healer and exorcist was such that long after his ministry was concluded, his name was still invoked by Christians and non-Christians alike, thus attesting to his lasting reputation and power. We'll look at each of these in turn.

JESUS' EXORCISMS AND HEALINGS

Everyone agrees that the essence of Jesus' proclamation was the kingdom (or rule) of God. What is not always clear, however, is that in the thinking of Jesus *the onset of the kingdom of God means the collapse of the kingdom of Satan.* And the collapse of the kingdom (or rule) of Satan is seen in the exorcisms and healings. The exorcisms and healings cannot be ignored or discounted if we are to understand fully the significance and import of Jesus' bold proclamation that the rule of God has indeed arrived, and that it is the time to repent and embrace it.

THE MIRACLES OF JESUS IN THE SYNOPTICS

Healing a leper	Matthew 8:1-4; Mark 1:40-45; Luke 5:12-16
Healing a centurion's servant	Matthew 8:5-13; Luke 7:1-10
Healing Peter's mother-in-law	Matthew 8:14-15; Mark 1:29-31; Luke 4:38-39
Calming of the storm	Matthew 8:23-27; Mark 4:35-41; Luke 8:22-25
Demoniacs among the tombs	Matthew 8:28-34; Mark 5:1-20; Luke 8:26-39
Healing of the paralytic lowered from the roof	Matthew 9:1-8; Mark 2:1-12; Luke 5:17-26
Raising of Jairus's daughter	Matthew 9:18-19, 23-26; Mark 5:21-24, 35-43; Luke 8:40-42, 49-56
Healing the bleeding woman	Matthew 9:20-22; Mark 5:25-34; Luke 8:43-48
Healing two blind men	Matthew 9:27-31
Healing the man with the mute spirit	Matthew 9:32-34
Healing the man with the withered hand	Matthew 12:9-14; Mark 3:1-6; Luke 6:6-11
Healing the blind and mute demoniac	Matthew 12:22-37; Mark 3:20-30; Luke 11:14-23
Feeding the five thousand	Matthew 14:13-21; Mark 6:30-44; Luke 9:10-17
Walking on the water	Matthew 14:22-33; Mark 6:45-51
Demons from the Canaanite woman's daughter	Matthew 15:21-28; Mark 7:24-30
Feeding the four thousand	Matthew 15:32-39; Mark 8:1-10
Healing the blind man at Bethsaida	Mark 8:22-26
Demons from the boy	Matthew 17:14-20; Mark 9:14-29; Luke 9:37-43
Healing the blind men at Jericho	Matthew 20:29-34; Mark 10:46-52; Luke 18:35-43
Cursing the fig tree	Matthew 21:18-22; Mark 11:12-14, 20-24
Demons from the man in the synagogue	Mark 1:21-28; Luke 4:31-37
Healing the deaf and mute man	Mark 7:31-37
Full net of fish	Luke 5:1-11
Raising the widow of Nain's son	Luke 7:11-17
Healing the crippled woman on the sabbath	Luke 13:10-17
Healing the man with dropsy	Luke 14:1-6
Healing the ten lepers	Luke 17:11-19
Healing of Malchus's ear	Luke 22:49-51

Adapted from Rex Koivisto

The association of the proclamation of the rule of God with exorcism and healing is evident in the New Testament Gospels:

And he called to him his twelve disciples and gave them authority over unclean spirits, to cast them out, and to heal every disease and every infirmity. (Mt 10:1)

These twelve Jesus sent out, charging them, "Go nowhere among the Gentiles, and enter no town of the Samaritans, but go rather to the lost sheep of the house of Israel. And preach as you go, saying, 'The kingdom of heaven is at hand.' Heal the sick, raise the dead, cleanse lepers, cast out demons." (Mt 10:5-8)

Similar commissionings of Jesus' disciples can be found in Mark 3:13-15; 6:7; Luke 6:12-19; 9:1-6.

Just as Jesus proclaimed the good news of God's rule and demonstrated its reality by attacking Satan's rule, so also his disciples are to go out (as *apostles*—that is, ones "sent") and do the same thing. The rule of God and the rule of Satan cannot coexist peacefully. The advance of the one means the retreat of the other.

That Jesus understood exorcism in this way is seen in a number of important sayings. When charged with tapping into the power of Satan himself in order to perform his exorcisms (more on this in a moment), Jesus retorted:

How can Satan cast out Satan? If a kingdom is divided against itself, that kingdom cannot stand. And if a house is divided against itself, that house will not be able to stand. And if Satan has risen up against himself and is divided, he cannot stand, but has an end. But no one can enter a strong man's house and plunder his goods, unless he first binds the strong man; then indeed he may plunder his house. (Mk 3:23-27)

But if it is by the finger of God that I cast out demons, then the kingdom of God has come upon you. (Lk 11:20)

Two features stand out. First, when Jesus says that Satan "has an end" (in Mk 3:26, which is how the Greek text literally reads), we have an exact verbal parallel with the *Testament of Moses*, a fictional work scholars are pretty sure was written in Palestine right around A.D. 30, at about the same time Jesus was at the height of his ministry. According to this writing, which is concerned with priestly corruption and the soon appearance of the kingdom of God:

> And then [God's] kingdom will appear in his whole creation.
> And then the Devil will have an end,
> And sorrow will be led away with him. (*Testament of Moses* 10:1)

This parallels Jesus' understanding closely. That is, when the kingdom of God appears, the devil will have an end. What is longed for and seen in futuristic terms in the *Testament of Moses* has begun to happen in the ministry of Jesus. The future "will have an end" in *Moses* has become the present "has an end" in the proclamation and deeds of Jesus.

Jesus' linkage of his proclamation of the rule of God with the demise of Satan would have been readily understood by his contemporaries. Indeed, it would have been welcomed by many of his contemporaries, though feared by others. Accordingly, when Jesus speaks of Satan having an end, the people hearing him would get the point: The rule of God has come; it's over for Satan.

The second important feature in the sayings of Jesus that link the rule of God with the exorcisms and healings is the reference to the "finger of God" (Lk 11:20). This is an allusion to the contest between Moses and Pharaoh's magicians (Ex 7—8). Initially the magicians could duplicate the feats of Moses and Aaron. But in the end they had met their match:

> The magicians tried by their secret arts to bring forth gnats, but they could not. So there were gnats on man and beast. And the magicians said to Pharaoh, "This is the finger of God." (Ex 8:18-19)

The expression, "the finger of God," understood in context means that Moses and Aaron were not magicians, pulling off clever tricks. They themselves possessed no power, for no human power, no matter how well trained in the magical arts (and Egypt was regarded in antiquity as the capital of magic), could do what Moses and Aaron were able to do. The magicians rightly concluded that what was at work in the two Hebrew brothers was "the finger of God."

This is also the idea in Jesus' saying. His ability to cast out demons is not through magic or gimmickry, but it is "by the finger of God," the same power that had worked long ago through Moses and Aaron. This is an astonishing claim, for Jesus not only has distanced himself from magic; he has claimed that the greatest power that God ever worked through a human being was at work through him. His opponents could criticize him if they wished, but it was difficult to deny what was happening right before their eyes. Hence their desperate argument that Jesus was in league with Satan (Beelzebul).

Some interpreters try to bracket off the healings from the exorcisms. No doubt some illness and infirmities had nothing to do with evil spirits, but some apparently did. We have an instructive example of this in the Gospel of Luke:

> And there was a woman who had had a spirit of infirmity for eighteen years; she was bent over and could not fully straighten herself. And when Jesus saw her, he called her and said to her, "Woman, you are freed from your infirmity." And he laid his hands upon her, and immediately she was made straight, and she praised God. But the ruler of the synagogue, indignant because Jesus had healed on the sabbath, said to the people, "There are six days on which work ought to be done; come on those days and be healed, and not on the sabbath day." Then the Lord answered him, "You hypocrites! Does not each of you on the sabbath untie his ox or his ass from the manger, and lead it away to water it? And ought not this woman, a daughter of Abraham whom Satan bound for eighteen years, be loosed from this bond on the sabbath day?" As he said this, all his adversaries were put to shame; and all the people rejoiced at all the glorious things that were done by him. (Lk 13:11-17)

What is interesting in this healing miracle is that the main point seems to be a legal one: Was Jesus or anyone else permitted to heal on the sabbath (that is, the traditional day of rest) or not? Contrary to Jewish piety and practice, Jesus says that it is permissible. The point isn't the miracle itself. But for the present purposes the important thing is to observe that the woman's infirmity is viewed in terms of satanic bondage. Jesus wishes to give her freedom (or rest) from this bondage, so what better day to do this but the sabbath? The healing of this woman is one more example of the liberating power that the rule of God brings. Among other things, God's rule dismantles the rule of Satan, whether in terms of casting out unclean spirits or bringing physical healing.[7]

JESUS' MIRACLES OF HEALING

A second important reason why the mighty deeds of Jesus need to be taken fully into account, if we are to understand his person and ministry, is that the miracles provided important evidence for Jesus and his contemporaries that his ministry was of God and fulfilled prophecy. The miracles were not some sort of sideshow by which Jesus impressed crowds or silenced critics. The miracles were essential, not only to prove the truth of the proclamation that God's rule had truly come (the point of "Jesus' Exorcisms and Healings") but to prove that the ministry of Jesus was in fulfillment of ancient prophecy.

We looked at the exchange between Jesus and the imprisoned and discouraged John the Baptist before. But let's take another, more in-depth look. The passage reads as follows:

> Now when John heard in prison about the deeds of the Christ, he sent word by his disciples and said to him, "Are you he who is to come, or shall we look for another?" And Jesus answered them, "Go and tell John what you hear and see: the blind receive their sight and the lame walk, lepers are cleansed and the deaf hear, and the dead are raised up, and the poor have good news preached to them. And blessed is he who takes no offense at me." (Mt 11:2-6; see Lk 7:18-23)

The criterion of embarrassment strongly supports the authenticity of this exchange. Why would an early Christian invent a story about John the "forerunner" expressing doubt about Jesus? Make no mistake; John's question, "Are you he who is to come?" means that he is no longer sure that Jesus is that special one raised up by God for the deliverance of Israel. John has doubts because he remains in prison. The significance of this point will become clear in a moment.

What is of great importance is the reply that Jesus gives. Most of it draws on the language of the prophecy of Isaiah. Jesus' words "the blind receive their sight" alludes to Isaiah 35:5 ("the eyes of the blind shall be opened") and perhaps also Isaiah 61:1 (which in the Greek version reads, "recovery of sight to the blind"). Jesus' declaration "the lame walk" alludes to Isaiah 35:6 ("then shall the lame man leap"), while his "the deaf hear" alludes to Isaiah 35:5 ("the ears of the deaf unstopped") and his "the dead are raised up" alludes to Isaiah 26:19 ("your dead shall live, their bodies shall rise"). The last phrase, "the poor have good news preached to them," alludes to Isaiah 61:1 ("the Lord has anointed me to bring good tidings to the poor"), a prophetic passage that probably underlies Jesus' well known beatitude: "Blessed are the poor, for yours is the kingdom of God" (Lk 6:20; see Mt 5:3).

These allusions to words and phrases from Isaiah strongly suggest that Jesus saw his ministry of mighty deeds as in *fulfillment of prophetic expectations.* Accordingly, his mighty deeds give us important insight into how Jesus himself understood his ministry.

Recognizing the allusive presence of Isaiah 61 also helps us understand why John the Baptist had his doubts. According to Isaiah 61:1, the anointed one of the Lord is "to bind up the brokenhearted, to proclaim liberty to the captives, and the opening of the prison to those who are bound." John was still locked up in prison, so how was Jesus the Lord's anointed (or Messiah)? Jesus knew that this was what lay at the heart of John's doubts and question, so he pointed out to his colleague that many of the things spoken about in Isaiah's prophecy were being fulfilled. John and everyone else need to recognize this. If they do, they are blessed.

Interpreters all along suspected that Jesus' reply implied that he saw himself as the Messiah. This was because it was an affirmative response to the question, "Are you he who is to come?" which was a way of speaking of the expected Messiah. But also because Isaiah 61, alluded to in Jesus' reply, speaks of one "anointed" (or made "Messiah") by the Lord.

Thanks to the discovery of a scroll from Qumran's fourth cave (that is, 4Q521), we now know that Jesus' appeal to the various words and phrases

THE COMING MESSIAH

An important fragmentary scroll from Qumran envisions the appearance of God's Messiah as follows:

> [. . . For the hea]vens and the earth shall listen to his Messiah [and all t]hat is in them shall not turn away from the commandments of the holy ones. Strengthen yourselves, O you who seek the Lord, in his service. (*vacat*) Will you not find the Lord in this, all those who hope in their heart? For the Lord seeks the pious and calls the righteous by name. Over the humble his spirit hovers, and he renews the faithful in his strength. For he will honor the pious upon the th[ro]ne of the eternal kingdom, setting prisoners free, opening the eyes of the blind, raising up those who are bo[wed down.] And for [ev]er (?) I (?) shall hold fast [to]the [ho]peful and pious [. . .] . . . [. . .] . . shall not be delayed [. . .] and the Lord shall do glorious things which have not been done, just as he said. For he will heal the injured, he shall make alive the dead, he shall proclaim good news to the afflicted, he shall . . [. . . the . . .], he shall lead the [. . .], and the hungry he shall enrich (?). (4Q521 frags. 2 + 4, col. ii, lines 1-13)

from Isaiah was indeed a messianic reply. This scroll, called by some *The Messianic Apocalypse,* alludes to some of the same words and phrases from Isaiah and related Scriptures, all under the heading of God's "Messiah whom heaven and earth will obey."[8]

We see then that Jesus' mighty deeds were not only viewed as in fulfillment of prophetic Scripture, they also attested Jesus' messianic identity.[9] Jesus and his followers were not the only ones who understood them this way; others did too.

Jesus' Mighty Deeds

Through the mighty deeds of Jesus the disciples gained important insight into who their Master was and the nature of the authority that he possessed. To neglect this dimension of Jesus' ministry cannot help but distort his portrait.

It was through his power to heal that Jesus demonstrated to skeptics that he possessed the authority to forgive sin:

And they came, bringing to him a paralytic carried by four men. And when they could not get near him because of the crowd, they removed the roof above him; and when they had made an opening, they let down the pallet on which the paralytic lay. And when Jesus saw their faith, he said to the paralytic, "My son, your sins are forgiven." Now some of the scribes were sitting there, questioning in their hearts, "Why does this man speak thus? It is blasphemy! Who can forgive sins but God alone?" And immediately Jesus, perceiving in his spirit that they thus questioned within themselves, said to them, "Why do you question thus in your hearts? Which is easier, to say to the paralytic, 'Your sins are forgiven,' or to say, 'Rise, take up your pallet and walk? But that you may know that the Son of man has authority on earth to forgive sins" — he said to the paralytic — "I say to you, rise, take up your pallet and go home." And he rose, and immediately took up the pallet and went out before them all; so that they were all amazed and glorified God, saying, "We never saw anything like this!" (Mk 2:3-12)

This is an important passage, for it sheds light on the meaning of "Son of Man," which was Jesus' preferred way of referring to himself. Although some scholars demur, it is likely that "Son of Man," which in Aramaic is an idiom that simply means "a human," derives from Daniel 7. I say this because Jesus consistently says "*the* Son of Man." The definite article, *the,* denotes specificity. That is, Jesus has in mind a specific "Son of Man," not simply a human. Because in a few places Jesus links "the Son of Man" with actual words and phrases from Daniel 7 (for example, Mk 10:45; 14:62) it is likely that "*the* Son of Man" refers to the figure in Daniel's vision.

In the vision of Daniel 7 the Son of Man figure receives authority and kingdom (or rule) *in heaven.* Jesus heals the paralyzed man to prove that as "the Son of Man" he has authority *on earth* to forgive sins. Jesus' "on earth" finds its counterpart in the heavenly scene of Daniel 7.

This heavenly authority is what distinguishes the mighty deeds of Jesus from the healings and exorcisms attributed to others. Jesus' other miracles leave the disciples and crowds awestruck and wondering who and what

THE SON OF MAN IN DANIEL'S VISION OF HEAVEN
AND IN JESUS' REPLY TO THE HIGH PRIEST

I saw in the night visions, and behold, with the clouds of heaven there came one like a son of man, and he came to the Ancient of Days and was presented before him. And to him was given dominion and glory and kingdom, that all peoples, nations, and languages should serve him; his dominion is an everlasting dominion, which shall not pass away, and his kingdom one that shall not be destroyed. (Dan 7:13-14)

But he was silent and made no answer. Again the high priest asked him, "Are you the Christ, the Son of the Blessed?" And Jesus said, "I am; and you will see the Son of man seated at the right hand of Power, and coming with the clouds of heaven." (Mk 14:61-62)

kind of man he is. We see this clearly in the great catch of fish:

Getting into one of the boats, which was Simon's, he asked him to put out a little from the land. And he sat down and taught the people from the boat. And when he had ceased speaking, he said to Simon, "Put out into the deep and let down your nets for a catch." And Simon answered, "Master, we toiled all night and took nothing! But at your word I will let down the nets." And when they had done this, they enclosed a great shoal of fish; and as their nets were breaking, they beckoned to their partners in the other boat to come and help them. And they came and filled both the boats, so that they began to sink. But when Simon Peter saw it, he fell down at Jesus' knees, saying, "Depart from me, for I am a sinful man, O Lord." For he was astonished, and all that were with him, at the catch of fish which they had taken; and so also were James and John, sons of Zebedee, who were partners with Simon. And Jesus said to Simon, "Do not be afraid; henceforth you will be catching people." (Lk 5:3-10)

Peter's recognition of his sinfulness and the need to put distance between himself and Jesus is reminiscent of the similar reaction of the prophet when he finds himself in the presence of God (for example, Is 6:5-7).

Remember also the miracle of the stilling of the storm:

And a great storm of wind arose, and the waves beat into the boat, so that the boat was already filling. But he was in the stern, asleep on the cushion; and they woke him and said to him, "Teacher, do you not care if we perish?" And he awoke and rebuked the wind, and said to the sea, "Peace! Be still!" And the wind ceased, and there was a great calm. He said to them, "Why are you afraid? Have you no faith?" And they were filled with awe, and said to one another, "Who then is this, that even wind and sea obey him?" (Mk 4:37-41)

The disciples' question, "Who then is this, that even wind and sea obey him?" alludes to the mighty deeds of God himself:

Some went down to the sea in ships,
　　doing business on the great waters;
they saw the deeds of the LORD,
　　his wondrous works in the deep.
For he commanded, and raised the stormy wind,
　　which lifted up the waves of the sea.
They mounted up to heaven, they went down to the depths;
　　their courage melted away in their evil plight;
they reeled and staggered like drunken men,
　　and were at their wits' end.
Then they cried to the LORD in their trouble,
　　and he delivered them from their distress;
he made the storm be still,
　　and the waves of the sea were hushed. (Ps 107:23-29)

The story as told in Mark 4 may well have been colored by details from Psalm 107. But even so, the impulse to portray Jesus in such terms speaks of the stunning impression his deeds had on his followers. To see Jesus in action, we can say, is to see God in action. Therefore, to tell the story adequately required appropriation of the language of Old Testament Scripture that spoke of the mighty and saving deeds of God himself. Jesus has impressed himself on his disciples in such a manner that only the language normally reserved for God could convey the full reality of their experience.

JESUS' MIRACLES

Scholars rightly compare Jesus with other Jewish exorcists and holy men. This is entirely appropriate, for comparative study is vital in doing historical and interpretive work. It helps us see more clearly how someone like Jesus would have been viewed by his contemporaries. Would he have been viewed as a magician? a prophet? a holy man? Or perhaps in another category altogether?

Josephus, the first-century Jewish historian, tells us of one Eleazar, an exorcist, who could "release people possessed by demons." This exorcist made

---

JOSEPHUS ON ELEAZAR THE EXORCIST

I have observed a certain Eleazar, of my race, in the presence of Vespasian, his sons, tribunes and a number of other soldiers, release people possessed by demons. Now this was the manner of the cure: Placing to the nostrils of the demon possessed person the ring which had under the seal a root which Solomon had prescribed, he then, as the person smelled it, drew out the demon through the nostrils. When the person fell down, he adjured the demon, speaking Solomon's name and repeating the incantations that he had composed, never to re-enter him. Then, wishing to persuade and to prove to those present that he had this ability, Eleazar would place at a small distance either a cup full of water or a foot basin and command the demon while going out of the human to overturn it and to make known to those watching that he had left him. And when this happened, the understanding and wisdom of Solomon were clearly revealed, on account of which we felt compelled to speak in order that all might know of the greatness of his nature and divine favor, and that the surpassing virtue of the king might not be forgotten by anyone. (*Antiquities of the Jews* 8.46-49)

---

use of various paraphernalia, including a smoldering root, a ring with a special seal, the name of Solomon and incantations said to have been handed down from the wise king of old. Jesus himself alludes to Jewish exorcists in his own time (see Lk 11:19). We probably should assume that the procedure they followed was much the same as that of Eleazar.

We are also told stories of other healers who were near contemporaries of Jesus. One, from the first century B.C., was known as Honi the Circle-Drawer. He earned this interesting sobriquet by praying, on one occasion, for rain. When none came he drew a circle on the ground and told God that he would not leave the circle until proper rain fell. Another was known as Hanina ben (or son of) Dosa. He was born a decade or two after Jesus. Several remarkable stories are told about him. In one story we are told that he used to pray and squeeze his head between his knees. If his prayer came fluently, then he knew that the person for whom he prayed would live; if it did not come fluently, he knew that the person for whom he prayed would die.

These examples are instructive to a point. A holy man, probably an early form of rabbi, who is pious and is known for having his prayers answered, sometimes in amazing ways, provides a general framework in which Jesus himself may well have been compared by many of his contemporaries. But the behavior of Jesus was significantly different from these men. Jesus did not pray in order to bring about healing. He never bargained with God (for example, "I will not leave this circle until this poor child recovers"). And in contrast to Eleazar the exorcist, Jesus made no use of paraphernalia—no ring with a seal, no smoldering root, no incantations handed down from Solomon and no appeal to the name of Solomon. Jesus simply touched someone or spoke a word and the healing or exorcism took place. It is no wonder that the crowds exclaimed, "What is this? A new teaching! With authority he commands even the unclean spirits, and they obey him" (Mk 1:27; see Mt 7:29; 9:8; Mk 1:22; Lk 4:32, 36).

The story of the exorcist who made use of Jesus' name provides strong evidence that Jesus was viewed by his contemporaries as a man of extraordinary power.

John said to him, "Teacher, we saw a man casting out demons in your name, and we forbade him, because he was not following us." But Jesus said, "Do not forbid him; for no one who does a mighty work in my name will be able soon after to speak evil of me. For he that is not against us is for us. (Mk 9:38-40)

It is not easy to explain this story as a creation of the early church. Indeed, the story stands somewhat in tension with the story of the professional exorcists mentioned in Acts 19. What is astonishing here is that Jesus' mighty deeds have become so well known that a professional exorcist has begun making use of Jesus' name, (presumably) just as he had been previously making use of the name of Solomon. In his own relatively brief ministry,

HONI THE CIRCLE DRAWER

According to Josephus (c. A.D. 90):

> Now there was a certain man named Honi, who was righteous and beloved of God, who at one time during a rainless period prayed to end the drought; and hearing, God sent rain. (*Antiquities of the Jews* 14.22)

According to the Mishnah (c. A.D. 200):

> Once they said to Honi the Circle-Drawer, "Pray that rain may fall." . . . He prayed, but rain did not come down. What did he do? He drew a circle and stood within it and said, "Lord of the universe, your sons have turned their faces to me, for I am as a son of the house before you. I swear by your great name that I will not move from here until you have mercy on your sons." Rain began dripping. He said, "Not for this have I prayed, but for rain [that fills] cisterns, pits, and caverns." It began to come down violently. He said, "Not for this have I prayed, but for rain of goodwill, blessing, and plenty." It came down in moderation until Israel went up from Jerusalem to the Mount of the House because of the rain. (Mishnah *Ta'anit* 3:8)

Jesus had become ranked with the best healers and exorcists.[10] Indeed, Jesus himself said, and evidently without challenge: "Behold, something greater than Solomon is here" (Mt 12:42; Lk 11:31).

Jesus' ability to heal and exorcize became so well known that it was difficult for him to move about the countryside or find time alone (Mk 1:28, 32-33, 45; 5:21; 6:53-56; 7:24). On one occasion we are told that Jesus found it necessary to teach the crowds from a boat, pushed away from the shore (Mk 4:1), thus creating a barrier between himself and those he taught. We all remember the poignant story of the woman with a hemorrhage who, hoping for healing, reached out and touched the hem of Jesus' coat (Mk 5:24-34).

JESUS' REPUTATION BEYOND EASTER

Jesus' reputation as healer and exorcist was such that at least one Jewish exorcist invoked his name to cast out unclean spirits. But this reputation did not fade after the conclusion of Jesus' ministry; in fact, it grew. Non-Christian Jews and pagans made use of Jesus' name, though not always with the results hoped for. A dramatic example of this is seen in the following story in the book of Acts:

> And God did extraordinary miracles by the hands of Paul, so that handkerchiefs or aprons were carried away from his body to the sick, and diseases left them and the evil spirits came out of them. Then some of the itinerant Jewish exorcists undertook to pronounce the

---

HANINA BEN DOSA

According to the Mishnah (c. A.D. 200):

> They say about Rabbi Hanina ben Dosa that he used to pray over the sick and say, "This one will live," or "That one will die." They said to him, "How do you know?" He said to them, "If my prayer is fluent in my mouth, I know that he is accepted; and if it is not, I know that he is rejected." (Mishnah *Berakot* 5:5)

According to the Talmud (c. A.D. 500):

> The deed happened again when Rabbi Hanina ben Dosa went to study Torah with Rabbi Yohanan ben Zakkai, that the son of Rabbi Yohanan ben Zakkai became ill. He said to him, "Hanina my son, pray for him that he may live." He put his head between his knees and prayed for him and he lived. Rabbi Yohanan ben Zakkai said, "If ben Zakkai had stuck his head between his knees for the whole day, no notice would have been taken of him. His wife said to him, "Is Hanina greater than you?" He said to her, "No; but he is like a servant before the king (and so goes in before him without waiting), and I am like a nobleman before the king (and therefore I must make an appointment)." (Babylonian Talmud *Berakot* 34b)

name of the Lord Jesus over those who had evil spirits, saying, "I adjure you by the Jesus whom Paul preaches." Seven sons of a Jewish high priest named Sceva were doing this. But the evil spirit answered them, "Jesus I know, and Paul I know; but who are you?" And the man in whom the evil spirit was leaped on them, mastered all of them, and overpowered them, so that they fled out of that house naked and wounded. And this became known to all residents of Ephesus, both Jews and Greeks; and fear fell upon them all; and the name of the Lord Jesus was extolled. Many also of those who were now believers came, confessing and divulging their practices. And a number of those who practiced magic arts brought their books together and burned them in the sight of all; and they counted the value of them and found it came to fifty thousand pieces of silver. So the word of the Lord grew and prevailed mightily. (Acts 19:11-20)

This story fits the pattern that has already been seen. The name of Jesus is recognized as so potent that professional exorcists (and probably healers too) make use of it, even if they are not Christians. Their use of the name of Jesus is purely pragmatic, even commercial. However, the name of Jesus is not to be trifled with. As in the New Testament Gospel stories, so here we have a powerful demon that recognizes the name of Jesus and the name of Paul, an apostle of Jesus. The evil spirit knows and respects Jesus and Paul, but it has no regard for the seven sons of Sceva. The power of the demon is seen in how it overpowers these men and drives them out.

Even in pagan traditions the name of Jesus was believed to be powerful. Let's examine a portion of a well-known exorcism formula from the Greek Magical Papyrus published many years ago.

A tested charm of Pibechis [a legendary magician from Egypt] for those possessed by demons: Take oil of unripe olives with the herb mastigia and the fruit pulp of the lotus, and boil them with colorless marjoram, while saying, "IOEL OS SARTHIOMI. . . . Come out of ____ (add the victim's name)." The Phylactery: On a tin lamella write "IAEO ABRAOTH . . ." and hang it on the patient. It is terrifying to every demon, a thing he fears. After placing the patient opposite you, conjure as follows: "I conjure you by the God of the Hebrews, Jesus, IABA IAE ABRAOTH . . . who appears in fire, who is in the midst of land, snow, and fog . . . let your angel, the implacable, descend and let him assign the demon flying around this form, which God formed in his holy paradise, because I pray to the holy God . . . who saved his people from Pharaoh and brought upon Pharaoh ten plagues because of his disobedience. . . . I conjure you by the seal that Solomon placed on the tongue of Jeremiah." (lines 3007-3041).[11]

Here we see Jesus' name invoked, right along with magical names and names of deities. We also see reference to the "seal" associated with Solomon. But what is astonishing is that Jesus is referred to as "the God of the Hebrews." A pagan exorcist, familiar with various Jewish traditions, was aware of the power of Jesus' name (through firsthand observation?) and probably knew that Jesus was Jewish and that early Christians confessed him as God's Son. Accordingly, from this pagan's point of view Jesus could be described as the God of the Hebrews.

Finally, even in rabbinic tradition recorded in the Talmud, we find discussion over the legitimacy of being healed in the name of Jesus. Evidently, some rabbis believed it was better to die than to be healed in the name of Jesus. A discussion such as this attests to the the ongoing reputation of Jesus as healer and exorcist.

The conclusion to be drawn from the evidence is that Jesus was known as a healer and exorcist throughout his ministry and beyond, and that these mighty deeds clarified in important ways the significance of his proclamation of the rule of God and the significance of his own person. If we hope to understand the historical Jesus fully and accurately, his mighty deeds must be given their proper place. Mighty deeds diminished is a Jesus distorted.

Dubious Uses of Josephus

Understanding Late Antiquity

Another way modern scholars distort the picture of Jesus in the New Testament Gospels is through questionable use of Josephus and related sources from late antiquity. Some scholars doubt the veracity of the New Testament Gospels because of their apparent lack of agreement with narratives related by Josephus, the well-known first-century Jewish historian and apologist. This lack of agreement, some say, is evidence that the Gospels are historically inaccurate. The alleged differences between the Gospels and Josephus often are exaggerated and sometimes—and this is important—the bias of Josephus is overlooked. But before exploring these issues further, a few things need to be said about Josephus and his writings.

Josephus and His Writings

Joseph bar Matthias was born into an aristocratic priestly family in A.D. 37, the year that Pontius Pilate was removed as governor of Judea and Samaria. Joseph (later known as Josephus) was educated in Rome, and on returning in the 60s he recognized the beginnings of unrest that would eventually lead to revolt. Josephus would have us believe that he tried to talk his countrymen out of revolt—because he rightly recognized Rome's great power. But when the revolt finally came, Joseph was given command of the Jewish rebel forces in Galilee. It is surprising that such authority would be entrusted to someone opposed to war. We probably have here an example of the self-serving, disingenuous side of the man Joseph. It is not the only such example.[1]

Defeated and in hiding, Joseph managed to save his life by prophesying the accession of Vespasian as emperor of Rome. This was a shrewd guess on the part of Joseph, who in A.D. 67 knew that Nero's days were numbered, that he had no successor and that Romans loved victorious generals. The odds favored General Vespasian. In due course, Nero died (in 68), three would-be successors (Galba, Otho and Vitellius) failed, and Vespasian (in 69) was proclaimed emperor of the Roman Empire. The prophecy of Joseph was fulfilled. Shortly after, he was liberated and assisted Titus, son of Vespasian, in bringing the Jewish rebellion to an end. Joseph accompanied Titus to Rome, adopted the imperial family name Flavius, Latinized his given name to Josephus, married a Roman aristocrat, took up residence in Italy, and wrote a series of books defending the Jewish people, explaining his life and role in the great revolt, and extolling the virtues of the Romans, especially his benefactors the Flavians.

Four of Josephus's works survive. These include *Jewish Wars* (7 vols.), *Antiquities of the Jews* (20 vols.), *Against Apion* (2 vols.), and *Life of Flavius Josephus*. *Jewish Wars,* composed in the mid-70s, describes the Jewish revolt from Rome, from A.D. 66 until the capture and destruction of Jerusalem in 70 and the later capture in 73 or 74 of Masada, Herod's mountain fortress that had been occupied by Jewish rebels. *Antiquities of the Jews* was first published around 90 and went through two or three subsequent editions. In this work Josephus tells the history of the Jewish people, from the book of Genesis to his own time. *Against Apion* is a polemical and apologetical work directed against Apion, an anti-Semite who among other things claimed that the Jewish race was neither ancient nor distinguished. *Life* is Josephus's autobiography. *Against Apion* and *Life* were probably published in the 90s.

In these works we hear of Pharisees and Sadducees, of scribes and priests (including high priests Annas and Caiaphas), and of familiar rulers and political figures, such as Herod the Great; his sons Archelaus, Herod Antipas and Philip; his grandson Agrippa; and various Roman authorities such as Pontius Pilate, Felix and Festus. Many of the places mentioned in the New Testament are found in the narratives of Josephus, including Galilee, Caesarea, Jericho, the Mount of Olives and Jerusalem. Josephus has much to say about the temple, about Israel's biblical and postbiblical history, and about various nationalities and ethnic groups, such as Greeks, Romans, Nabateans and Samaritans. In a few places Josephus actually mentions figures that play an important role in the founding of the Christian movement. These include Jesus, his brother James and John the Baptist.

Today some scholars believe that Josephus's account of the preaching, imprisonment and death of John the Baptist differs significantly with the accounts of the New Testament Gospels. In addition to this, some scholars think that the portrait of Pontius Pilate in the New Testament Gospels differs with what we are told in Josephus (and also in Philo, an older Jewish contemporary). These scholars suspect that the accounts of the New Testament Gospels are theologically motivated and therefore probably are not historically reliable. Is this skepticism justified? Do the narratives of Josephus and Philo necessarily lead to this conclusion?

JOSEPHUS ON JOHN THE BAPTIST

Although scholars from time to time have expressed doubts about the authenticity of the passages in Josephus's writings that speak of Jesus (*Antiquities* 18.63-64) and James (*Antiquities* 20.200-201), Josephus's account of the preaching and death of John the Baptist is widely accepted as authentic. Most scholars believe that this account is independent of the narrative preserved in the New Testament Gospels. What Josephus says about John is important because it not only offers us an independent perspective but places

JOSEPHUS ON JESUS OF NAZARETH

At this time there appeared Jesus, a wise man, *if indeed one ought to call him a man*. For he was a doer of amazing deeds, a teacher of persons who receive truth with pleasure. He won over many Jews and many of the Greeks. *He was the Messiah*. And when Pilate condemned him to the cross, the leading men among us having accused him, those who loved him from the first did not cease to do so. *For he appeared to them the third day alive again, the divine prophets having spoken these things and a myriad of other marvels concerning him.* And to the present the tribe of Christians, named after this person, has not disappeared. (*Antiquities* 18.63-64)

The words placed in italics are likely later Christian insertions into Josephus's account.

John into a broader political and historical context. Part of this broader political and historical context involves other public figures who attracted crowds and ran afoul of the authorities.

John the Baptist is, of course, familiar to readers of the New Testament Gospels. The public ministry of Jesus begins with the Baptist, who calls on the Jewish people to repent, to be baptized (that is, immersed) in the Jordan River (Mk 1:4-5), and, according to material found only in Luke (see 3:10-14), the Baptist urges people to be honest and generous. In the Gospels the message of John is given a distinctly eschatological orientation. That is, John's message is understood to be a call to prepare for changes God is about to bring about in Israel and in the world. The prophecy of Isaiah 40:3 ("Prepare the way of the Lord") is linked to his ministry. Moreover, John warns of coming judgment and predicts the coming of one "mightier" than himself who will baptize the people in spirit and fire (Mk 1:7-8).

The New Testament Gospels go on to say that John criticized Herod Antipas, the tetrarch of Galilee (ruled 4 B.C.-A.D. 39), for divorcing his wife (the

JOSEPHUS ON JAMES, THE BROTHER OF JESUS

He [Ananus] convened the council of judges and brought before it the brother of Jesus—the one called "Christ"—whose name was James, and certain others. Accusing them of transgressing the law he delivered them up for stoning. But those of the city considered the most fair-minded and strict concerning the laws were offended at this and sent to the king secretly urging him to order Ananus to take such actions no longer. (*Antiquities* 20.200-201)

daughter of Aretas IV, the king of Nabatea to the east) and marrying Herodias, the wife of his half-brother Herod Philip (Mk 6:18). Incensed, Herod imprisons John (Mk 6:17). Later, to make good on a boast before distinguished guests, Herod has John beheaded (Mk 6:16, 27-28).[2]

While some of this story appears in Josephus's account, the emphasis is different. Josephus focuses on the tensions between Galilee and Nabatea, which reached a crisis when the Nabatean king, in response to Herod's treatment of the king's daughter, attacked and destroyed Herod's army. The destruction of Herod's army was widely believed among the Jewish people to be divine retribution on Herod for putting John to death. Here is what Josephus has to say of John:

> Now it seemed to some of the Jews that the destruction of Herod's army was by God, and was certainly well deserved, on account of what he did to John, called the Baptist. For Herod had executed him, though he was a good man and had urged the Jews—if inclined to exercise virtue, to practice justice toward one another and piety toward God—to join in baptism. For baptizing was acceptable to him [God], not for pardon of whatever sins they may have committed, but in purifying the body, as though the soul had beforehand been cleansed in righteousness. And when others gathered (for they were greatly moved by his words), Herod, fearing that John's great influence over the people might result in some form of insurrection (for it seemed that they did everything by his counsel), thought it much better to put him to death before his work led to an uprising than to await a disturbance, become involved in a problem, and have second thoughts. So the prisoner, because of Herod's suspicion, was sent to Machaerus, the stronghold previously mentioned, and there was executed. But to the Jews it seemed a vindication of John that God willed to do Herod an evil, in the destruction of the army. (*Antiquities* 18.116-19)

Some critics think this account of John's preaching and activities contradicts the accounts that we have in the New Testament Gospels. But does it really? I don't think so. In fact, when we allow for Josephus's avoidance of eschatology and messianism, and for his attempt to portray Jewish religious parties in philosophical dress, we find that what Josephus says about John coheres with what the New Testament says.

According to Josephus, John "urged the Jews—if inclined to exercise virtue, to practice justice toward one another and piety toward God—to join in baptism." This, of course, is what the New Testament Gospels say. Josephus also says that baptism is acceptable to God, "not for pardon of whatever sins they may have committed, but in purifying the body, as though the soul had beforehand been cleansed in righteousness." Surely this also agrees with what the New Testament Gospels say. According to them, "John the baptizer appeared in the wilderness, preaching a baptism of repentance for the forgiveness of sins" (Mk 1:4; see Mt 3:1, 6; Lk 3:3). But baptism without repentance and a change in behavior was not acceptable to the John of the New Testament Gospels. He warns the people who come to him: "Bear fruit that befits repentance, and do not presume to say to yourselves, 'We have Abraham as our father'; for I tell you, God is able from these stones to raise up children to Abraham" (Mt 3:8-9; Lk 3:8-9). Josephus says that John called for the practice of "justice toward one another and piety toward God" (and here we hear a form of the Great Commandment—to love God and to love one's neighbor). In the New Testament Gospels, John insists on the same: "He who has two coats, let him share with him who has none; and he who has food, let him do likewise" (Lk 3:11).

When carefully compared and when allowance is made for what Josephus wished to withhold and what the New Testament Evangelists wished to emphasize, the accounts found in Josephus and in the New Testament Gospels complement one another.

Nevertheless, some scholars think there is a major discrepancy. Some critics say that according to the New Testament John was put to death for daring to criticize Herod Antipas for divorcing his wife and marrying his brother's wife, but according to Josephus John was put to death because of his popularity and influence over the crowds. Is this a genuine discrepancy? Again, I think not.

As a digression, Mark relates the story of John's imprisonment and his eventual execution (Mk 6:14-29). John's execution is said to have been the result of his criticism of the ruler's marriage to his sister-in-law:

> Herod had sent and seized John, and bound him in prison for the sake of Herodias, his brother Philip's wife; because he had married her. For John said to Herod, "It is not lawful for you to have your brother's wife." And Herodias had a grudge against him, and wanted to kill him. (Mk 6:17-19)

Mark's narrative goes on to tell of the banquet and the request to have John's head presented on a platter.

Some scholars point out that Josephus says that Herod seized John because of his "great influence over the people," which "might result in some form of insurrection," and that this explanation contradicts the Gospels. But Josephus has hardly supplied a reason for Herod's action. What is missed is that Mark, followed by Matthew and Luke, supplies the reason that Herod feared John's influence over the people. John's criticism of the tetrarch of Galilee reflects ideas current at this time; namely, the ruler is to have but one wife and is to set a proper moral example for the people. We have some important teaching on this topic in the Dead Sea Scrolls. One of these scrolls, the Temple Scroll, says: "No man is to marry his brother's ex-wife, for that would violate his brother's rights, even if the brother shares only the same father or only the same mother. Surely that would be unclean" (11QTemple 66:12-13).[3]

Herod found himself in a difficult position. His first wife became aware of his intentions and fled to her father, King Aretas of Nabatea. Herod's action shattered the fragile truce between Roman Galilee in the west and Na-

HERODIAN KINGS AND PRINCES

Antipater the Idumaean (63-43 B.C.)
Herod the Great (37-4 B.C.)
Herod Archelaus (4 B.C.-A.D. 6)
Herod Philip (4 B.C.-A.D. 34)
Herod Antipas (4 B.C.-A.D. 39)
Herod Agrippa I (A.D. 41-44)
Herod Agrippa II (A.D. 49-93)

batea in the east. Hostilities were almost certain and Herod needed the full support of his people. John's condemnation of his actions was the last thing he needed. As it turned out, Herod's fears were fully justified, for Aretas attacked Galilee and destroyed Herod's army, as mentioned in the quotation from Josephus.[4]

The New Testament Gospels say nothing of Herod's political problems. They only mention John's criticism of the tetrarch and his subsequent arrest and execution. Eventually, Josephus also mentions this dimension of the story. He too refers to Herodias's leaving her husband and—in violation of Jewish custom—marrying his half-brother Herod. Thus, the turning point of both accounts is the same. According to Josephus:

> But Herodias, their sister, was married to Herod [Philip], the son of Herod the Great, a child of Mariamme, daughter of Simon the high priest; and to them was born Salome. After her birth Herodias, thinking to violate the ways of the fathers, abandoned a living husband and married Herod [Antipas]—who was tetrarch of Galilee—her husband's brother by the same father. (*Antiquities* 18.136)

The respective accounts differ in the description of John's message. The New Testament Gospels emphasize John's fiery call for repentance and warning of coming judgment. Josephus says none of this, emphasizing instead John's ministry of purification for those committed to righteousness. As the numbers drawn to John swelled, Herod became alarmed, eventually imprisoning the Baptist. But Josephus never directly explains why Herod would want to silence the Baptist. After all, urging Galileans to "exercise virtue" and to "practice justice toward one another" should hardly occasion alarm. But if these exhortations are seen in the context of condemning a tetrarch who was not exercising virtue and was not practicing justice (especially with regard to his first wife, the daughter of Aretas), then Herod's actions against John occasion no surprise at all.

Josephus's noneschatological portrait of John as ethicist or moralizer is probably colored by a desire to present the Baptist in Greco-Roman philosophical dress. But the portrait may not be wholly inaccurate, for in Luke 3:10-14 we are told that John urged people to live just lives. What prompted Josephus to mention John at all was the widespread opinion among Jews that the catastrophe that overtook Herod (and contributed to Rome's eventual removal of him from office) came about because of his treatment of the Baptist. Evidently Josephus agrees with this assessment and so portrays John as a "good man" who urged righteous Jews to join him in baptism. But Josephus must be careful in what he says about John's message. Any hint of an agenda of reform or restoration would create in Roman minds sympathy for

Herod, whose actions would then seem appropriate.

Whether Josephus knew more about John's preaching and suppressed it—out of his reluctance to divulge to the Roman public Jewish interest in eschatology and messianism—is difficult to say. But what Josephus tells us does complement in important ways the portrait in the New Testament Gospels, especially when viewed in the context of the activities and promises made by other men of this time.

When the respective narratives of the New Testament Gospels and Josephus are read in full context and allowance is made for the respective theological and apologetical views, the supposed contradiction between Josephus and the Gospels disappears. Josephus and the New Testament Gospels are telling the same story, but emphasizing different elements of it.

JOSEPHUS ON PONTIUS PILATE

In recent years critics have argued that the New Testament Gospel portraits of a wavering, uncertain Pilate, who finds no guilt in Jesus and is willing to release him, is fiction and part of early Christian apologetic in the face of a threatening Roman government and perhaps in the aftermath of the Jewish revolt, which resulted in Christians trying to distance themselves from their Jewish cousins. Pilate, we are told, was bloodthirsty and insensitive to justice in general and to Jewish concerns in particular. He would never have proclaimed Jesus innocent and would never have offered to release him. The New Testament Gospels—so goes the argument—give us apologetic and propaganda, not history.[5] Why do some scholars think this? Are they correct?

Scholars are ready to think the worst of Pilate because of the negative criticisms of him in the writings of two Jewish contemporaries: Philo of Alexandria (c. 20 B.C.-c. A.D. 50) and Josephus (A.D. 37-c. 100). In his invective against the Roman emperor Gaius Caligula, Philo describes Pilate the governor of Judea as a "man of an inflexible, stubborn, and cruel disposition," adding that "briberies, insults, robberies, outrages, wanton injuries, executions without trial, and endless and supremely grievous cruelty" marked his administration (*Legatio ad Gaium* 301-2). Philo's remarks are primarily in reference to the incident of the golden shields that Pilate had placed in

Herod's palace in Jerusalem. These criticisms are politically motivated and probably exaggerate the governor's faults.[6] At the time that Philo wrote (in A.D. 39 or 40), Pilate had already been removed from office and was disgraced, thus making him an easy target for vilification. And of course, portraying Pilate in the worst possible light served the larger purpose of Philo's treatise.

Josephus, who also has no praise for Pilate, relates an incident in which one night Pilate transferred, from Caesarea Maritima to Jerusalem, military standards bearing the image of the Roman emperor (possibly another version of the same event described by Philo). A large group of Jews went to

---

THE PILATE INSCRIPTION

Unearthed during an excavation of the ancient theater at Caesarea Maritima was an inscription in which Pontius Pilate dedicates a building:

Latin	Translation
[NAUTI]S TIBERIEVM	[Seamen']s Tiberieum
[PON]TIVS PILATVS	[Pon]tius Pilate,
[PRAEF]ECTVS IVDA[EA]E	[Pref]ect of Jude[a]
[REF]E[CIT]	[restor]e[s . . .]

See Geza Alfödy, "Pontius Pilatus und das Tiberieum von Caesarea Maritima," *Studia classica Israelica* 18 (1999): 85-108.

Caesarea imploring the governor to remove the standards. Only their willingness to die, unresisting, compelled Pilate to have the offensive standards returned to Caesarea (*Jewish Wars* 2.171-74; *Antiquities* 18.55-59).

Josephus relates another incident whereby Pilate dipped into the temple treasury to secure additional funding for a municipal project. The account from which the money was taken was the "sacred treasure known as *korbonas*" (*Jewish Wars* 2.175; *Antiquities* 18.60-62). Josephus is here referring to the dedicated offering known as "korban," that is, a gift given to God (" 'korban,' that is, 'gift' " [Mk 7:11]; "It is not lawful to put them [that is, Judas's pieces of silver] into the *korbonas*" [Mt 27:6]). To take such consecrated

JOSEPHUS ON ANNAS AND CAIAPHAS

Quirinius had now liquidated the estate of Archelaus. . . . Since the high priest Joazar had now been overpowered by a popular faction, Quirinius stripped him of the dignity of his office and installed Annas the son of Seth as high priest. (*Antiquities* 18.26)

[Caesar] dispatched Valerius Gratus to succeed Annius Rufus as governor over the Jews. Gratus deposed Annas from his sacred office, and proclaimed Ishmael, the son of Phiabi, high priest. Not long afterwards he removed him also and appointed in his stead Eleazar the son of the high priest Annas. A year later he deposed him also and entrusted the office of high priest to Simon, the son of Camith. The last mentioned held this position for not more than a year and was succeeded by Joseph, who was called Caiaphas. After these acts Gratus retired to Rome, having stayed eleven [sic] years in Judaea. It was Pontius Pilate who came as his successor. (*Antiquities* 18.33-35)

Vitellius, on reaching Judaea, went up to Jerusalem, where the Jews were celebrating their traditional feast called the Passover. Having been received in magnificent fashion, Vitellius remitted to the inhabitants of the city all taxes on the sale of agricultural produces and agreed that the vestments of the high priest and all his ornaments would be kept in the temple in custody of the priets, as had been the privilege before. . . . Vitellius was guided by our law in dealing with the vestments, and instructed the warden not to meddle with the question where they were to be stored or when they should be used. After he had bestowed these benefits upon the nation, he removed from his sacred office the high priest Joseph surnamed Caiaphas, and appointed in his stead Jonathan, son of Annas the high priest. (*Antiquities* 18.90-91, 95)

Upon learning of the death of Festus, Caesar sent Albinus to Judaea as governor. The king removed Joseph from the high priesthood, and bestowed the succession to this office upon the son of Annas, who was ikewise called Ananus. It is said that the elder Annas was exremely fortunate. For he had five sons, all of whom, after he himself had previously enjoyed the office for a very long time, became high priests of God—a thing that had never happened to any other of our high priests. (*Antiquities* 20.197-98) items and put them to a secular use would have been highly offensive to the Jewish people. Once again, the Jewish people protest and offer no resistance. Pilate sent soldiers, dressed as civilians, among the people. At a prearranged signal, these disguised soldiers began beating the people with clubs, killing some, injuring many others and finally dispersing the crowd.

In both of the incidents related by Josephus, the ruling priests are conspicuous by their silence. This is especially startling in the case of taking money from the *korbanas*, for Pilate could not have done this, nor would he have dared to do this, without permission and assistance from the ruling priests themselves. Evidently, Caiaphas the high priest and Pilate the governor worked well together. It is not surprising that when Pilate was removed from office in early A.D. 37, after his brutal assault on the Samaritans, Caiaphas was also removed from office shortly after (*Antiquities* 18.88-89, 95).

The Evangelist Luke also alludes to a grisly event, when Jesus is told "of the Galileans whose blood Pilate had mingled with their sacrifices" (Lk 13:1). This may be yet one more instance of the governor's violence against his subjects.[7]

From episodes such as these and from the negative descriptions in Philo and Josephus, many scholars assume that Pilate had little regard for Jewish sensitivities and reacted violently against any disturbance or defiance of his authority. Therefore, because the New Testament Gospels portray Pilate as weighing his options and showing a measure of reluctance before condemning Jesus to death, scholars mistrust the testimony of the Gospels. I think this interpretation of Pilate and the Gospels, however, needs some rethinking.

Pilate's record is not nearly as bloody as it seems. Moreover, every confrontation with his subjects likely took place after consultation with Jewish leaders. Pilate was neither rash nor particularly violent. And the idea that he had no regard for Jewish sensitivities is based on an uncritical reading of Philo and Josephus, both of whom had axes to grind against the former governor. Let's review these points.

Pilate's record. Is Pilate's record a bloody one? Some think so; one popular writer refers to Pilate's approach to crowd control in one word: *slaughter!* However, I think this is an uncritical and overheated reading of the records. In the case of the shields, Pilate backed down. He killed no one.

The peaceful Jewish protest was successful. In the case of the use of sacred funds for the municipal project, Pilate must have acted with at least tacit support from the ruling priests, for he could never have dipped into a temple treasury without permission. The public protest was in all probability as much directed against the ruling priests, especially the captain of the treasury, for allowing this sacrilege as it was directed against the Roman governor. Pilate's cowardly stratagem of disguising his soldiers and starting a riot, which his troops could then put down violently, is just the sort of unprincipled craftiness we see at work during the hearing and plebiscite involving Jesus of Nazareth. It is possible that the attack on the crowd protesting the misuse of sacred monies is the attack mentioned in Luke 13. If so, then we have only one bloody encounter between Pilate and his Jewish subjects. The other bloody encounter—the one with the Samaritans—would prove to be Pilate's undoing.

Pilate's assault on the Samaritans in A.D. 36 and his subsequent removal from office, along with the removal of Caiaphas, are instructive. A Samaritan prophet persuaded many of his countrymen that God had shown him the location of the lost temple vessels. Accordingly, many gathered to this prophet at the foot of Mount Gerizim, where the Samaritan temple once stood. Why would Pilate take notice of a Samaritan prophet who was concerned with the location of the vessels that once were part of the Samaritan temple at the foot of Mount Gerizim? Josephus casts the event in as much political light as possible, suggesting that part of the Samaritan prophet's agenda was national renewal and insurrection. National and religious renewal may well have been part of the prophet's agenda, but was his preaching to the Samaritan people really a prelude to insurrection? If it was, why was Pilate summarily removed from office? And why was Caiaphas also removed?

Although Josephus withholds vital information, a plausible answer to these questions is not hard to find. The Samaritan prophet did not hope to find the lost sacred vessels as a prelude to insurrection but as a prelude to rebuilding the Samaritan temple, which the Hasmoneans—the Jewish high-priestly rulers—destroyed in the second century B.C. The Jewish ruling priests destroyed the Samaritan temple as part of their effort to re-Judaize the traditional land of Israel. The Samaritans never forgave their Jewish cousins. In fact, they retaliated by sneaking into the Jewish temple one night and scattering human bones in the sacred precincts. As a result of these bad acts there was bad blood between Jews and Samaritans, and Josephus recounts tales of violence and antagonism. Jesus' teaching presupposes this ill will (for example, the parable of the good Samaritan or the story of the grateful Samaritan leper).

If the Samaritan prophet only hoped to find the sacred vessels in order to renew Samaritan interest in rebuilding their temple, why then did Pilate attack them? I think it is likely that the governor was encouraged to take this action by his ranking Jewish collaborator, Caiaphas the high priest. And why did Caiaphas encourage Pilate to attack the Samaritan prophet and his following? Because Caiaphas was not about to stand by and allow the Samaritans to rebuild a rival temple, a temple that the high priest's predecessors rightly destroyed a century and a half earlier. It is most likely that Caiaphas interpreted the Samaritan's goals in the most alarming way and encouraged Pilate to take action. Once the vessels were found, the temple would be rebuilt. And once the temple was rebuilt, rebellion would soon follow. Pilate took the bait. After the attack, the Samaritans bitterly complained, and Pilate was removed from office. When Caiaphas's role in the affair was discovered, he too was removed.

We have evidence that other Roman governors acted on intelligence and advice provided to them by the ruling priests. During the administration of Cuspius Fadus (A.D. 44-46) Josephus tells us of a man named Theudas who urged the people to take up their possessions and meet him at the Jordan River, where at his command the waters would be parted (*Antiquities* 20.97-98). The Roman governor dispatched the cavalry, which scattered Theudas's following. The would-be prophet was himself decapitated and his head put on display in Jerusalem. It is likely that Theudas's association with the Jordan River was an attempt to reenact the story of Joshua and the crossing of the Jordan at the beginning of the conquest of the Promised Land (Josh 4). Thus Theudas's summons to the populace was indeed a prelude to a reconquest of the land of Israel and the overthrow of the land's current rulers. This is quite clear to people who know the stories of Israel's Scriptures, but how did the Roman governor know any of this? The best explanation is that the ruling priests, acting in their advisory and collaborative role, informed the governor.

Let's consider another example. During the administration of the Roman governor Antonius Felix (A.D. 52-60), a Jewish man from Egypt made an appearance in Jerusalem (*Jewish Wars* 2.259-63; *Antiquities* 20.169-70). He stationed himself on the Mount of Olives, which overlooks the Temple Mount, and summoned people to himself, claiming that at his command the walls of the city would fall down, permitting him and his following to enter the city and presumably to take control of it. Governor Felix promptly dispatched the cavalry, which routed and dispersed the following. However, the Egyptian himself escaped. Here again, we have a man acting out Joshua typology, in this case hoping that the walls of Jerusalem would fall, just as the walls of Jericho had centuries earlier. Again, in all probability ruling priests informed the Roman governor as to the meaning of the Jewish man's activities and words.

My point here is to show that Roman governors usually acted after consultation with the local, native authorities. In the case of Pontius Pilate, it is likely that he took action against the Jewish people who protested profane use of the sacred *korban* money and later against the Samaritans only after consultation with Caiaphas and his associates. These two incidents may well have been the lone violent actions taken against the public during Pilate's administration.

Pilate's tenure. There is another point here to consider. Pilate is usually thought to have assumed office in A.D. 25 or 26. His removal in early 37 means that he was governor about eleven years. But there is evidence (from coins and from Josephus) that Pilate's tenure in office may have begun as early as 19 or 20. If so—and this is not the place to debate a complicated question—then Pontius Pilate may have been governor of Judea and Samaria for seventeen years. By standards of the time, to have been a governor so long in a place such as Judea, with significant elements of the population that deeply resented the presence and authority of foreigners, Pilate's administration was remarkably stable and peaceful. We might compare Pilate to two of his successors: (1) the two-year administration of Fadus (and the slaughter of Theudas), and (2) the eight-year administration of Felix (and the slaughter of the Egyptian Jew's following). If Pilate had only two bloody clashes with his subjects in a seventeen-year period (or even eleven-year period, for that matter), his administration seems no worse than the administrations of others and may even have been better than most.

I am not trying to rehabilitate Pilate, much less canonize him (as indeed he is in the Coptic Church!). I have no doubt that by today's standards the governor was corrupt and had little or no commitment to justice or human rights. I doubt that he had any genuine concern whatsoever with regard to Jesus of Nazareth and whether he lived or died.

In the case of Jesus, Pilate's motives were thoroughly political. On the eve of the Passover, the most sacred holiday in the Jewish calendar, with Jerusalem swollen with Jews who took their faith seriously and longed for Israel's redemption, Pilate found himself confronted with a potentially dangerous situation. Pilate's Jewish collaborators—Caiaphas and his priestly associates—were calling for the immediate execution of Jesus. But is a public execution in the vicinity of Jerusalem at Passover time a smart move? And was Jesus, who talked of God's rule but had no armed following, a serious threat? Pilate's hesitation had nothing to do with justice; it had everything to do with politics. Pilate knew the primary motivation of Caiaphas and his temple associates was that Jesus had insulted them, implying in his teaching that they were unworthy of their office and faced divine judgment. Pilate did not want to execute a popular preacher and healer in public and on the eve of Passover for no more reason than that he had angered an aristocratic priesthood that many Jews regarded with contempt. Pilate the shrewd politician was a survivor and was not about to be harried into making a rash decision.

Jesus' refusal to deny the accusation that he had either claimed or had allowed his following to believe that he was Israel's anointed king persuaded Pilate that Jesus should be put to death. Because Jesus was found guilty of high treason and not simply disturbance of the peace, he was condemned to crucifixion, with the charge that he had claimed to be "king of the Jews" (Mk 15:26; see Mt 27:37; Lk 23:38; Jn 19:19). So in the end, Pilate yielded to the demands of the ruling priests (as evidently he did on other occasions, finally resulting in his removal from office), but only after he shifted responsibility to the ruling priests by washing his hands and declaring, "I am innocent of this man's blood" (Mt 27:24). From a legal point of view, this was not necessary, for Jesus' tacit acknowledgment of his role in the awaited kingdom of God provided sufficient grounds in the eyes of Rome for his execution. But from a political point of view the wily governor wanted to be sure that, in the eyes of the Jewish public, the decision to have Jesus put to death was not his, at least not alone.

Far from unhistorical apologetic, as some critics assert, this is Pilate in true form. This is the Pilate who tries to sneak images of Caesar into Jerusalem, but when confronted by an angry public backs down. This is the Pilate who wants to break up the mob protesting a serious violation in the use of dedicated funds, but does so through deception and trickery. This is the Pilate who is guided by high-priestly counsel and eventually—after a long tenure in office—finds himself recalled. The Pilate of the New Testament Gospels is consistent with the Pilate known to us from other sources—when the Gospels and these other sources are read critically and in full context.[8]

When Pilate is understood better—and this means that we not accept at face value the vilified presentations in Philo and Josephus—the objections sometimes lodged against the historicity of the governor's Passover pardon are also answered. According to the New Testament Gospels, it was Pilate's custom at Passover to release a prisoner: "Now at the feast he used to release for them one prisoner for whom they asked" (Mk 15:6; see Mt 27:15; Jn 18:39). Some critics argue that because nothing is said in other sources of Pilate's offer of a pardon at Passover, the Gospels cannot be trusted. This is hardly good historical argumentation. On the contrary, it smacks of scholarly bias.

All four Gospels know of Pilate's custom, and other sources in fact do mention the release of prisoners on various occasions, including at Passover. The Mishnah (Jewish oral law and tradition committed to writing at the beginning of the third century) says that "they may slaughter [the Passover lamb] for one . . . whom they have promised to bring out of prison" on the Passover (m. *Pesahim* 8:6). Who the "they" are is not made clear (Jewish authorities? Roman authorities?), but it is interesting that the promised release from prison is for the express purpose of taking part in the Passover observance. A papyrus (P.Flor 61, c. A.D. 85), quotes the words of the Roman governor of Egypt: "You were worthy of scourging . . . but I give you to the crowds." In his letters Pliny the Younger (early second century) says, "It was asserted, however, that these people were released upon their petition to the proconsuls, or their lieutenants; which seems likely enough, as it is improbable any person should have dared to set them at liberty without authority" (*Epistles* 10.31). An inscription from Ephesus relates the decision of the proconsul of Asia to release prisoners because of the outcries of the people of the city. Livy (writing early first century) speaks of special dispensations whereby chains were removed from the limbs of prisoners (*History of Rome* 5.13.8). Josephus tells us that when governor Albinus prepared to leave office (A.D. 64), he released all prisoners incarcerated for offenses other than murder (*Antiquities* 20.215). He did this hoping to gain a favorable review from the inhabitants of Jerusalem. And finally, years earlier Archelaus hoped to appease his countrymen, and so gain his late father's kingdom, by acquiescing to their demands that those imprisoned be released ("Some demanded the release of the prisoners who had been put in chains by Herod" [*Antiquities* 17.204]).

The evidence as a whole suggests that Roman rulers, as well as at least one Herodian prince, on occasion did release prisoners (so apparently did other rulers in the eastern Mediterranean). This was done for purely political reasons: to satisfy the demands of the crowds and to curry their favor. Another factor that supports the historicity of the Gospel narratives is the improbability of asserting such a custom if there had been none. If Pilate had not released prisoners on the Passover or on other holidays, or at least on one occasion, the Evangelists' claim that he did so could have been quickly and easily shown to be false and would therefore have occasioned embarrassment for the early church. That all four of the Evangelists report this episode (and the Fourth Evangelist probably did so independent of the three Synoptic Gospels) argues that no such embarrassment clung to the story.[9]

Josephus supplies us with further information that lends significant support to the New Testament Gospel narratives of the sequence of events, or judicial process, that led up to Jesus' death. According to the Gospels, Jesus was (1) seized by the ruling priests, (2) interrogated by the ruling priests and members of the Jewish council (or Sanhedrin), (3) handed over to the Roman governor, (4) interrogated by the governor, and then (5) condemned to death.

Some radical critics in recent years have called into question this sequence of events, suggesting that the Evangelists have invented it, either to vilify the Jewish people or to try to find a meaningful connection between Jesus' preaching and his execution. (One scholar actually suggested that in visiting Jerusalem Jesus simply got caught up in a riot and was put to death.) This skepticism is hardly warranted, and the alternative explanations are far from convincing, not least because the same sequence of events is attested in Josephus.

In the passage about Jesus (*Antiquities* 18.63-64), Josephus describes Jesus as a teacher and "doer of amazing deeds." But what is important is that Josephus says the "leading men among us" accused Jesus and that as a result Pilate condemned him to the cross. Elsewhere in Josephus, "leading men" refers to the ruling priests (see *Antiquities* 11.140-41; 18.121). Thus Josephus provides, in bare outline, the same sequence as we have it in the New Testament Gospels. But there is more.

Josephus also tells us of a prophet named Jesus ben Ananias, who in the year A.D. 62 began to proclaim the doom of the city of Jerusalem and the temple. The parallels between Jesus of Nazareth and Jesus ben Ananias are quite interesting. The relevant portions of the passage in Josephus's account of the Jewish rebellion read as follows:

> Four years before the war . . . there came to the feast, at which is the custom of all Jews to erect tabernacles to God, one Jesus son of Ananias, an untrained peasant, who, standing in the Temple, suddenly began to cry out, "A voice from the east, a voice from the west, a voice from the four winds, a voice against Jerusalem and the sanctuary, a voice against the bridegroom and the bride, a voice against all the people" [Jer 7:34]. . . . Some of the leading citizens, angered at this evil speech, arrested the man and whipped him with many blows. But he, not speaking anything in his own behalf or in private to those who struck him, continued his cries as before. Thereupon, the rulers . . .

brought him to the Roman governor. There, though flayed to the bone with scourges, he neither begged for mercy or wept. . . . When Albinus the governor asked him who and whence he was and why he uttered these cries, he gave no answer to these things. . . . Albinus pronounced him a maniac and released him. . . . He cried out especially at the feasts. . . . While shouting from the wall, "Woe once more to the city and to the people and to the sanctuary . . ." a stone . . . struck and killed him. (*Jewish Wars* 6.300-309)

We see in this passage the same judicial process that overtook Jesus of Nazareth years earlier. Both men entered the temple precincts. Both men uttered prophetic threats against the temple, with both alluding to Jeremiah 7, a scathing passage threatening the temple with destruction. (Jesus of Nazareth alluded to Jer 7:11 and Jesus ben Ananias alluded to Jer 7:34.) Both men were arrested by Jewish authorities (the ruling priests). Both men were interrogated by these authorities. Both men were subsequently handed over

---

JERUSALEM TEMPLE WARNING

A nineteen-inch-high limestone fragment contains a warning to Gentiles to stay out of the temple. The fragment was found in 1935 outside the wall around Jerusalem's Old City. A complete version of the same inscription is in the Archaeological Museum in Istanbul, Turkey. The inscription reads:

Let no Gentile enter
within the partition and barrier
surrounding the Temple; whosoever
    is caught shall be responsible
    for his subsequent
    death

This is probably the warning described by Josephus: "Upon [the partition wall of the Temple court] stood pillars, at equal distances from one another, declaring the law of purity, some in Greek, and some in Roman letters, that 'no foreigner should go within that sanctuary' " (*Jewish Wars* 5.193-94).

to the Roman governor. Both men were interrogated further by the Roman governor. Both men were scourged. The only significant difference is that whereas Pilate condemned Jesus of Nazareth to the cross, Albinus released Jesus ben Ananias, having found him a harmless maniac.

Accordingly, in two passages—one directly concerned with Jesus of Nazareth and the other concerned with another man who entered the temple precincts a generation later—Josephus corroborates the sequence of events recounted in the New Testament Gospels. On any fair reading of the Gospels the narrative of Jesus' arrest, Jewish and Roman interrogations, and eventual condemnation to the cross should be regarded as fully historical and trustworthy.

The New Testament Gospels also say that Jesus was mocked by the Roman soldiers:

> And the soldiers led him away inside the palace (that is, the praetorium); and they called together the whole battalion. And they clothed him in a purple cloak, and plaiting a crown of thorns they put it on him. And they began to salute him, "Hail, King of the Jews!" And they struck his head with a reed, and spat upon him, and they knelt down in homage to him. And when they had mocked him, they stripped him of the purple cloak, and put his own clothes on him. And they led him out to crucify him. (Mk 15:16-20)

The mockery of Jesus as a Jewish king finds an approximate parallel in one of Philo's writings. It was on the occasion of King Agrippa's visit to Alexandria, where the people seized a lunatic named Carabas, a street person who was often made sport of. According to Philo, they

> drove the poor fellow into the gymnasium and set him up high to be seen by all and put on his head a sheet of byblus spread out wide for a diadem, clothed the rest of his body with a rug for a royal robe, while someone who had noticed a piece of the native papyrus thrown away in the road gave it to him for his scepter. And when as in some theatrical farce he had received the insignia of kingship and had been tricked out as a king, young men carrying rods on their shoulders as

spearmen stood on either side of him in imitation of a bodyguard. Then others approached him, some pretending to salute him, others to sue for justice, others to consult him on state affairs. Then from the multitudes there rang out a tremendous shout hailing him as *Mari* [Aramaic, "My lord"], which is said to be the name for "lord" with the Syrians. (*In Flaccum* 36-39)

Other sources relate incidents that approximate the mockery of Jesus. There is an account of harsh and humiliating treatment of deposed would-be emperor Vitellius (A.D. 69) at the hands of Roman soldiers, who mockingly made the former emperor revisit various stations where at one time he was held in honor (see Dio Cassius *Roman History* 64.20-21). In a fragmentary deposition recording the words of the new emperor Hadrian and a Jewish embassy, with reference to the Jewish revolt that occurred toward the end of Trajan's reign (A.D. 115-117), mention is made of the mockery of a would-be monarch: "Paulus (spoke) about the king, how they brought him forth and (mocked him?); and Theon read the edict of Lupus ordering them to lead him forth for Lupus to make fun of the king" (P.Louvre 68.1.1-7). Plutarch (writing c. A.D. 100) relates a story in which Pirates mocked a prisoner who had claimed the rights of Roman citizenship. They dressed him up ("threw a toga on him"), extended to him various honors (including falling to their knees), then finally made him walk the plank (*Pompey* 24.7-8).[10]

Fair and careful study of Josephus, Philo and other sources from late antiquity shows that the New Testament Gospels offer accurate and plausible accounts of the actions of historical figures like Pontius Pilate. There are no compelling reasons to view the New Testament Gospel narratives as theologically or apologetically driven fictions that either misrepresent Pilate or vilify the ruling priests. Indeed, the narratives of the New Testament Gospels supplement in important ways our knowledge of first-century Palestine.

ANACHRONISMS AND EXAGGERATED CLAIMS

Christianities Lost and Otherwise

Lately it has become fashionable to speak of multiple "Christianities" and hosts of lost Gospels.[1] One of the fictional characters in Dan Brown's *The Da Vinci Code* declares that there were some eighty Gospels circulating in the first century, which is simply preposterous. This whole confusion is made worse when scholars attempt to smuggle second-century writings into the first century, thus "proving" that Christianity was indeed quite diverse from the beginning, and that all of these Christianities are more or less of equal merit, equal antiquity and equal authority. Sometimes these remarkable tours de force conclude with pleas for greater tolerance and openness to new forms of Christian experience. This may be politically correct, but is it historically correct?

In chapters three and four we looked at the problems encountered in trying to assign early dates to texts that bear all the markings of the second century—sometimes markings that point to the end of the second century, if not beyond. Yet these are some of the writings that a few scholars would like to convince us actually were composed in the first century—perhaps in slightly different, earlier hypothetical forms—and reflect ideas older still, perhaps reaching back to the first generation of Christians. As we have seen, there simply is no convincing evidence for the early dating of these extracanonical writings.

Even apart from the question about how early these writings can be dated, there is still the assumption held by some that there were many "Christianities" and that only one of them—the one that would eventually emerge as "orthodox" Christianity—happened to triumph, overpowering and pushing aside the other forms. This whole approach is deeply flawed and, as is the case in so much of this debate, reflects anachronism and exaggeration.

THE ORIGIN AND BELIEFS OF EARLY CHRISTIANITY

Jesus died on the eve of Passover (or Good Friday), in A.D. 30 or 33.[2] So far as his followers were concerned, the movement that John the Baptist and Jesus had launched was finished. As one of these followers was remembered

---

AN ANCIENT TESTIMONY

Papias, bishop of Hierapolis (in Asia Minor, today's Turkey), flourished in the early second century A.D. He authored five volumes of a work called *Expositions of the Sayings of the Lord*. Unfortunately, only a few fragments of this work survive in quotations in the works of later writers (such as Eusebius, the great church historian of the fourth century). In one of these surviving fragments, Papias tells of meeting followers of the "elders," that is, the apostles of Jesus:

> And if by chance someone who had been a follower of the elders should come my way, I inquired about the words of the elders—what Andrew or Peter said, or Philip, or Thomas or James, or John or Matthew or any other of the Lord's disciples, and whatever Aristion and the elder John, the Lord's disciples, were saying. For I did not think that information from books would profit me as much as information from a living and abiding voice. (Quoted by Eusebius *Ecclesiastical History* 3.39.4; see a similar report in Jerome *Famous Men* 18)

See J. B. Lightfoot, J. R. Harmer and M. W. Holmes, *The Apostolic Fathers,* rev. ed. (Grand Rapids: Baker, 1989), p. 314.

---

to have remarked, "We had hoped that he was the one to redeem Israel" (Lk 24:21). But, as it turned out, their disappointment was short-lived. What a difference a weekend can make!

Christian faith began Sunday, the first Easter, with the discovery of an empty tomb and the appearances of the risen Jesus. Of the New Testament Gospels, the Gospel of Mark provides us with the earliest account. It reads as follows:

And when the sabbath was past, Mary Magdalene, and Mary the mother of James, and Salome, bought spices, so that they might go and anoint him. And very early on the first day of the week they went to the tomb when the sun had risen. And they were saying to one another, "Who will roll away the stone for us from the door of the tomb?" And looking up, they saw that the stone was rolled back—it was very large. And entering the tomb, they saw a young man sitting on the right side, dressed in a white robe; and they were amazed. And he said to them, "Do not be amazed; you seek Jesus of Nazareth, who was crucified. He has risen, he is not here; see the place where they laid him. But go, tell his disciples and Peter that he is going before you to Galilee; there you will see him, as he told you." And they went out and fled from the tomb; for trembling and astonishment had come upon them; and they said nothing to any one, for they were afraid. (Mk 16:1-8)

Most Bibles continue with verses 9-20, usually in brackets or in a note at the bottom of the page. This is done because these verses (known as Mark's "Long Ending") are not found in the oldest manuscripts. Scholars suspect—rightly so—that they were added two to three centuries after the publication of Mark. The Gospel of Mark did not originally end at verse 8 but contained at least one more paragraph (which may have been known to Matthew) in which the appearance of Jesus to the women and to the disciples was described. What happened to Mark's original ending, we will probably never know.

The Gospels of Matthew and Luke follow Mark's account. What is provided here is limited to what goes beyond the narrative in Mark. Matthew says:

Now after the sabbath, toward the dawn of the first day of the week, Mary Magdalene and the other Mary went to see the sepulcher. . . . So they departed quickly from the tomb with fear and great joy, and ran to tell his disciples. And behold, Jesus met them and said, "Hail!" And they came up and took hold of his feet and worshiped him. Then Jesus said to them, "Do not be afraid; go and tell my brethren to go to Galilee, and there they will see me." (Mt 28:1, 8-10)

Now the eleven disciples went to Galilee, to the mountain to which Jesus had directed them. And when they saw him they worshiped him; but some doubted. And Jesus came and said to them, "All authority in heaven and on earth has been given to me. Go therefore and make disciples of all nations, baptizing them in the name of the Father and of the Son and of the Holy Spirit, teaching them to observe all that I have commanded you; and lo, I am with you always, to the close of the age." (Mt 28:16-20)

Luke says:

And returning from the tomb they told all this to the eleven and to all the rest. Now it was Mary Magdalene and Joanna and Mary the mother of James and the other women with them who told this to the apostles; but these words seemed to them an idle tale, and they did not believe them. (Lk 24:9-11)[3]

That very day two of them were going to a village named Emmaus, about seven miles from Jerusalem, and talking with each other about all these things that had happened. While they were talking and discussing together, Jesus himself drew near and went with them. But their eyes were kept from recognizing him. And he said to them, "What is this conversation which you are holding with each other as you walk?" And they stood still, looking sad. Then one of them, named Cleopas, answered him, "Are you the only visitor to Jerusalem who does not know the things that have happened there in these days?" And he said to them, "What things?" And they said to him, "Concerning Jesus of Nazareth, who was a prophet mighty in deed and word before God and all the people, and how our chief priests and rulers delivered him up to be condemned to death, and crucified him. But we had hoped that he was the one to redeem Israel. Yes, and besides all this, it is now the third day since this happened. Moreover, some women of our company amazed us. They were at the tomb early in the morning and did not find his body; and they came back saying that they had even seen a vision of angels, who said that he was alive.

Some of those who were with us went to the tomb, and found it just as the women had said; but him they did not see." And he said to them, "O foolish men, and slow of heart to believe all that the prophets have spoken! Was it not necessary that the Christ should suffer these things and enter into his glory?" And beginning with Moses and all the prophets, he interpreted to them in all the scriptures the things concerning himself.

So they drew near to the village to which they were going. He appeared to be going further, but they constrained him, saying, "Stay with us, for it is toward evening and the day is now far spent." So he went in to stay with them. When he was at table with them, he took the bread and blessed, and broke it, and gave it to them. And their eyes were opened and they recognized him; and he vanished out of their sight. They said to each other, "Did not our hearts burn within us while he talked to us on the road, while he opened to us the scriptures?" And they rose that same hour and returned to Jerusalem; and they found the eleven gathered together and those who were with them, who said, "The Lord has risen indeed, and has appeared to Simon!" Then they told what had happened on the road, and how he was known to them in the breaking of the bread. (Lk 24:13-35)

The Gospel of John says:

Now on the first day of the week Mary Magdalene came to the tomb early, while it was still dark, and saw that the stone had been taken away from the tomb. So she ran, and went to Simon Peter and the other disciple, the one whom Jesus loved, and said to them, "They have taken the Lord out of the tomb, and we do not know where they have laid him." Peter then came out with the other disciple, and they went toward the tomb. They both ran, but the other disciple outran Peter and reached the tomb first; and stooping to look in, he saw the linen cloths lying there, but he did not go in. Then Simon Peter came, following him, and went into the tomb; he saw the linen cloths lying, and the napkin, which had been on his head, not lying with the linen cloths but rolled up in a place by itself. Then the other disciple, who reached the tomb first, also went in, and he saw and believed; for as yet they did not know the scripture, that he must rise from the dead. Then the disciples went back to their homes.

But Mary stood weeping outside the tomb, and as she wept she stooped to look into the tomb; and she saw two angels in white, sitting where the body of Jesus had lain, one at the head and one at the feet. They said to her, "Woman, why are you weeping?" She said to them, "Because they have taken away my Lord, and I do not know where they have laid him." Saying this, she turned round and saw Jesus standing, but she did not know that it was Jesus. Jesus said to her, "Woman, why are you weeping? Whom do you seek?" Supposing him to be the gardener, she said to him, "Sir, if you have carried him away, tell me where you have laid him, and I will take him away." Jesus said to her, "Mary." She turned and said to him in Hebrew, "Rabboni!" (which means Teacher). Jesus said to her, "Do not hold me, for I have not yet ascended to the Father; but go to my brethren and say to them, I am ascending to my Father and your Father, to my God and your God." Mary Magdalene went and said to the disciples, "I have seen the Lord"; and she told them that he had said these things to her. (Jn 20:1-18)

These Gospel narratives are interesting, not least because of the primacy given to Mary Magdalene and other women. Let's review the data. (1) According to Mark, Mary Magdalene, Mary the mother of James, and Salome went to the tomb of Jesus and found it empty. They met a mysterious person, who told them that Jesus of Nazareth was risen and they are to report this to Peter. The account abruptly breaks off. (2) According to Matthew, Mary Magdalene and the "other Mary" (presumably the mother of James, as stated in Mark) went to the tomb. They encountered a strange figure that Matthew calls "an angel of the Lord," and they were told essentially the same thing narrated in Mark. But Matthew's narrative does not break off. It goes on to describe the appearance of Jesus to the women, who "took hold of his feet and worshiped him." The risen Jesus repeats the instructions of the angel. He later meets all of the apostles and commissions them to make disciples of all peoples.

We have some new and interesting details in Luke's version. (3) According to this Gospel, Mary Magdalene, Joanna, Mary the mother of James, and "other women with them" visited the tomb, found it empty, encountered two men in dazzling apparel, and received the commission to report the resurrection of Jesus to the apostles, who found the report idle and without credibility. Luke goes on to narrate the interesting story of the two men on their way to the village of Emmaus. One of these men is named Cleopas. They met the risen Jesus. Later, the two men found the eleven apostles (that is, the twelve apostles minus Judas Iscariot), who told the two men that the "Lord has risen indeed, and has appeared to Simon" (Peter or Cephas).[4] Luke's Gospel goes on to describe Jesus' farewell to his disciples, which in somewhat different form is repeated in Acts 1.

John's version offers a few differences also. (4) According to this Gospel, Mary Magdalene went to the tomb early Sunday morning. There is no mention of other women. When she found the stone rolled back and the tomb empty, she went and reported this to Simon Peter and the other disciple (that is, the "Beloved Disciple"). These two ran to the tomb and found it as Mary had said. Sometime later, and John's narrative is not clear on this point, Mary Magdalene returned to the tomb, still thinking that Jesus' body is missing, and there met the risen Jesus. Jesus told her, "Do not hold me," which makes us think of Matthew's version (at Mt 28:9). Mary then returned to the disciples and said, "I have seen the Lord."

These details are admittedly tangled, but a fairly clear outline does emerge: (1) Women—among whom Mary Magdalene is preeminent—are the first to find the empty tomb. (2) Mary Magdalene seems to be the first person to see the risen Jesus. (3) Peter (Cephas or Simon) sees the risen Jesus. (4) The eleven disciples, and apparently one or two others, see Jesus.

The resurrection of Jesus, as actually witnessed by the followers of Jesus, was what transformed Jesus' movement into what would become the Christian faith. All who identified themselves as a Christian in the early years of the new faith agreed.[5] There was no Christian group that discounted the resurrection and taught that Christian faith was centered on something else.

The resurrection of Jesus transformed his following, energizing it and renewing its sense of mission. It also gave rise to either new or heightened understandings of the significance of Jesus himself and his ministry. The two most important conclusions confirmed in the minds of Jesus' followers because of the resurrection were (1) the exalted status of Jesus (as Lord, Savior, Messiah, Son of God), and (2) the atoning significance of his death. The Scriptures of Israel (or what Christians call the Old Testament) were studied in the light of the resurrection and these new, deeply felt convictions.

We see this development in the other writings of the New Testament. I will focus on Paul because some claim that Paul's understanding of Jesus and the Christian faith was significantly different from the understanding of Jesus' original followers. Here is an important passage in Paul's letter to the Christians of Corinth, Greece, written in the early 50s.

> For I delivered to you as of first importance what I also received, that Christ died for our sins in accordance with the scriptures, that he was buried, that he was raised on the third day in accordance with the scriptures, and that he appeared to Cephas [Peter], then to the twelve. Then he appeared to more than five hundred brethren at one time, most of whom are still alive, though some have fallen asleep. Then he appeared to James, then to all the apostles. Last of all, as to one untimely born, he appeared also to me. (1 Cor 15:3-8)

Although Paul's "received" tradition does not match the Gospel reports exactly, there is important agreement.[6] According to Paul the risen Jesus appeared to Cephas (that is, Simon Peter), then to the Twelve. By "Twelve" Paul either means the surviving eleven apostles (that is, the Twelve minus Judas Iscariot) still referred to as the "Twelve," or he means the surviving eleven plus Matthias, who succeeded Judas (see Acts 1:23-26) and who had also seen the risen Jesus. (I think the latter option is more likely.) So far, Paul's list matches the reports of the Gospels. And, up to this point, we probably have the "official" tradition, to which Paul will add.

Paul continues by saying that Jesus appeared to more than five hundred of his followers "at one time." This appearance seems to go beyond the timeline of the New Testament Gospels. Then the risen Jesus appeared to James, the brother of Jesus, which may have been what brought James (and his brothers) into the Christian community, and to "all of the apostles," by which Paul probably means other apostles, in addition to the Twelve, such as Barnabas (see Acts 14:14; 1 Cor 9:5-6; Gal 2:9), Andronicus, Junia, and others whose names we do not know (see Rom 16:7).[7] And finally, Paul says, Jesus appeared to him.

The women are conspicuously missing in Paul's list. Not one woman is mentioned—not Mary Magdalene, not "the other Mary," no one. Why? Didn't Paul know that the women were actually the first to find the empty tomb and to see the risen Jesus? I am sure that he did. Interpreters have plausibly explained that Paul's received tradition in 1 Corinthians 15 is an "official list" of witnesses, trimmed and tightened up for apologetic purposes. Only the most important figures in the early church are mentioned by name, such as Peter and the Twelve (that is, the original eleven plus Matthias), and James the brother of Jesus. Women are doubtlessly included in the "more than five hundred" and probably are also included in "all the apostles."[8] By definition, an apostle must have seen the risen Jesus (but not all who saw the risen Jesus necessarily became apostles).

Paul's testimony is early and important. According to his letter to the churches of Galatia, in Asia Minor (today's Turkey), Paul was converted within two or three years of the resurrection of Jesus.[9] About three years later Paul went to Jerusalem to visit Peter (Gal 1:18). During that time he saw James, the brother of Jesus. Fourteen years later Paul, along with Barnabas and Titus, returned to Jerusalem (Gal 2:1). On this occasion Paul sets before the leaders of the Jerusalem church his understanding of Christian faith:

> I laid before them (but privately before those who were of repute) the gospel which I preach among the Gentiles, lest somehow I should be running or had run in vain. (Gal 2:2)

> And from those who were reputed to be something (what they were makes no difference to me; God shows no partiality)—those, I say, who were of repute added nothing to me; but on the contrary, when they saw that I had been entrusted with the gospel to the uncircumcised, just as Peter had been entrusted with the gospel to the circumcised (for he who worked through Peter for the mission to the

circumcised worked through me also for the Gentiles), and when they perceived the grace that was given to me, James and Cephas [Peter] and John, who were reputed to be pillars, gave to me and Barnabas the right hand of fellowship, that we should go to the Gentiles and they to the circumcised; only they would have us remember the poor, which very thing I was eager to do. (Gal 2:6-10)

The context makes clear that Paul's understanding of the gospel did not require Gentiles to observe Jewish law. The leaders of the Jerusalem church agreed (Gal 2:3). This is an important piece of information to bear in mind. According to Paul, his understanding of the Christian message was in agreement with the understanding of the original disciples and apostles of Jesus ("who were reputed to be pillars"), among them Peter.[10] Paul was not developing a new version of Christianity, over against the older, more Jewish form of Christianity promoted by the leaders of the church in Jerusalem.[11] The only thing that the pillars impressed on Paul was that he "remember the poor," which Paul says he was eager to do. Accordingly, Paul's understanding of the Christian message and his apostolic authority to proclaim it were confirmed by the leaders of the Jerusalem church.

The point that I want to make here is that there is absolutely no evidence of a significant difference in opinion with regard to the *core message* of the Christian faith. Both Paul and Peter affirm the death and resurrection of Jesus, and the need for a response in faith if one is to be saved. Compare the following passages.

Selections from Paul's letters:

Now I would remind you, brethren, in what terms I preached to you the gospel, which you received, in which you stand, by which you are saved, if you hold it fast—unless you believed in vain. For I delivered to you as of first importance what I also received, that Christ died for our sins in accordance with the scriptures, that he was buried, that he was raised on the third day in accordance with the scriptures, and that he appeared to Cephas, then to the twelve. (1 Cor 15:1-5)

Paul, a servant of Jesus Christ, called to be an apostle, set apart for the gospel of God which he promised beforehand through his prophets in the holy scriptures, the gospel concerning his Son, who was descended from David according to the flesh and designated Son of God in power according to the Spirit of holiness by his resurrection from the dead, Jesus Christ our Lord. (Rom 1:1-4)

For I am not ashamed of the gospel: it is the power of God for salvation to every one who has faith, to the Jew first and also to the Greek. (Rom 1:16)

If you confess with your lips that Jesus is Lord and believe in your heart that God raised him from the dead, you will be saved. For man believes with his heart and so is justified, and he confesses with his lips and so is saved. (Rom 10:9-10)

Selections from tradition associated with Peter:

Men of Israel, hear these words: Jesus of Nazareth, a man attested to you by God with mighty works and wonders and signs which God did through him in your midst, as you yourselves know—this Jesus, delivered up according to the definite plan and foreknowledge of God, you crucified and killed by the hands of lawless men. But God raised him up. . . . This Jesus God raised up, and of that we all are witnesses. . . . Repent, and be baptized every one of you in the name of Jesus Christ for the forgiveness of your sins. (Acts 2:22-24, 32, 38)

Blessed be the God and Father of our Lord Jesus Christ! By his great mercy we have been born anew to a living hope through the resurrection of Jesus Christ from the dead, and to an inheritance which is imperishable, undefiled, and unfading, kept in heaven for you, who by God's power are guarded through faith for a salvation ready to be revealed in the last time. (1 Pet 1:3-5)

For Christ also died for sins once for all, the righteous for the unrighteous, that he might bring us to God, being put to death in the flesh but made alive in the spirit. (1 Pet 3:18)

PAPIAS ON MARK AND PETER

The church historian Eusebius passes on an interesting tradition relating to the composition of the Gospel of Mark, under the influence of Peter:

> And the Elder used to say this: "Mark, having become Peter's interpreter, wrote down accurately everything he remembered, though not in order, of the things either said or done by Christ. For he neither heard the Lord nor followed him, but afterward, as I said, followed Peter, who adapted his teachings as needed but had no intention of giving an ordered account of the Lord's sayings. Consequently Mark did nothing wrong in writing down some things as he remembered them, for he made it his one concern not to omit anything which he heard or to make any false statement in them." (Quoted by Eusebius *Ecclesiastical History* 3.39.15)

See J. B. Lightfoot, J. R. Harmer and M. W. Holmes, *The Apostolic Fathers*, rev. ed. (Grand Rapids: Baker, 1989), p. 316.

Christian faith began with the resurrection of Jesus, whose death was interpreted (in Jewish terms) as atoning and saving and in fulfillment of prophecy. There was no disagreement on this point. All who believed in Jesus and were numbered among his followers concurred on these essential beliefs. There was no other "Christianity" that thought otherwise. The Gospels written in the first century, that is, the New Testament Gospels (Matthew, Mark, Luke, and John), narrate the discovery of the empty tomb and appearances of the risen Jesus to his followers. The resurrection of Jesus and its saving power become the central truth of Christian preaching and missionary activity, to which Peter and Paul give emphatic witness. There simply is no evidence of any other Christian movement in the first generation following Easter that preached something else.

Before concluding this section we might consider the titles used in reference to Jesus. Twenty-six of the twenty-seven writings of the New Testament refer to Jesus as the *Christ* (or Messiah), the word that means one anointed of God or by God's Spirit (as in Is 61:1). The only writing in the New Testament that does not refer to Jesus this way is the tiny letter 3 John. Nineteen

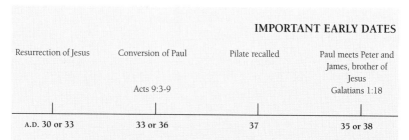

IMPORTANT EARLY DATES

Resurrection of Jesus	Conversion of Paul	Pilate recalled	Paul meets Peter and James, brother of Jesus
	Acts 9:3-9		Galatians 1:18
A.D. 30 or 33	33 or 36	37	35 or 38

For discussion of Paul's chronology, see Robert Jewett, *A Chronology of Paul's Life* (Philadel Mass.: Hendrickson, 1998), pp. 390-97; Ben Witherington III, *The Paul Quest: The Renewed*

of the twenty-seven writings of the New Testament refer to Jesus as the *Lord Jesus*. The number of writings increases if we include the writings that simply say, in reference to Jesus, "the Lord." Twelve of the writings of the New Testament refer to Jesus as *Son of God*. Again, the number of writings increases if we include examples where Jesus is referred to simply as "the Son." All of these titles appear in Paul's letters and in other writings in the New Testament, such as James, 1-2 Peter, Jude, Hebrews, the Gospel of John and the letters of John, which are the writings thought to reflect the Jewish Christian perspective.

Jesus is also widely confessed as *Savior* in the New Testament, again representing the earliest Christian writings. Jesus is Savior in Luke-Acts (Lk 2:11; Acts 5:31; 13:23), Paul (Phil 3:20; Eph 5:23), and the traditions linked to Peter (2 Pet 1:1, 11; 2:20; 3:18), John (Jn 4:42; 1 Jn 4:14) and Jude (Jude 25). This list grows if we include instances of the verb *save*, which have the same meaning and function as Savior (for example, Mt 1:21; Heb 7:25; 9:28).

Jesus is Savior of Jews and non-Jews alike, primarily because of the atoning value of his death on the cross. In short, by dying on the cross, Jesus paid for the sins of humanity. This is the teaching of all of Christianity's earliest teachers and writers. Not every New Testament writing speaks to this topic, of course, but most do, and not one suggests an alternative understanding of Jesus' death.

In sum, the essence of the Christian faith is found in Christianity's earliest writings, all of them originating in the first century, many within two or

IN CHRISTIAN ORIGINS

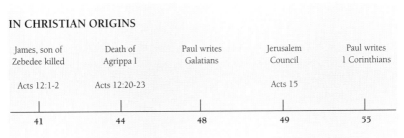

James, son of Zebedee killed	Death of Agrippa I	Paul writes Galatians	Jerusalem Council	Paul writes 1 Corinthians
Acts 12:1-2	Acts 12:20-23		Acts 15	
41	44	48	49	55

phia: Fortress Press, 1979); Jack Finegan, *Handbook of Biblical Chronology,* rev. ed. (Peabody, *Search for the Jew of Tarsus* (Downers Grove, Ill.: InterVarsity Press, 1998), pp. 304-31.

three decades of Jesus' death and resurrection. Not only that, the core beliefs and values of early Christianity grew out of Jesus' pre-Easter teaching, and out of the Easter and Pentecost experiences of the first generation of believers.[12] Claims that in the middle of the first century several "Christianities" existed side by side—holding to different views of Jesus' person and mission, and different ideas of what it meant to be his follower—exaggerate the differences and distort the evidence. Admittedly, there were disagreements among Jesus' earliest followers. But do these disagreements justify speaking of "lost Christianities"? To this issue we turn next.

UNITY AND DIVERSITY IN EARLY CHRISTIANITY

Whereas the first generation of Christians were unified with respect to the core beliefs that Jesus—Israel's Messiah and God's Son—had died on the cross for the sin of humanity and that on the third day he had been raised, there were disagreements over questions pertaining to the validity and application of the law of Moses, either with regard to Jews or to Gentiles. This thorny issue was never completely settled and eventually led to a decline in Jewish membership in the church, which resulted in a lasting division in the church.

The New Testament writings do not hesitate to air the church's dirty linen. Although Luke the Evangelist labors hard to portray Christian unity, the disagreements in the first generation of the church are plain to see in the book of Acts. The disagreements do not focus on Jesus himself. He is universally regarded among his followers as Israel's Messiah, God's Son and the world's Savior. The point of disagreement concerns whether non-Jews (or

Gentiles) must become Jewish proselytes (or converts) in order to be saved by Jesus Messiah. Some said yes; others said no.

This debate unfolds in the book of Acts and is alluded to in several places in Paul's writings. This is not surprising, since Paul's mission to non-Jews—outlined in Acts and mentioned from time to time in his letters—was a major contributing factor.

In Acts the first indication of the coming debate is seen in the mention of the spread of the Christian movement to Samaria. We are told that Philip—a deacon, not an apostle—began preaching Messiah Jesus to Samaritans. Many believed and were baptized (Acts 8:1-13). Next we are told: "Now when the apostles at Jerusalem heard that Samaria had received the word of God, they sent to them Peter and John, who came down and prayed for them that they might receive the Holy Spirit" (Acts 8:14-15). For Luke, the reception of the Holy Spirit offers tangible proof of genuine conversion.

We see this again, two chapters later, in the story of the conversion of Cornelius the Roman centurion. Peter proclaimed the Christian message to this man: "And we are witnesses to all that [Jesus] did. . . . God raised him on the third day. . . . To him all the prophets bear witness that every one who believes in him receives forgiveness of sins through his name" (Acts 10:39-40, 43). Cornelius and his household presumably believed what Peter is saying, for while Peter was still speaking, "the Holy Spirit fell on all who heard the word" (v. 44). The Jewish believers with Peter "were amazed, because the gift of the Holy Spirit had been poured out even on the Gentiles" (v. 45). Peter then ordered these new converts to be baptized (vv. 47-48).

What we now have in Acts is the spread of the Christian message to Samaritans (who were regarded by Jews, more or less, as half Jewish, half Gentile) and to Gentiles. Each time representatives from Jerusalem observed and confirmed the reality of the conversions. Why? Observation and confirmation are needed because many Jewish believers did not think Gentiles could become believers unless their conversion included full adoption of Judaism (that is, becoming proselytes). Of course, in telling the story the way he did, Luke prepared for the ministry of Paul in order to show that Paul's evangelizing of Gentiles was not only legitimate, it actually followed the example of Peter himself, the leader of the church.

The church convened a council in Jerusalem to deal with this disturbing development. Peter and others were accused by some, who asked: "Why did you go to [the Gentiles] and eat with them?" (Acts 11:3). This may sound odd to us moderns, but for first-century Jews who took the law of Moses seriously this was an important question. In recent times the Jewish people had faced deadly oppression, designed to force them to eat and live as Gentiles. In the second century B.C. devout Jews (the "Maccabean martyrs") suffered torture and execution for refusing to eat pork (2 Maccabees 6–7). To eat pork and adopt other Gentile customs was understood as abandoning Jewish law and faith.

How is it, then, that Peter, who leads the Jesus movement, a movement that will eventually redeem and restore Israel, can enter the house of a Gentile and eat the food that is set before him? Good question. The question was answered by telling how God's Holy Spirit took possession of the Gentiles who had believed in Jesus (Acts 11:4-18). The unstated but implied logic of this affirmation was clear enough: If *God* can live with Gentiles (who do not follow Jewish food laws), then surely *Peter and other Jewish believers* can. The larger question was not entirely answered, but for now Jewish believers seemed satisfied.

Not much later in the Acts narrative Paul was commissioned to take the Christian message abroad. In Acts 13–14 we have a recounting of his well-known first missionary journey. Although he first entered synagogues in every city that he and his companions visited ("to the Jew first"), when rejected he turned to the Gentiles ("then to the Greek").[13] Paul did not require his Gentile converts to adopt Jewish practices, much less become full-fledged Jewish proselytes. This precipitated the next Jerusalem council, which is narrated in Acts 15. Here is how the story gets under way:

> But some men came down from Judea and were teaching the brethren, "Unless you are circumcised according to the custom of Moses, you cannot be saved." And when Paul and Barnabas had no small dissension and debate with them, Paul and Barnabas and some of

the others were appointed to go up to Jerusalem to the apostles and the elders about this question. So, being sent on their way by the church, they passed through both Phoenicia and Samaria, reporting the conversion of the Gentiles, and they gave great joy to all the brethren. When they came to Jerusalem, they were welcomed by the church and the apostles and the elders, and they declared all that God had done with them. But some believers who belonged to the party of the Pharisees rose up, and said, "It is necessary to circumcise them, and to charge them to keep the law of Moses." (Acts 15:1-5)

Some people today are puzzled by the position of the Pharisees. I am not puzzled at all; it makes sense. In fact, the concern here is the same concern expressed during Jesus' ministry. Pharisees were critical because from their perspective Jesus did not seem to take the Jewish laws of purity and sabbath seriously. In fact, he often ate with sinners. As Israel's Messiah, so went the reasoning, shouldn't Jesus be more careful to observe faithfully the law of Moses, a law for which many devout Jews gave their lives? Of course, Jesus replied to these criticisms, pointing out that it is the sick who need a doctor (thus implying that the sinners with whom he fellowshiped were indeed sinners) and that what defiles a person is what comes out of the heart, not what goes into the stomach (Mk 2:15-16; 7:14-23). As for picking grain and eating it on the sabbath, didn't David and his men eat consecrated bread on the sabbath? So why can't Jesus and his disciples follow this scriptural precedent? And isn't the "Son of Man" (who received heavenly authority) the lord of the sabbath? (Mk 2:23-28).

Replies such as these, buttressed by the remarkable event of Easter, seem to have satisfied some Pharisees, who in time joined the Christian movement. This is not too surprising, since they were known for their belief in resurrection (Acts 23:6-8; Josephus, *Jewish Wars* 2.163). A resurrected Messiah was something that many of them may well have found compelling. But they were still Pharisees, and by definition that meant they took the law of Moses seriously.[14] So what was this about Gentiles, who were not observant of the law and apparently were not planning to become Jewish proselytes, joining the movement? Surely this cannot be right, they reasoned. Jesus may have eaten with sinners (at least he regarded them as *sinners!*), but they were circumcised and so at least were marginally within the bounds of the law of Moses. But Gentiles entering the community of the Messiah?

The controversy addressed by the Jerusalem Council, described in Acts 15, was the issue that divided the early church. Although the decision reached gives the impression that Paul and supporters of the mission to the Gentiles were vindicated, the problem was not fully resolved and simply never went away. But even if the church remained divided on the question of how Jewish the Gentile believers should become, is there justification for speaking of "Christianities" in the first century? I don't think so.[15]

In Acts 11 Peter had spoken and settled the matter. Yes, even Gentiles can be saved by Messiah Jesus. Now, here in Acts 15, James the brother of Jesus spoke. No, Gentiles do not have to become Jewish proselytes. As believers in God and his holy Son, however, Gentiles must abandon pagan practices. The advice of James was accepted and the problem, at least for the time, seemed to be settled.

It is important to note that the recommendation of James was not an endorsement of Old Testament law (whether the old pre-Abraham code associated with Noah, or the law of Moses). It was rather a charge that Gentiles who convert to the faith not continue in their heathen ways. James is remembered to have said:

> Therefore my judgment is that we should not trouble those of the Gentiles who turn to God, but should write to them to abstain from the pollutions of idols and from unchastity and from what is strangled and from blood. For from early generations Moses has had in every city those who preach him, for he is read every sabbath in the synagogues. (Acts 15:19-21)

Three important points need to be underscored. First, James has said that "we [Jewish believers] should not trouble those of the Gentiles who turn to God," that is, who repent and believe in Messiah Jesus. What "not trouble" means is that the Gentiles should not be required to become Jewish proselytes as part of their conversion to the messianic faith. This was Paul's position also, as seen in Galatians 2:11-14, where Paul sharply criticized Peter for his inconsistent and hypocritical behavior with respect to Gentile believers.

Second, James charges Gentile believers to abstain from idolatrous and immoral behavior, which was all too common in pagan lifestyle and religious practices. Turning to God meant turning away from paganism. Part of this charge concerned idolatry and food: "abstain from the pollutions of idols . . . and from what is strangled and from blood." This too was Paul's position, as he himself states when confronted with this issue in the church of Corinth (1 Cor 8:7-13; 10:7-8, 14-28), portions of which read:

> I wrote to you not to associate with any one who bears the name of brother if he is guilty of immorality or greed, or is an idolater, reviler, drunkard, or robber—not even to eat with such a one. (1 Cor 5:11)

> For if any one sees you, a man of knowledge, at table in an idol's temple, might he not be encouraged, if his conscience is weak, to eat food offered to idols? And so by your knowledge this weak man is destroyed. (1 Cor 8:10-11)

> Do not be idolaters as some of them were. . . . We must not indulge in immorality as some of them did. . . . Therefore, my beloved, shun the worship of idols. (1 Cor 10:7-8, 14)

And finally, James charges Gentile believers to abstain "from unchastity." Again, Paul is completely in agreement with this recommendation:

> For this is the will of God, your sanctification: that you abstain from unchastity. (1 Thess 4:3)

> I wrote to you in my letter not to associate with immoral men. (1 Cor 5:9)

> The body is not meant for immorality. (1 Cor 6:13)

> Shun immorality. Every other sin that a man commits is outside the body; but the immoral man sins against his own body. (1 Cor 6:18)

We must not indulge in immorality as some of them did. (1 Cor 10:8)

In some of Paul's instructions and prohibitions, he too combines idolatry, immorality and eating, as did James in his Council letter.

Third, James says that "from early generations Moses" has been proclaimed "in every city" and "is read every sabbath in the synagogues." What James means here is that Gentiles who turn to God and believe in his Messiah in fact already know that pagan practices, such as idolatry and immorality (including temple prostitution), are wrong and are condemned. They have already heard the basics of the law of Moses, even if they have not frequented the local synagogue. Injunctions to refrain from such practices should not come as a big surprise.

In sum, we find that the principal disagreement within the early church concerned the question of Gentiles and the Jewish law. Were they required to obey it? And, if so, how much of it?[16] What we see in both James and Paul is essentially the same position. Gentiles neither have to adopt the Jewish law nor become Jewish proselytes; but they must refrain from immoral and idolatrous pagan practices.

There is one more issue that must be addressed. New Testament interpreters have for centuries wrestled with the apparent tension between James and Paul regarding the question of works and justification. For Paul, no one can be justified by "works of the law" (Gal 2–3; Rom 4). To prove it, he cites the example of Abraham. Here are two brief parts of Paul's argument:

A man is not justified by works of the law but through faith in Jesus Christ, even we have believed in Christ Jesus, in order to be justified by faith in Christ, and not by works of the law, because by works of the law shall no one be justified. (Gal 2:16)

Does he who supplies the Spirit to you and works miracles among you do so by works of the law, or by hearing with faith? Thus Abraham "believed God, and it was reckoned to him as righteousness." So you see that it is men of faith who are the sons of Abraham. (Gal 3:5-7)

But James seems to say something else:

Do you want to be shown, you shallow man, that faith apart from works is barren? Was not Abraham our father justified by works, when he offered his son Isaac upon the altar? You see that faith was active along with his works, and faith was completed by works, and the scripture was fulfilled which says, "Abraham believed God, and it was reckoned to him as righteousness"; and he was called the friend of God. You see that a man is justified by works and not by faith alone. (Jas 2:20-24)

What is interesting is that James has appealed to the same Scripture from Genesis to which Paul appealed. For Paul, Genesis 15:6 ("Abraham believed God, and it was reckoned to him as righteousness") proves his point: God justifies, or reckons as righteous, those who respond to him in faith. Abraham, whose father was a Gentile, believed God's promise and became the father of the Jewish people. For Paul this passage served as theological template for understanding faith, works and righteousness. But for James, Scripture shows that "Abraham our father was justified by works" and that therefore a person "is justified by works and not by faith alone."

Ever since Martin Luther, the great Reformer, referred to James as a "strawy epistle" (German, *strohern Epistel*), the apparent disagreement between Paul and James has been notorious and has resisted solution. Some interpreters simply say that one writer corrected the other and that therefore we have evidence of two divergent forms of Christianity. I do not agree.

What James was trying to counter is the notion that faith in God does not necessarily call for works of righteousness and compassion. What use is that kind of faith? James says, "You believe that God is one" (Jas 2:19). Without any works, this faith proves nothing. Why? The clue is found in the verse of Scripture that James quotes. He quotes the first part of the Shema: "Hear, O Israel! The LORD is our God, the LORD is one!" (Deut 6:4). The Shema goes on to say, "You shall love the LORD your with all your heart and with all your soul and with all your might" (Deut 6:5). Does this sound familiar? According to Jesus, we are to love God and our neighbor as ourself (Mk 12:28-31). In James's letter, he is complaining of those who readily confess the Shema ("God is one, and I love God") but do not put into practice what Jesus required and is taught in the law of Moses: "You shall love your neighbor as yourself" (Lev 19:18).

Therefore, if someone is in need of clothing or food and all that the so-called believer extends is a greeting, "Be warmed and filled," then the faith of this person is dead. James appeals to Genesis 15:6, but in connection with the great story of Abraham's willingness to offer up his son Isaac (Gen 22). James's point is that Abraham's faith is demonstrated to be real in his action.

None of this contradicts Paul. Indeed, Paul did fundraising for the poor of Jerusalem (1 Cor 16:1-3; Gal 2:10), thus putting into practice what James regards as a faith proven by works. Paul also agrees that faith results in "good works" (for example, Eph 2:10). This is why elsewhere he speaks of the "obedience of faith" (Rom 1:5; 16:26). The question is one of emphasis and situation.

In my view the letter of James is early and authentic. It is not a late, fictive writing that pretends to have been written by James, the brother of Jesus, written perhaps to counter Paul. I can find no convincing explanation for such a scenario, and neither can recently published experts on James.[17]

The admonitions in James 2 are completely in step with church practice and discipline, with respect to the treatment of the poor and the distribution of resources (see Acts 2; 4–6). The letter of James serves a pastoral function, urging (Jewish) believers to demonstrate the living reality of their faith through good works. It was not written to deal with teaching that claimed good works and self-made righteousness complete the saving work of Messiah Jesus. That was the problem Paul addressed.

What Paul challenges in his letters, written shortly after the letter of James, is the idea that Gentiles must adhere to the law of Moses if their Christian walk is to mature. The idea that Paul attacks is not the teaching of James. The differences that we see in the respective writings of these men are due to different sets of problems that each one in his own way had to address.[18]

So once again the differences and disagreements attested in the New Testament writings do not constitute evidence of divergent "Christianities" in the first generation of the church. Of course, there are still some who have argued that this is the case, claiming that the New Testament represents a body of writings that has been screened, thus filtering out the writings that may have championed a different view of the Christian faith. But what writings are these? In earlier chapters in this book we have taken a hard look at the top contenders—*Gospel of Thomas, Gospel of Peter, Gospel of Mary* and others. None of these writings can be dated earlier than the middle of the second century.

The only way someone can come up with a divergent "Christianity" is to import a second-century writing or teacher into the middle of the first century. The examples cited by Bart Ehrman in his *Lost Christianities* are second-century persons and movements. He discusses Ebionites, Marcion and his following, and Gnosticism. All of these individuals and groups arose in the second century. Ebionites were Jews who believed in Jesus but rejected some of the claims about Jesus and the Jewish law. The Ebionite Gospels were apparently revisions of Matthew, thus bringing the Gospel story in line with Ebionite theology. No Ebionite writing or fragment dates before A.D. 120. Marcion was a second-century extremist who wished to delete the Old Testament and most of the overtly Jewish writings from the New Testament. He was happy with Paul's letters, but with little else. The church rightly rejected

PROPOSED DATES FOR NEW TESTAMENT GOSPELS

Early Dates
Mark (A.D. 55-60)
Matthew (A.D. 60-65)
Luke (A.D. 60-65)
John (A.D. 85-90)

Late Dates
Mark (A.D. 65-70)
Matthew (A.D. 75-80)
Luke (A.D. 75-80)
John (A.D. 90-95)

The dates of the New Testament Gospels are disputed. Most scholars accept the late dates, with some variations. For studies that favor the early dates see John A. T. Robinson, *Redating the New Testament* (Philadelphia: Westminster, 1976); John W. Wenham, *Redating Matthew, Mark and Luke: A Fresh Assault on the Synoptic Problem* (Downers Grove, Ill.: InterVarsity Press, 1992).

his ideas. Gnosticism, as we saw in chapters three and four, likely did not arise until the second century, and not one of this movement's writings that we possess, either in whole or in part, dates before the middle of the second century. (I especially have in mind the *Gospel of Thomas*, which evidence suggests was not written before A.D. 175.)

In short, Ehrman and others who speak of "lost Christianities" are talking about individuals and groups who moved away from the earlier, widely attested teaching of Jesus and the first generation of his followers. These hypothetical Christianities did not exist in the middle of the first century.

But lack of evidence and anachronism need not prevent the creation of novel scenarios. All one needs is imagination and an uninformed readership. We turn to this odd dimension of the problem in chapter ten.

HOKUM HISTORY AND BOGUS FINDINGS

Jesus Between the Lines

Just when the reading public thought that speculative reconstructions of the historical Jesus and Christian beginnings could not get any sillier than what was put forward in Dan Brown's *The Da Vinci Code,* along comes Michael Baigent's utterly ludicrous *The Jesus Papers,* with its theory of a faked death and letters written by Jesus to the Jewish Sanhedrin. Beam me up, Scotty.

Unfortunately, these ridiculous books are not the only ones published in recent years; they have been preceded by many others, and the pace, I regret to say, seems to be quickening. Why? No one knows for sure. Our postmodern, irrational society, where truth is subjective and negotiable, probably has something to do with it. As one reviewer put it: The success of *The Da Vinci Code* says more about the gullibility of modern society than it does about Dan Brown's skills.

The authors of the books we will look at in this chapter derive inspiration from some of the radical theories propounded by scholars. Some of these theories we have already examined. What I think happens is that once credentialed scholars attempt to smuggle quirky Jesuses of the second- and third-century Gospels into the first century as rivals to the more familiar first-century Jesus of the New Testament, then new possibilities open up to popular writers, who—not restrained by mundane things like evidence and plausibility—rely on imagination and speculation, and in some cases mystical insights.

In what follows we will look at a sampling of this hokum history and bogus findings, which has resulted in a series of grossly distorted images and histories of Jesus and Christian beginnings. Some of these writers treat ancient documents as coded material that must be unpacked of its "true meaning." Others accept legends, hoaxes and forged documents as fact, and are quite ready to draw conclusions from unsubstantiated rumors. Still others blend together legitimate archaeology with highly speculative guesswork. It is no wonder that nonexperts today are bewildered and would like to know what is going on.

INTERPRETATION BY CODES AND CIPHERS

Most books concerned with history and interpretation support arguments and conclusions with evidence, the kind of evidence other people can examine and evaluate for themselves. But some of the books concerned in the present chapter defy conventional scholarly assessment. Mystical intuition, psychic knowledge and convoluted schemes that treat what appear to be normal texts as encoded ciphers cannot be assessed in any kind of objective manner. When the average intelligent reader says, "I don't see it," the author of hokum history and bogus findings says, "You lack my insight" or "You haven't learned the rules yet."

Let me illustrate this point with the astounding conclusions reached by retired Australian lecturer and writer Barbara Thiering in her books *The Qumran Origins of the Christian Church* (1983), *Jesus the Man: A New Interpretation from the Dead Sea Scrolls* (1992; U.S. edition: *The Riddle of the Dead Sea Scrolls*), *Jesus of the Apocalypse: The Life of Jesus After the Crucifixion* (1995), and *The Book That Jesus Wrote: John's Gospel* (1998). Here are some of her findings:

- Sunday March 1, 7 B.C., Jesus was born at Mird, near the Dead Sea, not far from Qumran.

- At age twelve Jesus was separated from his mother.

- As a teen Jesus may have traveled to Alexandria, Egypt, where he was influenced by Buddhism.

- On Monday March 25, A.D. 15, at the age of twenty-one, Jesus was baptized in Jerusalem.

- In A.D. 20 Joseph, the father of Jesus died.

- On March 1, A.D. 29, on his thirty-fifth birthday, Jesus begins preparation for ministry; John the Baptist revokes Jesus' authority to baptize.

- On Tuesday, June 6, A.D. 30, Jesus and Mary Magdalene are betrothed. They marry on Saturday, September 23, A.D. 30. Simon Magus officiates. This is a trial marriage. A second, binding marriage takes place March 18, A.D. 33.

- On Friday, March 20, A.D. 33, Jesus is crucified, along with Simon Magus and Judas Iscariot. However, Jesus was drugged, swooned, fooled the Romans, and was taken down from the cross still alive (though badly injured). His life is saved by special medicines smuggled into the tomb with him. Jesus recovers.

- On Saturday, September 15, A.D. 36, Jesus returns on the scene.

- On Monday, February 29, A.D. 40, Saul (Paul) meets Jesus, to decide what to do about the Roman emperor Gaius Caligula.

- On September 3, A.D. 45, Jesus teaches in Antioch.

- On Tuesday, March 17, A.D. 50, at Philippi, Jesus marries again, this time Lydia.

- On Tuesday, March 7, A.D. 58, Jesus, Luke and Paul assemble in Thessalonica to celebrate the twenty-fifth anniversary of the Last Supper and the crucifixion.

This is only part of Thiering's findings. The former lecturer of the University of Sydney School of Divinity has uncovered a great deal more. And yes, Jesus has children by his wives Mary and Lydia. How are these amazing "facts" discovered, you ask? According to Thiering: By carefully reading the Dead Sea Scrolls and the writings of the New Testament, and of course assuming that they are all in code and that they therefore need to be decoded. This means that, that means this and so on. Rarely does the text actually mean what it says on the surface.[1]

Thiering finds in this code some amazing things. It turns out the "Teacher of Righteousness" of the Scrolls is none other than John the Baptist, and the "Wicked Priest"—the Teacher's archenemy—is, of course, Jesus. The raising of Lazarus (in Jn 11), who is really Simon Magus, turns out to be code for being excommunicated from the Qumran community. Turning the water into wine (in Jn 2) means that Gentiles, previously only permitted water baptism, may now become full members in the community and may partake of bread and wine. We even hear of "popes" and "cardinals," and so on. I am not aware of a single competent scholar on the planet who agrees with Thiering's conclusions.[2] One can read every line in the New Testament, the Dead Sea Scrolls and any other literature from this period of time and not find any of the things that Thiering thinks she has found. Why not? Because none of it is there.

Of course, we need not be limited to texts, whether in code or not. Hypnosis, says Dolores Cannon, can lead to new discoveries about Jesus too. In *Jesus and the Essenes: Fresh Insights into Christ's Ministry and the Dead Sea Scrolls* (1992) Cannon, a psychic and past-life hypnotist, describes for readers how through regressive hypnosis she was able to recover one of her subject's previous lives. In this particular life the person had been an Essene and had known Jesus. Well, why bother with Hebrew and the study of the Scrolls, when a long-lost spirit can tell you all you want to know? Through this procedure, it might be added, Cannon claims that she has learned a lot about the prophecies of Nostradamus, UFOs and Wicca.

The writings of Thiering and Cannon are among the strangest in print. Of course, many readers will readily agree. They want history based more on historical investigation and less on séance. But let readers beware; there are some books that have been published that pretend to engage in research and investigation, but all they offer is another approach to hokum history and bogus findings.

LEGENDS AND HOAXES BECOME HISTORY

In recent years the public has been bombed with theories regarding the Holy Grail, that is, the cup from which Jesus and his disciples drank at the Last Supper. For more than one thousand years the church took no interest in this cup. Then in the late twelfth century a poet named Chrétien de Troyes (died c. 1185) wrote a poem, *Le Roman de Perceval ou le Conte du Graal* (c. 1175), for Philip the Count of Flanders. He died before the poem was finished, leaving behind more than 9,000 lines. Other poets stepped in to complete it, such as Robert de Boron and Wolfram von Eschenbach. Out of these literary efforts arose the legend of the Holy Grail. The Anglo world knows the legend well, in the version of King Arthur and the Knights of the Round Table. Germans and French have their own versions of it also.

This is, of course, the stuff of myth and legend. There is no historical evidence of the existence or knowledge of the existence of the cup Jesus drank from. Apart from its mention in the New Testament, there is none whatsoever. Nor is there any evidence that the Knights Templar, who served primarily as armed escorts to and from Europe and the Holy Land, ever had any connection to the Holy Grail or found hidden documents or lost treasures or whatever. But lack of evidence is no problem—if you have imagination and interpret legends as historical fact. Throw in an anti-Christian agenda, complete with an imagined truth-suppressing Vatican, and you are ready to write some hokum history.

And this is what Michael Baigent, Richard Leigh and Henry Lincoln have done in their *The Holy Blood and the Holy Grail* (1982; U.S. title: *Holy Blood, Holy Grail*). They would have us believe that they have done careful, critical research and have discovered the truth: Jesus and Mary Magdalene were lovers, had children, and these children, or their children, reached southern France and married into noble families, from which would eventually emerge the French Merovingians. The Knights Templar and the Priory of Sion, a secret society founded in 1099, knew of all this and did all in their power to keep it secret and thus protect the descendants of Jesus and Mary. Grand Masters of the Priory of Sion included Leonardo da Vinci, Sir Isaac Newton and Victor Hugo. How on earth did Baigent and company discover this? They found some of the Priory's secret papers, hidden away in the Bibliothèque Nationale of France. They also found important clues in artwork and legends associated with Rennes le Château. No credible historian believes any of it. And for good reason.

As it turns out, the whole thing is a hoax, and the hoaxers have themselves admitted it. Baigent had been informed that it was a hoax some time before publishing *The Holy Blood and the Holy Grail*, but that did not stop him from going ahead. The hoax began in 1956 with rumors of treasure and valuable documents found at Rennes le Château. Pierre Plantard, along with some friends, exploited the rumors, creating a full-blown hoax, complete with French and Latin documents relating to the nonexistent Priory of Sion, some of which were planted in the Bibliothèque Nationale. (Images of these documents can be downloaded from the Internet.) The hoaxers would eventually admit to what they had done, including Plantard, under oath in a French court of law. Plantard served time in prison for fraud. He died in 2000. The matter was investigated by Jean-Luc Chaumeil, a French journalist, and a book exposing the hoax has been published by archaeologist Bill Putnam and John Edwin Wood, *The Treasure of Rennes-le-Château: A Mystery Solved* (2003).

Along the way, Michael Baigent and Richard Leigh also published *The Dead Sea Scrolls Deception* (1991). This book too is fraught with problems, inaccuracies and misleading rumors and innuendo. In it the authors capitalize on the controversy surrounding the delay of the publication of the last of the Dead Sea Scrolls, most from cave 4, mostly consisting of thousands of fragments. The delay in publication was a scandal, to be sure, but it had nothing to do with hiding truths that would be embarrassing to the church.

According to Baigent and Leigh, the unpublished scrolls contained facts that lend support to their earlier theory about Jesus. Only months after the book appeared, photographs of the remaining scrolls were published. Shortly after that, the text of all of the Dead Sea Scrolls—in Hebrew and Aramaic as well as English translation—became available. As it turned out, none of the controversial allegations in *The Dead Sea Scrolls Deception* were true.

In short, what Michael Baigent and Richard Leigh have given the public is pseudohistory. From rumors, legends and outright hoaxes they have fashioned a fairytale about Jesus and Mary and much of the history of the church. Unfortunately, these books have sold well, and they have deceived many, among them Margaret Starbird and Dan Brown.

Following the lead of *The Holy Blood and the Holy Grail,* whose theories initially offended her, popular writer Margaret Starbird came to embrace the idea of a romantic relationship between Jesus and Mary. She embellishes the Mediterranean legend of Mary Magdalene, who supposedly arrived on the shores of Gaul (today's France) in A.D. 42 in the company of a little girl named Sarah. Because the Hebrew name Sarah means "princess," Starbird tells us, we may suspect that this little princess was none other than the daughter of Jesus. In her books, *The Woman with the Alabaster Jar* (1993), *The Goddess in the Gospels* (1998), *The Tarot Trumps and the Holy Grail* (2000), *Magdalene's Lost Legacy: Symbolic Numbers and the Sacred Union in Christianity* (2003), *The Feminine Face of Christianity* (2003), and *Mary Magdalene, Bride in Exile* (2005), Starbird combines legends of mermaids, the Christian symbol *ichthys* ("fish"), Merovingian legends, gematria (finding meaning in numbers), the root meaning of "Magdalene," and a verse or two of Scripture (for example, Lam 4:8) and comes up with her own version of the utterly unfounded belief that Mary Magdalene gave birth to Jesus' child and then fled with this child to France. Again, no qualified historian, living or dead, gives any credence to this scenario. But no matter; the books sell and Starbird continues to give talks at spiritual retreats.

More than any other, it is the work of Michael Baigent and Richard Leigh—and of Margaret Starbird to a lesser degree—that influenced Dan Brown. *The Da Vinci Code* accepts virtually all of the conclusions put forward in *The Holy Blood and the Holy Grail,* as well as most everything in the *Dead Sea Scrolls Deception* (which is why Baigent and Leigh sued Brown and his publisher for theft of intellectual property). Brown also borrows some questionable material from other doubtful sources and adds a bit of his own to the mix. The errors in his book are egregious and legion. Let's review a few of them.

We need not revisit the Priory of Sion and Rennes le Château hoaxes, which Brown accepts as gospel. (See his "Fact" page at the beginning of the book.) But something needs to be said about Da Vinci's portrait of the "Last Supper" (c. 1497), which adorns the wall of the convent Santa Maria delle Grazie in Milan. In the book much is made about the figure to the right of Jesus. Brown argues that the figure, who is beardless and has a full head of long, flowing hair, is Mary Magdalene. Art historians disagree; they say it is the youthful Beloved Disciple of the Gospel of John.

The art historians, of course, are correct. In the time of Leonardo youthful men were portrayed in art with beardless faces and long tresses. We see this in Leonardo's portrait of the youthful "John the Baptist" (painted 1513-1516). We also see this in Raphael's portrait of "St. Sebastian" (painted 1502-1503), in Piero della Francesca's "St. Julian" (painted 1455-1460), in Andrea del Verrocchio's "Tobias and the Angel" (painted 1470-1480) and in many others. The youthful men in all of these Renaissance portraits do appear to us moderns as young women. But those who have studied the art from this period know that they are indeed youthful men, including the Beloved Disciple to the right of Jesus in Leonardo's "Last Supper."[3]

So if the Priory of Sion is a modern hoax and the person on Jesus' right is the Beloved Disciple, not Mary Magdalene, just where does the idea that Jesus and Mary were lovers come from? There are only two texts from antiquity that could be interpreted as suggesting some sort of romance. They are the *Gospel of Philip* and the *Gospel of Mary*.

The *Gospel of Philip* survives in the Coptic language in codex 2 of the Nag Hammadi Library (discovered in Nag Hammadi, Egypt, in 1945). The *Gospel of Philip* probably was first composed in Greek or Syriac, perhaps as early as A.D. 150. On page 63 of codex 2, lines 32-36, we read:

> The companion of the [. . .] Mary Magdalene. [. . .] her more than [. . .] the disciples [. . .] kiss her [. . .] on her [. . .].

The brackets indicate holes in the text. Most of the missing words and letters can be restored with some confidence. Restored, the text probably read something like this:

> The companion of the [Savior is] Mary Magdalene. [But Christ loved] her more than [all] the disciples [and used to] kiss her [often] on her [. . .].

With reference to the last missing element, some scholars have suggested restoring "mouth" or "lips." These proposed words are possible, but other words are possible also, such as "head," "cheek" or "hand." However it is restored, romantic love is not in view. A kiss showed respect in the time of Jesus and his disciples. Remember, on the night of the betrayal Judas kissed Jesus, just as a disciple would kiss his master. The point that is being made in the *Gospel of Philip* is that Jesus showed Mary more respect and honor than he did the other disciples. This means that Jesus may well have taught Mary things that he did not teach the others. This in turn means that Mary may well be a source for new truth about Jesus, which is the whole point of these second-century writings. The author of the *Gospel of Philip* is not trying to suggest that Jesus and Mary were lovers. He only wants to elevate Mary to the level, or even beyond the level, of the other disciples.

The same point is being made in the *Gospel of Mary*. It dates from the same period of time as the *Gospel of Philip* and holds a similar mystical, Gnostic understanding of the world and of Jesus and his mission. The *Gospel of Mary* survives in two Greek fragments and in a large Coptic fragment. Mary Magdalene is invited to share with the disciples those things Jesus taught her that the other disciples have not heard:

> Peter says to Mary, "Sister, we know that you were much loved by the Savior, as no other woman. Therefore tell us what words of the Savior you know, what we have not heard." (6:1-2)

For the next several pages Mary relates to the disciples ideas similar to those of many Gnostic writings. When she ends her discourse, Andrew, the brother of Peter, expresses disbelief. He does not think Jesus ever said such things. Peter agrees, suggesting that Mary may have lied. Then Mary begins to weep and say:

> "[Do you think that I have told lies] about the Savior?" Levi says to Peter, "Peter always does anger lie within you; and now thus you question the woman as opposing her. If the Savior regarded her worthy, who are you to despise her? For that one, having known her, loved her always and assuredly." (10:5-10)

Again, the point here has to do with Mary's qualifications as a disciple of Jesus, not a lover of Jesus. Peter is angry that Jesus had more regard for Mary than he had for him. The phrase "having known her" carries no sexual connotation (and in any event, the Greek and Coptic versions read somewhat differently). It should be understood in the Gnostic sense of possessing full knowledge. What is at stake is Mary's right to contribute to the teaching and theology of the community. This is the burden of the *Gospel of Mary;* it has nothing to do with romance.[4] So, what evidence is there of romance between Jesus and Mary? Not much; in fact, there is none.

Dan Brown's character Sir Leigh Teabing, whose name derives from Richard *Leigh* and Michael *Baigent* (with Teabing as an anagram of Baigent), is the principal instructor in *The Da Vinci Code,* helping Professor Robert Langdon of Harvard University interpret the clues pertaining to the true meaning of the Grail. Teabing is a veritable fountain of misinformation. He wrongly credits the contents of the Bible to Emperor Constantine (fourth century A.D.); claims that the emperor pressured Christian theologians into viewing Jesus as divine, instead of human; and claims that there were eighty Gospels, many of which the emperor ordered burned. As for the *Gospel of Philip,* we are wrongly told that it is written in Aramaic. Teabing wrongly refers to the Coptic codices, which are books, as "scrolls." He seems to think that all of the Dead Sea Scrolls were found in one cave, in the 1950s. In fact, eleven caves were found, beginning in 1947. He wrongly asserts that the scrolls tell the "true Grail story" and depict the ministry of Jesus, "in very human terms." All of this is utter nonsense, especially since the Dead Sea Scrolls contain no Christian texts or references whatsoever. Nothing more needs to be said. Many books have appeared in the last two or three years, that point out these and dozens more errors.[5]

THE ABSENCE OF EVIDENCE IS NOT A PROBLEM

Michael Baigent, coauthor of *The Holy Blood and the Holy Grail* and *The Dead Sea Scrolls Deception,* has come up with another amazing tale. This one is called *The Jesus Papers: Exposing the Greatest Cover-Up in History* (2006). In the Grail books Baigent believed he had proven that Jesus had a child through Mary Magdalene. In *The Jesus Papers* Baigent, who holds a graduate degree in mysticism and describes himself as an expert in the field of arcane knowledge, thinks he has proven that Jesus survived his crucifixion and wrote letters in which he denies his divinity. Well, if that doesn't beat all.

There are three major elements to Baigent's latest theory. First, he says that he, Richard Leigh and Henry Lincoln received a letter from an Anglican vicar, the Reverend Douglas Bartlett, in which he says he knows of "a document containing incontrovertible evidence that Jesus was alive in the year A.D. 45." The letter goes on to say that this is the real treasure of Rennes le Château, whose discovery had resulted in the sudden wealth of the Abbé Béranger Saunière at the beginning of the twentieth century. Eventually our intrepid authors visited the old vicar, who told them that in the 1930s, while living in Oxford, he learned from Canon Alfred Lilley (1860-1948) of the existence of a manuscript that proves that Jesus was indeed still living in A.D. 45. Lilley saw this manuscript in France in the 1890s. The old vicar couldn't remember what the document said exactly. The document is gone; no one has seen it since. And so there is no opportunity to examine it. Baigent suspects that the Vatican (of course) bribed the Abbé of Rennes le Château, which would account for the Abbé's wealth, and then either hid the document or destroyed it.

Let me get this straight. Baigent is asking us to believe a story he says he heard from an elderly man in the 1980s, about a conversation this elderly man had with another elderly man in the 1930s, about a document the older elderly man says he saw in the 1890s, but which no one today can produce. And this is evidence of what? Quite apart from the utter flimsiness of this whole chain of hearsay, we have already seen that the legend of the treasure of Rennes le Château is a 1950s-era hoax and has been laid to rest. The good Abbé earned some extra money through the sale of masses, got caught and was disciplined. His journals and ledgers (unlike Baigent's mysterious document) still exist and list the names of those who paid the Abbé money and how much they paid. No treasure, no mystery; no mysterious lost document either.

The second major element put forward by Baigent is no better. Based on his interpretation of the image that depicts the body of Jesus at the tomb, which serves as station 14 of the "Stations of the Cross"[6] in the church at Rennes le Château, Baigent has concluded that Jesus did not die on the cross but was drugged, with the help of Pontius Pilate, quickly placed in a tomb and then at night, with no one about, Jesus' friends removed him from the tomb, nursed him back to health, and then Jesus departed from Judea and headed for Egypt.[7] And just how does the image of station 14 in the church at Rennes le Château reveal this startling truth? The moon is up. Yes, that's right—the moon is up. You see, according to Jewish burial traditions, bodies are supposed to be in the tomb before nightfall, *before the moon comes up*. Yet, in the painting that depicts station 14, a full moon is seen high in the night sky. Baigent deduces from this anomaly that in the painting Jesus is not being placed *in* the tomb dead; he is being taken *from* the tomb alive!

That is quite a lot to deduce from a moon in a painted depiction of station 14. Is it likely, moreover, that Pilate would take part in a plot to assist Jesus in escaping his fate, since, after all, the governor had ordered Jesus' execution in the first place? Perhaps there is a simpler explanation. I wonder if the artist who painted station 14 was influenced by the Gospel story? It reads: "When it was evening, there came a rich man from Arimathea, named Joseph, who also was a disciple of Jesus" (Mt 27:57; Mk 15:42-43). Joseph requested the body of Jesus, hastily prepared it for burial and then placed it in a tomb. Notice that the story begins with the words, "When it was *evening*" (emphasis added). Not knowing Jewish burial traditions, the artist of station 14 in the church in Rennes le Château misunderstood what was meant by "evening" (which in the Gospels means *end of day,* not *nightfall*) and so exercised artistic license and depicted the burial as taking place *at night,* with a full moon in the sky.

I suspect this is a better explanation than the one Baigent provides. And there is one other thing: Jesus' friends in the painting of station 14 are depicted as *grieving,* which is what you would expect them to do if their friend and teacher is being placed in the tomb *dead,* not if their friend and teacher is being taken from the tomb *alive.*

Baigent's third major element is the weakest of all and proves that Baigent needs no evidence whatsoever to cook up a good cover-up. He tells us that he was able to track the source of rumors in the Holy Land of the existence of documents that would be dangerous to the Vatican. His investigation led him to a collector of biblical antiquities who lives in a "large European city." (Baigent will not name this city or this collector.) The collector told Baigent that in 1961, while excavating in the cellar of an old house in Jerusalem, he found two papyrus documents bearing Aramaic text. Items found with these documents led the collector to date the documents to A.D. 34. The documents are letters, and the writer identifies himself as "the Messiah of the children of Israel." This must be Jesus, he reasoned. Who else could it be? The letters, which are addressed to the Jewish Sanhedrin, explain that the writer did not intend to claim divine status in saying that he possessed the Spirit of God. Initially unwilling to unveil these letters, eventually the collector showed them to Baigent.

Although Baigent cannot read Aramaic, and so does not personally know what these documents actually say (or even if the text is Aramaic), he believes what the collector told him. He tells us that the collector showed the letters to Yigael Yadin and Nahman Avigad, two respected Israeli archaeologists and biblical scholars, and they confirmed the antiquity and authenticity of the texts. Unfortunately, one of them must have leaked the existence of the letters to Catholic authorities, the collector surmises, for it wasn't long before pressure was applied to the collector. To get the authorities to back off he promised to keep the documents under wraps. Baigent also promised not to say anything about them, at least not right away.

Well, here we go again. Baigent asks us to believe that Jesus of Nazareth, having faked his death on the cross and having fled to Egypt, wrote two letters in Aramaic to the Sanhedrin in Jerusalem, in which he explains that he is not divine, at least not any more divine than anyone else who has been touched by God's Spirit. We are to trust Baigent, even though he cannot read Aramaic, cannot name the collector who possesses the alleged Aramaic letters, and cannot even name the city in which the collector resides. We are to trust Baigent and the anonymous collector when we are assured that the Aramaic letters were authenticated by two prominent archaeologists, who just happen to be unavailable for comment. (Yadin died in 1984; Avigad, in 1992.) We are to believe all this, even though no living, qualified expert has seen these documents, and the two who say they have seen them—and are still living—cannot read them.

I might also mention that Baigent neglects to mention that archaeologists and papyrologists will tell you that no papyrus (plural: papyri) can survive buried in the ground, in Jerusalem, for two thousand years. The only papyrus documents that have survived from antiquity have been found in arid climates, such as the area surrounding the Dead Sea and the sands of Egypt.[8] No ancient papyri have been found in Jerusalem itself. Jerusalem receives rainfall every year; papyri buried in the ground, beneath houses or wherever, decompose quickly. So whatever Baigent saw, they were not ancient papyri found beneath somebody's house in Jerusalem, and they were not letters Jesus wrote.

And there you have it. The greatest cover-up in history exposed.

What lesson have we learned from Baigent's research into the arcane? When you have a hot new theory, who needs evidence?

ARCHAEOLOGY ON THE EDGE

Sometimes there *is* evidence, and that is good. But evidence of what? This is the troubling question that keeps coming to mind when we consider carefully and critically the evidence and claims proposed by James Tabor in his latest book, *The Jesus Dynasty: The Hidden History of Jesus, His Royal Family, and the Birth of Christianity* (New York: Simon & Schuster, 2006). Let's take a look at a couple of its claims.

It needs to be stated at the outset that Tabor is no Michael Baigent or Dan Brown. Tabor is a legitimate, properly trained archaeologist and biblical scholar who received his Ph.D. from the University of Chicago and currently serves on the faculty of the University of North Carolina at Charlotte. Moreover, his book *The Jesus Dynasty* has a lot of good material in it. I have no doubt serious students of the Bible and Christian origins will read it with profit. However, I worry about nonexperts who read it and fail to see how tenuous some of the speculation and conclusions are.

My first major problem with Tabor's book concerns the suggestion that Jesus' human father was a Roman soldier, perhaps Jewish by birth. (Tabor discounts out of hand any thought that Jesus' conception might have been miraculous.) Tabor thinks he may have located this soldier's tomb in Germany. He speculates that Jesus may have visited this man, in the region of Sidon (on the north coast of the Mediterranean), as may be hinted in Mark 7:24: "And from there he arose and went away to the region of Tyre and Sidon. And he entered a house, and would not have any one know it." What evidence does Tabor have for any of this?

In the late second century A.D. a philosopher by the name of Celsus wrote a polemical work against Christianity. This work survives in numerous quotations in a rebuttal *(Contra Celsum)* written by Origen, a Christian biblical scholar, in the middle of the third century A.D. Among other things, Celsus says Jesus sojourned in Egypt, where he learned magic, returned to Israel, dazzled everyone with what appeared to be miracles, claimed to be God and so forth. But here is the interesting part: Celsus also says that Mary, the mother of Jesus, was impregnated by a Roman soldier named Pantera (or Panthera), a slur that is repeated in the later rabbinic literature (for example, such as in the Tosefta, which dates no earlier than A.D. 300; see Tosefta *Hullin* 2.22-24). Tabor rightly notes that Pantera was a real name used by real Roman soldiers in the time of Jesus. He believes that a tombstone, bearing an inscription of one Pantera, discovered in 1859 in Bingerbrück, Germany, may actually be in reference to Jesus' father. The inscription reads:

> Tiberius Julius Abdes Pantera
> of Sidon, aged 62
> a soldier of 40 years service,
> of the 1st cohort of archers,
> lies here.

Tabor plausibly suggests that the name Abdes is a Latin transliteration of the Hebrew (or Aramaic) *Ebed,* which means "servant." This possibility, plus the fact that the soldier of this inscription was from Sidon, which is not too far from Galilee, could well mean that this man was Jewish and could have come into contact with Mary. Accordingly, Tabor declares, "The mystery of Pantera [is] solved." Is it? Before anyone can declare anything *solved,* we must ask if the Pantera of the inscription was of the right age, in the vicinity of the village where Mary lived and in the year 5 or 6 B.C. if he has any chance to have impregnated Mary. Tabor is unable to show this, and other scholars who have discussed this inscription have expressed doubts.[9]

Tabor points out that some church fathers took the Pantera allegation seriously. For example, in *Against Heresies* (78.7.5) Epiphanius (A.D. 315-403) suggests that Joseph's father was Jacob Panthera. Tabor thinks this supports the historicity of the tradition. Otherwise, why would church fathers such as Epiphanius take it so seriously? But Epiphanius and later Christian writers are simply trying to fend off the slur, and to do so they throw out various proposals, some having no more merit than the allegations themselves. Accordingly, their fourth-century (and later) rebuttals provide no actual evidence that the Pantera proposal by Celsus actually has any history earlier than the time of Celsus himself.

In my view the allegation that Jesus' real father was a man named Pantera (or Panthera) exploits Christians' claim that Jesus was born of a "virgin" (Greek, *parthenos*). It was nothing more than a play on words. Pantera was the closest sound-alike name, and was a name of soldiers, so Jesus' conception was suggested to be not that of a virgin, a *parthenos,* but that of a soldier, a man named Panthera. We have here nothing more than slander and rebuttal. We have no actual archaeological evidence that can with any probability be linked to Jesus.

My second major problem with Tabor's book concerns the remarkable proposal that we may know where Jesus' remains lie buried. Of course, Tabor assumes here that Jesus died and stayed dead. He was not resurrected. So once again, as in the case of the conception and birth of Jesus, Tabor rules out any possibility of miracle.

According to Tabor the tomb of Jesus was found empty because the body of Jesus was removed and reburied elsewhere. This in itself is possible. After all, the body of Jesus had been placed in a tomb reserved for criminals. His body was not in his family's tomb. The authorities could move it if they wished. But Jewish burial law permitted the family to take possession of the skeletal remains about one year after death and rebury them in the family's tomb. It is not likely that Jesus' body would be moved without the family knowing of it. Indeed, when the tomb of Jesus was discovered empty, it was initially assumed that his body had been moved and this created great consternation (see Jn 20:13-15). Had the body of Jesus been removed and placed somewhere else, his family and disciples could have and would have discovered this. But they did not because the body had not been moved at all. There was no second tomb.

Nevertheless, Tabor is pretty sure that Jesus' body was removed, thus accounting for the empty tomb, and Tabor has an idea where the remains are buried to this day. The grave of Jesus is a little bit north of Tsfat (Safed) in Galilee. How does Tabor know this? It is a tradition passed on by a revered sixteenth-century mystic named Rabbi Isaac ben Luria. As a devotee of the kabbalah, ben Luria evidently had a vision, which revealed to him the locations of the tombs of various Jewish sages and saints, including the tomb of Jesus of Nazareth. I doubt any scholar will take this proposal seriously.[10]

I find it ironic that Tabor is willing to give credence to the vision of a sixteenth-century mystic and kabbalist, but is not willing to give credence to the vision of the first-century Saul of Tarsus. Saul did not believe Jesus was the Messiah and certainly did not believe that he had been raised from the dead—tomb or no tomb. Saul was hard at work trying to stamp out the new heresy. Then Saul met the risen Messiah. And we know the rest of the story. I'll take Saul's vision any day over ben Luria's. I urge Tabor to do the same.

IN SEARCH OF THE COSMIC PRINCIPLE

Not long ago Tom Harpur's *The Pagan Christ* created a sensation by presenting in new form the odd notion that Jesus did not exist.[11] I say odd because almost no serious academic—of any ideological, religious or nonreligious stripe—doubts that Jesus of Nazareth actually lived some time in the first century and was crucified by order of Pontius Pilate, governor of Judea. The evidence for the existence of Jesus—literary, archaeological and circumstantial—is overwhelming.

According to Harpur,

> There is nothing the Jesus of the Gospels either said or did—from the Sermon on the Mount to the miracles, from his flight as an infant from Herod to the Resurrection itself—that cannot be shown to have originated thousands of years before, in Egyptian Mystery rites and other sacred liturgies such as the Egyptian Book of the Dead.[12]

In short, the Gospel writers have transformed an important Egyptian theme of spirituality into a Jewish allegory of a man who never existed. In this way the fictive Jesus passes on an ancient religious legacy, a legacy that might be called the "Pagan Christ." It is hard to imagine how the evidence of history could be more forced and distorted than what we have in *The Pagan Christ*.

Harpur at one time believed that Jesus was a historical person. In fact, as seen in his earlier writings, Harpur believed that Jesus truly healed people and was raised from the dead. He now denies all of this in *The Pagan Christ*. What brought on the change? Judging by comments that he makes at the beginning of his book, his change in thinking had little to do with critical, historical work (though the work of "minimalists," that is, those who minimize the historical elements in the Bible, exerted some influence). It had more to do with adopting the theosophic views of Gerald Massey (1828-1907) and Alvin Boyd Kuhn (1880-1963). The work of these men, especially their reconstructions of ancient history and attempts to draw lines of continuity between Egyptian religion and Christianity, is deeply flawed. No qualified historian takes the theories of these men seriously. Anyone charmed by Harpur's *Pagan Christ* should beware. We are talking old, odd stuff here. Personal philosophy and introspection it may be; history in any responsible, recognized sense it is not.[13]

CONCLUSION

We have reviewed in this chapter some strange theories and bizarre reconstructions of the history—or nonhistory—of Jesus of Nazareth and Christian beginnings. Common to this hokum history and these bogus findings are eccentric approaches that competent, trained historians find utterly implausible. Legends, rumors, forged documents, hoaxes and psychic intuition hardly constitute the stuff from which sober historical truth will be found. I conclude this chapter with a plea that readers of books such as Brown's *Da Vinci Code,* Baigent's *Jesus Papers* and Harpur's *Pagan Christ* recognize them for what they really are. They are not based on credible evidence; they do not follow recognized standards of critical investigation; and they do not offer anything approaching genuine history.

WILL THE REAL JESUS PLEASE STAND UP?

Unfabricating His Aims and Claims

In chapter ten we examined some of the worst examples of hokum history and bogus research. This would be no proper way to conclude a book about Jesus of Nazareth, even if the primary purpose has been to expose the errors and shortcomings of radical and pseudoscholarship. Something more positive and edifying needs to be said. In this chapter I want to wrap up the discussion with a review of some of the most important aspects of Jesus and the movement that he founded, with emphasis on their proper setting and context.

In this final chapter I treat seven important topics: (1) Jesus' relationship with the Judaism of his day, (2) Jesus' claims, (3) Jesus' aims, (4) the factors that led to Jesus' death, (5) the resurrection of Jesus and the emergence of the Christian church, (6) the nature of the New Testament Gospels, and (7) Christian faith as part of the Jewish story. All of these items are related in one way or another to issues treated in previous chapters. But some of these ideas are not well understood even by professing Christians, and they should be. If they are not understood, then writers of hokum history and bad theology will continue to prey on the naive and credulous.

JESUS' RELATIONSHIP WITH THE JUDAISM OF HIS DAY

Down through the centuries, it has been fashionable to view Jesus as opposed to Judaism in various ways. Christian theologians have assumed that Jesus criticized the religion of his people for being legalistic (or "Pharisaic"), for being caught up with externals, and for having little or no place for grace, mercy and love. Jesus' action in the temple, which has been traditionally referred to as the "cleansing of the temple" (Mk 11:15-18 and parallel passages in other Gospels), was directed, we have been frequently told, against the system of sacrifice. Religion is supposed to be a matter of the heart, not rituals. Jesus understood this, but his Jewish peers did not. So goes this understanding.

Several scholars, both Jewish and Christian, have rightly complained against this caricature. Perhaps the most influential challenge in recent years has come from E. P. Sanders.[1] He rightly argues that there is no evidence that would suggest that Jesus opposed Judaism or criticized it as a religion of externals and rituals. Instead, there is substantial evidence to the contrary.

Jesus accepted all of the major tenets of the Jewish faith. These tenets include the unity and sovereignty of God, the value and sanctity of the temple of Jerusalem, the authority of the Jewish Scriptures, the election of the people of Israel, and the hope of Israel's redemption.

Jesus, moreover, observed many of the practices associated with Jewish piety of his day: alms, prayer and fasting (Mt 6:1-18). Jesus fasted in the wilderness during his period of temptation (Mk 1:12-13). He prayed and taught his disciples to pray (Mt 6:7-15; Lk 11:1-13; 22:39-46). He and his disciples gave alms, and he taught others to do likewise (Lk 11:41; 12:33; Jn 13:29). Jesus presupposed the validity of the temple, the sacrifices and Israel's holy days (Mt 5:23-24; Mk 14:14). He read and quoted from the Jewish Scriptures and clearly regarded them as authoritative (Mk 10:19; 12:24-34; Lk 4:16-22; 10:25-28). Apparently he attended synagogue services regularly (Lk 4:16); his style and interpretation of Scripture reflect at many points the style and interpretation that emerged within the synagogue.[2]

Predicting that Jerusalem faced disaster, Jesus wept over Israel's ancient city (Lk 19:41-44). Jesus loved his people and longed for their salvation. His original disciples—all of them Jewish—embraced the same hope.

Jesus accepted the authority of Torah (that is, the Law). He did not reject the Torah, as has sometimes been asserted. What Jesus opposed were certain interpretations and applications of the Law. In the so-called antitheses of the Sermon on the Mount (that is, "You have heard it said, but I say to you . . ."; see Mt 5:21-48), Jesus does not contradict the commands of Moses; he challenges conventional interpretations and applications of those laws. The antithetical "but I say to you" does not oppose the commandments themselves. For example, Jesus agrees that killing is wrong but adds that hatred is wrong too. He agrees that adultery is wrong but adds that predivorce lust (which often led to divorce and remarriage) is also sin. He agrees that swearing falsely is wrong but speaks against the practice of oath-taking in his time. Jesus does not oppose *restitution* ("an eye for an eye"), but he does oppose using this command as pretext for *revenge*. He agrees that people should love their own people but adds that they should love other people as well, even enemies.

Jesus may have believed that his own authority, which derived from God's Spirit and with which he had been anointed (Mk 1:10; Lk 4:18), equaled that of Torah. But his authority did not undermine the authority of Torah; it explained it and applied it in new ways conditioned by his strong sense of the dawning of the kingdom (rule) of God and the changes that it would bring.

Jesus' innovative interpretation is consistent with parallel innovations expressed by Israel's classical prophets. As did theirs, Jesus' interpretation challenged conventional interpretations and applications of Israel's sacred tradition. For example, in Isaiah 28 the prophet declares that the "LORD will rise up as on Mount Perazim, and he will be angry as in the Valley of Gibeon" (Is 28:21). Here Isaiah has alluded to stories of David's victory over the Philistines (see 2 Sam 5:17-21; 5:22-25 = 1 Chron 14:13-16), stories that no doubt Isaiah's contemporary opponents interpreted as guaranteeing victory in the face of a foreign threat. But Isaiah found in this sacred story no guarantee of Israel's victory in his day. On the contrary, the Lord will do a "strange deed" and an "alien work" (Is 28:21), by which the prophet means that God will give the victory to Israel's enemies. Isaiah says this because he rightly perceived that God was God of all people. God was not Israel's private deity.

Jesus also interpreted Israel's sacred story in this manner. In his Nazareth sermon (Lk 4:16-30) Jesus read Isaiah 61:1-2, a passage understood to promise blessing for Israel and judgment for Israel's enemies, and then appealed to the examples of Elijah and Elisha (Lk 4:25-27). From these examples, where these mighty figures of old ministered to Gentiles (1 Kings 17:1-16; 2 Kings 5:1-14), Jesus declared that his "anointed" task was to bless the marginalized and the suspect, not only the righteous of Israel. This kind of interpretation may have been daring—and surely would have been opposed by many teachers—but it presupposed the authority of Israel's Scriptures; it did not attack this authority. Jesus' respect for Jewish Scripture places him squarely within first-century Judaism.

JESUS' CLAIMS

Probably no feature has been more divisive than the question of the claims that Jesus made for himself. This topic is usually referred to as the question of Jesus' self-understanding. The main reason that this area of research has been so controversial is that Jesus says little about himself, at least directly. But there are many indicators that he understood himself as a special agent in God's service.

He evidently claimed to be a prophet. Jesus himself complained: "No prophet is without honor, except in his home country" (Mk 6:4). This tradition is likely authentic, for it is hard to understand why early Christians would make up a saying implying that Jesus' relatives and acquaintances did not treat him with respect. Apparently the public also regarded him as a prophet: "Some say you are one of the prophets" (Mk 8:28); "A great prophet has arisen among us!" (Lk 7:16); "If this man were a prophet . . ." (Lk 7:39). This tradition is in all probability historical, for early Christians spoke of Jesus as Savior, Lord and Son of God; they did not emphasize his identity as a (mere) prophet. And, of course, Jesus was remembered to have made predictions (Mk 13:2) and uttered what can probably be regarded as prophetic indictments against various persons, institutions or groups (Mk 12:1-11; 14:58; Mt 11:20-24; Lk 10:13-15).

Jesus was frequently addressed as "rabbi" (Mk 9:5; 10:51; 11:21; 14:45). He taught as a rabbi, even though his admirers affirmed that he taught as one having much greater authority than did other teachers of his day (Mk 1:22, 27). Those outside of his following addressed him as "rabbi" (which was understood at this time to mean teacher [Mk 5:35; 10:17; 12:14]). Some scholars have asserted that the appearance of *rabbi* in the Gospels reflects an anachronistic usage of the title, since it did not become a title until after A.D. 70. But the use of *rabbi* in the Gospels is informal and evidently reflects Jewish usage in the first century, before its later, formalized usage. Why would

Christians writing after 70 apply a formal title to Jesus, a title used of religious teachers who were becoming increasingly critical of Christianity? If anything, the title would have been avoided. That it is used so frequently suggests, in my judgment, that the Gospel tradition is primitive and authentic. Jesus is called "rabbi" in the Gospels because, like it or not, he was addressed as such during his public ministry.

Although there is not a hint that Jesus referred to himself as a priest or that any of his followers so regarded him, Jesus performed some actions usually understood as priestly functions. He declared persons "clean" (Mk 1:41; Mt 11:5; Lk 7:22) and "forgiven" (Mk 2:5; Lk 7:47-48). He also dared to challenge temple policy and practice put in place by the ruling priests. The most provocative challenge was the so-called cleansing of the temple. Only in the later theology of the church did Jesus' death and subsequent intercessory role in heaven come to be understood in sacrificial and priestly terms, as seen, for example, in the book of Hebrews.

Jesus regularly referred to himself as the "Son of Man," an epithet that has been hotly debated for many years. This is not the place to go into a detailed study of this complicated question, but I will hazard a few brief comments. In my judgment, this self-designation, which evidently was Jesus' favorite, alludes to the "son of man" of Daniel 7. Jesus saw himself as this figure, to whom kingdom, power and authority were to be given. This self-reference suggests that Jesus saw himself as God's vice-regent. In a saying that has good claim to authenticity, Jesus assures his disciples: "I assign to you, as my Father assigned to me, a kingdom, that you may eat and drink at my table in my kingdom, and sit on thrones judging the twelve tribes of Israel" (Lk 22:29-30). The disciples' self-interested request for the seats of honor when Jesus comes in his "glory" (Mk 10:35-45), which because of its embarrassing nature virtually guarantees its authenticity, in all probability arose out of the assumption that Jesus was indeed the "Son of Man" through whom Israel would be restored and the kingdom of God would be established.

Did Jesus regard himself as the Messiah? The evidence is ambiguous, but taken as a whole it supports the contention that he did. He was confessed as such by his disciples (Mk 8:29-30). When John the Baptist asked Jesus if he is "the one who is to come," Jesus' reply was full of allusions to

Isaiah 35:5-6 and Isaiah 61:1-2 (Mt 11:2-6; Lk 7:18-23). It is clear that by this Jesus answered John in the affirmative. But did John ask Jesus if he was the *Messiah*? He probably did, judging by a recently published scroll from Qumran (that is, 4Q521). This scroll contains parallel allusions to the passages from Isaiah and understands them as the works of the Messiah.[3] In other words, in his reply to John, Jesus has implied that he is the coming one (that is, the Messiah), as is evidenced by the fact that he is busy doing the works of the Messiah.

The blind son of Timaeus hailed Jesus as the "Son of David," which is probably a messianic designation (Mk 10:47-48). When Jesus entered Jerusalem, the crowd shouted for the coming of the kingdom of David (Mk 11:9-10). He rode the donkey (Mk 11:1-7), as did Solomon, the son of David (1 Kings 1:38-40; see Zech 9:9). Jesus also presumed to have authority within the temple precincts. This he could do only if he were a ruling priest or Israel's king. It is not likely that Jesus was viewed as a ruling priest, for reasons we have already looked into. Some commentators have argued that Jesus quoted and discussed Psalm 110:1 in such a way as possibly to distance himself from son of David tradition (Mk 12:35-37). But Jesus seems to be saying that the Messiah would be *greater than David*. Jesus was anointed (Mk 14:3-9), which was probably a messianic anointing by a devoted follower. When asked by the high priest if he was the Messiah, Jesus said he was (Mk 14:61-62). And, importantly, Jesus was crucified by the Romans as "king of the Jews" (Mk 15:26, 32).

The early and widespread belief among Christians that Jesus was Israel's Messiah, or Christ, suggests that Jesus was understood as such from the time of his public ministry and not simply from the time of the Easter proclamation. It is highly unlikely that the resurrection in itself would have led Jesus' disciples to confess Jesus as Messiah if he had never claimed or accepted such identification during his ministry. Would the followers of the well-known second-century Rabbi Aqiba have proclaimed their beloved teacher Messiah, had he been resurrected following his martyrdom (c. A.D. 135)? I doubt it. The post-Easter proclamation of Jesus as the Messiah strongly implies that Jesus was understood this way before Easter.

Did Jesus regard himself as God's Son? The evidence here also is ambiguous, and it is tied to the question of Jesus' messianic self-understanding. David is called "son" in relation to God (see 2 Sam 7:14; Ps 2:7). The Messiah is therefore in some sense the "son of God." In 1 Chronicles 29:23 Solomon is said to have "sat on throne of the LORD," so in a certain sense the son of David is expected to sit on the throne of God. This concept would add to the conviction that the Messiah would serve as God's vice-regent.

The most dramatic utterance, and one that ties together the Son of Man imagery with the Son of God identity, is found in Jesus' reply to Caiaphas. In the attempt to find incriminating evidence against Jesus, the high priest asks: "Are you the Messiah, the son of the Blessed [that is, God]?" Jesus answers: "I am; and you will see the son of man seated at the right hand of Power [that is, God], and coming with the clouds of heaven" (Mk 14:61-62). Because in this exchange Jesus confesses what the Evangelist Mark believes him to be (see Mk 1:1), some scholars doubt its authenticity. That is, they think Mark is the author of this confession, not Jesus. They also wonder how the disciples would have learned of it, since they were not present but had fled (see Mk 14:50). Others have pointed out the apparent inconsistency in having Jesus "seated at the right hand," which is to be stationary, yet "coming with the clouds," which is to be moving. Therefore, we may have distinctive traditions that have been clumsily (and inauthentically) juxtaposed. So goes the argument.

These objections, however, carry little weight. To assert that Jesus did not regard himself as in some sense God's Son makes the historian wonder why others did. From the earliest time Jesus was regarded by Christians as the Son of God. Why not regard him as the great Prophet, if that is all that he had claimed or had accepted? Why not regard him as the great Teacher, if that had been all that he had ever pretended to be? Earliest Christianity regarded Jesus as Messiah and as Son of God, I think, because that is how his disciples understood him and how Jesus permitted them to understand him.

The objection that the disciples were not present to hear the exchange between Jesus and Caiaphas and so could not have known what transpired is naive. Are we really to imagine that the disciples, who later became zealous proclaimers of their Master and his teaching, never learned what happened, that they had no idea on what grounds the Jewish authorities condemned him? This strains common sense. Even if the rules of the Mishnah (c. A.D. 220) were not in force in the early first century, it is likely that a capital verdict would have been made public, as the Mishnah in fact says was required. Jesus' claim to be Israel's Messiah would then account for the Roman crucifixion and for the posting of the placard (or *titulus*) that read, "king of the Jews." For the claim to be Messiah is a claim to be the Jewish king. It is almost beyond belief that the disciples would have learned nothing of this. The fact that his disciples were not present probably does explain, however, why the record of the exchange between Jesus and his accusers (Mk 14:55-65) is so brief and in places so vague.

Finally, the objection based on the odd juxtaposition of being *seated* and of *moving* among the clouds carries little weight when it is remembered that the throne on which God sits is a *chariot*. In fact, the throne described in Daniel 7:9, on which the Ancient of Days (God) takes his seat and to which the son of man figure approaches, is said to have wheels that "were burning fire." What apparently shocked Caiaphas was not only that Jesus boldly affirmed his messianic identity, but that he dared to assert that he would sit on *God's throne*.[4] Not only was Jesus' answer treason in the eyes of Rome, it was blasphemy in the eyes of devout Jews who did not hold to such messianic ideas—and the Sadducean high priesthood in the time of Jesus held to few messianic beliefs. Jesus has claimed that the day will come when Caiaphas and company will see Jesus, the "Son of Man," seated at God's right hand, on God's chariot throne, thundering through heaven and coming in judgment. That a man would dare claim such a thing was indeed blasphemous.[5]

JESUS' AIMS

Closely related to the question of Jesus' *claims* is the question of Jesus' *aims*. The "Old Quest of the Historical Jesus" (sometimes called the "Nineteenth-Century Quest") was launched when scholars began to question Jesus' intentions. Hermann Samuel Reimarus's posthumous writings (1774-1778) argued that Jesus attempted to have himself installed as Israel's earthly, political king.[6] This provocative thesis led to new, critical readings of the Gospels. The twists and turns of the Old Quest were eloquently reviewed and assessed by Albert Schweitzer in what has become a classic in its own right,

The Quest of the Historical Jesus.[7] With the emergence of form criticism in the 1920s, whose early practitioners thought that much of the Gospel material originated in the church and did not derive from Jesus, many abandoned the Quest. It was thought to be historically impossible—and theologically illegitimate, according to some theologians. But a New Quest, seeking to find the link between the Jesus of history and the "Christ of faith," was initiated in the 1950s and then yet another phase, now called the "Third Quest," emerged in the 1980s.[8]

What were Jesus' actual aims? They are closely bound up with the question of what his proclamation of the kingdom (or rule) of God meant. It is almost universally agreed that Jesus proclaimed the kingdom of God and that he recommended changes of thinking and behavior in view of its appearance.

Although it is disputed by some, it is likely that Jesus continued John the Baptist's call for repentance and that this call for repentance was preparatory for the appearance of the kingdom (see Mk 1:15; 6:12). Jesus believed that his miracles were evidence of its appearance: "If it is by the finger of God that I cast out demons, then the kingdom of God has come upon you" (Lk 11:20). Jesus urged his followers to have faith in God and to forgive one another (Mk 11:22-25; Mt 6:14-15). These urgings in themselves do not mark Jesus off from Judaism, of course, but they take on a somewhat different nuance in light of Jesus' announcement of the kingdom. Jesus urged his followers to serve one another and not to be like the mighty men or the rulers of their day, who lorded it over others and liked to be served (Mk 10:35-45).

Jesus promised his disciples that they would sit on thrones judging the twelve tribes of Israel (Mt 19:28; Lk 22:28-30). This saying gives us a clear insight into Jesus' aims. He and his disciples expected to set up a new administration, in God's own time, of course. This expectation coheres with the parable of the wicked vineyard tenants (Mk 12:1-11), which threatened Jerusalem's Jewish authorities with the loss of their position. The "vineyard," that is, Israel, will be "given to others," that is, to Jesus' disciples. This does not mean, contrary to some Christian and Jewish interpreters, that Gentiles or Christians are supposed to replace the Jewish people.

Such an interpretation is anachronistic and inaccurate. Jesus evidently expected his own disciples, at some time known only to God, to form a new government, to sit on thrones judging (in the sense of the ruling, not in the sense of condemning) the twelve tribes. The reference to the "twelve tribes" also implies that Jesus fully expected the restoration of Israel, *all Israel*. This coheres with his call for repentance. If all Israel will repent, then all Israel will be restored.

One of the shocking and offensive features of Jesus' ministry was his association with "sinners," that is, with people who either were not or at least did not appear to be Torah observant (Mt 9:10-13; Mk 2:15-17; Lk 15:1-2). It seems that Jesus believed that forgiveness could be readily and quickly extended to those who violated or neglected the law of Moses. But this forgiveness required repentance and faith (Mt 11:20-24; 12:39-42; Lk 7:47-50; 11:29-32; 13:1-5; 15:7).

Jesus' rejection led to a new element in his preaching and teaching. He was not greeted by the high priest when he entered Jerusalem (Mk 11:1-11). He criticized some aspect of temple policy and practice (Mk 11:15-19). Ruling priests challenged him and demanded to know by what authority he was doing these things (Mk 11:27-33). After his threatening parable of the wicked vineyard tenants, Jesus was challenged and questioned by various persons and religious parties (Mk 12:13-34). Jesus again went on the offensive, warning his disciples to beware the scribes who devour the estates of widows (Mk 12:38-40). Then, as a living illustration of this warning, he lamented the widow who gave her last penny to a wealthy and, in the opinion of some of his contemporaries, avaricious temple establishment (Mk 12:41-44).

When they left the temple precincts, Jesus told his disciples that the beautiful buildings of the temple mount would be leveled; not a stone would be left on another (Mk 13:1-2). His aims of national repentance (and restoration) resisted, Jesus evidently began to speak of coming judgment on the city of Jerusalem and its world famous temple (Lk 19:41-44; 21:20-24). It is in this context that Jesus probably uttered the words that were later used against him during his hearing before Caiaphas and the ruling council: "We heard him say, 'I will destroy this temple made with hands, and in three days I will build another, not made by hands' " (Mk 14:58).

JESUS' DEATH

Jesus was most likely put to death was because he made claims that his opponents understood as in some sense messianic. The placard that the Romans placed over or near his cross, which read "The King of the Jews" (Mk 15:26), is the principal evidence for this view.[9] There is other evidence that Jesus held to messianic ideas, even if he did not assert his messiahship explicitly (which would have been inappropriate, according to Jewish expectations). This evidence, such as entering Jerusalem on a donkey and being anointed, we have already looked at.

The Roman crucifixion of Jesus lends important support to the report that Jesus affirmed his messiahship in response to the high priest's question (Mk 14:61-64). Affirming messiahship in itself was probably not blasphemous, but claiming to sit on the divine throne, *next to God himself,* would surely have been regarded as blasphemous and would have added incentive to hand Jesus over to the Romans.

Another reason for desiring Jesus' death was his threat against the temple establishment. He not only hinted in his parable of the wicked vineyard tenants that the ruling priests would lose their place, he also predicted that because of them the temple would be destroyed. That the ruling priests could be deeply offended by such rhetoric is well illustrated in the experience of another Jesus, the son of Ananias, who some thirty years after the death of Jesus of Nazareth wandered around the city of Jerusalem, sometimes near the temple, uttering woes based on Jeremiah 7. (Remember that Jesus' criticism of temple polity also had been based on Jeremiah 7.) According to Josephus (*Jewish Wars* 6.300-309), this man was seized by the ruling priests, who interrogated him and beat him and then handed him over to the Roman governor with demands that he be put to death. The governor interrogated him further, beat him further and decided to release him as a harmless lunatic.

Jesus of Nazareth didn't die because he quarreled with Pharisees over matters of legal interpretation. He didn't die because he taught love, mercy and forgiveness. Jesus didn't die because he associated with "sinners." He didn't die because he was a good man. Jesus died because he threatened the political establishment with the prospects of undesired change. His contemporaries foresaw the real possibility of a serious riot, perhaps even a full-scale rebellion. The Jewish leaders (who were principally the high priest and the ruling priests) were responsible to the Roman governor to maintain law and order, and the governor was in turn answerable to Rome. Jesus was viewed as a troublemaker by both of these authorities; therefore he had to go. Because Jesus did not have an armed following, there was no need to seize any of his followers. Hence, there was no battle and no bloodshed beyond the crucifixion of Jesus himself.

THE EARLY CHURCH

Why did the early church begin? This question does not require a complicated or lengthy answer. The early church began because of its firm belief that Jesus had been resurrected and had appeared to dozens, even hundreds, of his followers. From its inception the early church proclaimed the resurrection of Jesus.[10] Apart from the resurrection there was no reason to develop and maintain a distinctive identity. Jesus' teaching had not condemned Judaism; so there would have been little reason for his followers, which at the time of his death probably consisted entirely of Jewish people, to abandon or modify aspects of Judaism, especially something as controversial as the evangelization of non-Jews, without following the norms involved in making proselytes.

It was the unshakable conviction that God had raised Jesus, who had in turn commanded his followers to continue to preach his vision of the kingdom, which ultimately led to the emergence of the church. The church took on the characteristics that it did in order to deal with the new challenges it faced in the years and decades following Jesus' death and resurrection. The church believed that its Lord and Savior would return. But what should it do until he returned? How would it survive, especially in view of its growing estrangement from Judaism, the parent faith, and in view of increasing persecution at the hands of the pagan state? The writings of the New Testament were produced, in part, to answer these questions.

THE GOSPELS

In my view, even though the Gospels are written from a perspective of faith in Jesus, they are reliable. Faith and truthful history are not necessarily at odds. Criteria of authenticity, which are remarkably vigorous in their application to the Gospels, confirm the essential core of Jesus' teaching. It is not necessary to claim that the Gospels are inerrant, though for theological reasons many Christians accept them as such, and that every saying and deed attributed to Jesus is true to history. But claims that the Gospels are unreliable, full of myth and legend, and so biased that knowledge of what Jesus really said and did cannot be recovered are excessive and unwarranted. Even the Jesus Seminar, as extreme as its conclusions have been and as mistaken and wrongheaded as many of its assumptions and methods are, has "authenticated" a good portion of this essential core. The Seminar has presented the public with a skewed view of Jesus, to be sure, but its members have concluded, nonetheless, that Jesus proclaimed the kingdom of God and associated with sinners.

It is true that the Gospels may tell us much about the concerns of their respective authors (which is the task of redaction criticism) and may even tell us something about early Christians who handed down the tradition (which is the task of form criticism), but the authors' principal concern was to publish the teachings and deeds of Jesus. His words and example were considered normative. Indeed, there is evidence early on that the words of Jesus were considered on par with Scripture, which in a Jewish context is remarkable.

Given such a high regard for Jesus' words, it is not likely that early Christians would have freely invented sayings and then attributed them to Jesus. In fact, the oft-heard assertion that many of the sayings were generated by questions and issues that the early church faced is called into doubt by the observation that many of these questions and issues (as seen in the New Testament letters) are nowhere addressed by the sayings of Jesus. There was disagreement over the question of circumcision, eating meat sacrificed to idols, spiritual gifts, Jew-Gentile relations, and qualifications for church office, but not a saying of Jesus speaks to any of these questions. This shows that the Gospel writers were not in the habit of making things up. There is every reason, then, to conclude (again, without invoking theological dogmas) that the Gospels have fairly and accurately reported the essential elements of Jesus' teaching, life, death and resurrection.

CHRISTIAN FAITH AND THE JEWISH STORY

The earliest followers of Jesus were Jews. The church was predominantly Jewish until after the first major war with Rome (A.D. 66-70), and not until after the catastrophic Bar Kokhba war (A.D. 132-135) did the Jewish church of Jerusalem come to an end and a Gentile bishop succeed the Jewish bishop there. It would be many centuries before the Ebionites (Jewish Christians) would finally cease as a distinct and viable denomination within Christianity. Accordingly, for Jewish and Christian scholars today, the origins of Judaism and Christianity constitute a complex and interesting story whose interwoven threads should not be unraveled.

The story of Christian origins is a Jewish story. Indeed, many Messianic Jews today believe that Christianity remains a Jewish story. The original Gospel proclamation—"Jesus is risen!"—was part of this Jewish story. Christianity was a Jewish movement rooted in the conviction that God had at last fulfilled his promises to Abraham and David, that he had at last fulfilled countless prophecies, and that he had at last inaugurated the kingdom of God. This new and energetic Jewish movement reached out to capture the Gentiles, to bring them into submission to the teachings of Jesus the Jew, the Messiah of Israel. Israel was now indeed the "light unto the nations" (Is 49:6) and was engaged in a task that would redound to its glory (Lk 2:32).

Ironically, the mighty Roman Empire, which smashed the state of Israel in a series of punishing wars (from A.D. 66-135), was itself overrun by a messianic faith rooted in Israel's sacred Scriptures and its ancient belief in the God of Abraham. Those Gentiles who have been invited to play a part in this exciting story should never forget its Jewish authors and players.

The true story of the historical Jesus is exciting and inspiring. The true story may well be an old story, but it is far more compelling than the newer, radical, minimalist, revisionist, obscurantist and faddish versions of the Jesus story that have been put forward in recent years. Ongoing archaeology and ongoing discovery and study of ancient documents will continue to shed light on this old story. These discoveries may require an adjustment here and there. But thus far these discoveries have tended to confirm the reliability of the Gospels and disprove novel theories. I suspect that ongoing honest, competent research will do more of the same.

Appendix 1

AGRAPHA

Free-Floating Sayings of Jesus

The so-called agrapha (or extracanonical sayings) were popularized many years ago in a small book by Joachim Jeremias.[1] Of the hundreds of candidates, Jeremias isolated eighteen sayings "whose authenticity admits of serious consideration." But Otfried Hofius's recent critical survey is much less optimistic, rightly judging many of these agrapha as representing nothing more than embellishments or variations of sayings extant in the Synoptic tradition or elsewhere in the New Testament writings.[2]

In the opinion of Hofius only nine agrapha—half the number proposed by Jeremias—have any hope of being authentic. They are as follows:

How is it then with you? For you are here in the temple. Are you then clean? . . . Woe to you blind who see not! You have washed yourself in water that is poured forth, in which dogs and swine lie night and day, and washed and scoured your outer skin, which harlots and flute girls also anoint, bathe, scour, and beautify to arouse desire in men, but inwardly they are filled with scorpions and with [all manner of ev]il. But I and [my disciples], of whom you say that we have not [bathed, have bath]ed ourselves in the liv[ing and clean] water, which comes down from [the father in heaven]. (P.Oxy. 840.2)

As you were found, so will you be taken away. (Syriac *Liber Graduum* 3.3; 15.4; 24.2; see Justin, *Dialogue with Trypho the Jew* 47.5: "In whatever things I take you, in these I shall judge you"; see *Apocalypse of Ezekiel* 4[?])

The kingdom is like a wise fisherman who cast his net into the sea; he drew it up from the sea full of small fish; among them he found a large (and) good fish; that wise fisherman threw all the small fish down into the sea; he chose the large fish without regret. (*Gospel of Thomas* 8)

Ask for the great things and God will add to you the little things. (Clement of Alexandria *Stromateis* 1.24.158; Origen *Commentary on Psalms* 4.4; *De Oratione* 2.2; 14.1; Eusebius *Commentary on the Psalms* 16.2)

Be approved money-changers. (Origen *Commentary on Job* 19.7; Jerome *Epistulae* 99.11.2; *Clementine Homilies* 2.51; 3.50; 18.20)

On the same day he saw a man performing a work on the sabbath. Then he said to him: "Man! If you know what you are doing, you are blessed. But if you do not know, you are cursed and a transgressor of the law." (Codex D, in place of Luke 6:5)

Whoever is near me is near the fire; whoever is far from me is far from the kingdom. (Origen *Homilies on Jeremiah* 20.3; see *Gospel of Thomas* 82; Didymus the Blind *Commentary on Psalms* 88.8)

And never be joyful, save when you look upon your brother in love. (*Gospel of Hebrews* 5; see Jerome *Commentary on Ephesians* 3 [on Eph 5:4])

[He that] stands far off [today] will tomorrow be [near you]. (P.Oxy. 1224.2)

The first five agrapha resemble the character and quality of the Synoptic tradition; they are probably no more than variations and conflations of it. For example, the first agraphon is probably modeled on the woe found in Matthew 23:27-28 (see Mt 7:6) and the sayings about living water in the Fourth Gospel (see Jn 4:10-12; 7:37). The second agraphon may represent a summary of apocalyptic warnings, such as those found in Matthew 24:27, 40-41; Luke 17:24, 26-30, 34-35. The third agraphon, which speaks of the "wise fisherman," has probably been modeled after the parables of the pearl and the dragnet, which are juxtaposed in Matthew 13:45-46, 47-48. The fourth agraphon probably represents a variation of Matthew 6:33 and its parallels. The fifth agraphon could be based on an interpretation of Paul's admonition in 1 Thessalonians 5:21-22. Evidently Dionysius of Alexandria, one of Origen's pupils, knew of the saying; but he derived it from an "apostolic voice" and not from Jesus (see Eusebius, *Ecclesiastical History* 7.7.3). Hofius regards the authenticity of this agraphon "quite improbable."

However, Hofius believes that "there are no well-founded objections against" the last four agrapha. None of these agrapha appears to be derivative from canonical or apocryphal sources. All have a Palestinian or Jewish flavor. Nevertheless, Hofius has strong reservations about the sixth agraphon. I have reservations about the seventh agraphon. It coheres with Synoptic sayings (Mk 9:49; Lk 12:49) and is reminiscent of a rabbinic saying: "Aqiba, he that separates himself from you separates himself from life" (Babylonian Talmud *Qiddushin* 66b; Babylonian Talmud *Zevahim* 13a). However, interesting parallels can also be found in Greek literature: "He who is near Zeus is near the lightning" (Aesop); "Far from Zeus and far from the lightning" (Diogenianus). Thus, the agraphon may be no more than an adaptation of a well-known proverb. The eighth agraphon appears to be independent of the love command (Mk 12:31), while there is no parallel to the ninth agraphon. Both the eighth and ninth agrapha are consistent with Jesus' teaching. Perhaps they are genuine. If they are, they really do not add anything new to what is known of Jesus' teaching.

From his review of the agrapha Hofius finds little evidence supporting the assumption held by some scholars that there was a substantial amount of material on a level of quality approximating that of the Synoptic tradition that survived independent of the canonical Gospels. Hofius quotes Jeremias with approval: "Our four canonical Gospels embrace with great completeness almost all the early Church knew of the sayings and deeds of Jesus in the second half of the first century."[3] Hofius further concludes that the evidence of the agrapha militates against the view that the early church freely invented dominical sayings.

It is apparent that the agrapha cannot be used to portray the historical Jesus as appreciably other than he is depicted in the New Testament Gospels. Our primary sources for Jesus research, in the attempt to reconstruct the life and times of Jesus of Nazareth, are the Gospels that were eventually canonized by the church.

Appendix 2

WHAT SHOULD WE THINK
ABOUT THE *GOSPEL OF JUDAS*?

Thursday April 6, 2006, the National Geographic Society held a press conference at its Washington, D.C., headquarters and announced to some 120 news media the recovery, restoration and translation of the *Gospel of Judas*. The story appeared as headline news in dozens of major newspapers around the world and was the topic of discussion in a variety of news programs on television that evening and subsequent evenings. A two-hour documentary aired on the National Geographic Channel on Sunday, April 9, and has aired several times since.

What is the *Gospel of Judas*? Why all the fuss, and what should Christians and others think about it?

THE DISCOVERY OF THE *GOSPEL OF JUDAS*

At the best investigators can determine, a leather-bound codex (or ancient book), whose pages consist of papyrus, was discovered in the late 1970s, perhaps in 1978, in Egypt, perhaps in a cave. For the next five years the codex, written in the Coptic language,[1] was passed around the Egyptian antiquities market. In 1983 Stephen Emmel, a Coptic scholar, acting on behalf of James Robinson, formerly of Claremont Graduate University and well known for his work on the similar Nag Hammadi codices, examined the recently discovered codex in Geneva. Emmel was able to identify four tractates, including one that frequently mentioned Judas in conversation with Jesus. He concluded that the codex was genuine (that is, not a forgery) and that it probably dated to the fourth century. Subsequent scientific tests confirmed Emmel's educated guess.

After the seller was unable to obtain his asking price, the codex journeyed to the United States, where it ended up in a safe deposit box in Long Island, New York, and it suffered serious deterioration. Another dealer placed it in a deep freezer, mistakenly thinking that the extreme cold would protect the codex from damaging humidity. Unfortunately, the codex suffered badly, with the papyrus turning dark brown and becoming brittle.

Happily, the codex was eventually acquired by the Maecenas Foundation in Switzerland and, with the assistance of the National Geographic Society, was recovered and partially restored. I say "partially restored" because an unknown number of pages are missing (perhaps more than forty) and only about 85 percent of the much talked about *Gospel of Judas* has been reconstructed.

The National Geographic Society wisely commissioned a series of tests to be undertaken, including carbon-14 dating, analysis of the ink and various forms of imaging, to ascertain the age and authenticity of the codex. Carbon 14 dates the codex to A.D. 220-340. At the present time most of the members of the team incline to a date between 300 and 320 (but Emmel thinks a bit later).

In 2005 the Society assembled a team of biblical scholars, in addition to Coptologists Rodolphe Kasser, Gregor Wurst and others, to assist with the interpretation of the *Gospel of Judas*. These added members included Bart Ehrman, Stephen Emmel, Marvin Meyer (who also assisted in the reconstruction of the codex), Elaine Pagels, Donald Senior and me.[2] With the exception of Rodolphe Kasser, who is ill, all of the Coptologists and consultants were present at the aforementioned press release and made statements.

PUBLICATION OF THE *GOSPEL OF JUDAS*

An English translation of the *Gospel of Judas* has been published by the National Geographic Society in an attractive volume by Rodolphe Kasser, Marvin Meyer and Gregor Wurst.[3] This volume includes helpful introductory essays by the editors and translators, including one by Bart Ehrman, explaining the condition of the codex and the relationship of the *Gospel of Judas* to early Christian literature, including other Gnostic texts.

The *Gospel of Judas* is found on pages 33-58 of Codex Tchacos, but there are three other tractates (or writings): pages 1-9 preserve a version of the *Let-*

ter of Peter to Philip, which is approximately the same text as the second tractate of Nag Hammadi's codex 8. Pages 10-32 preserve a book of *James,* which approximates the third tractate of Nag Hammadi's codex 5, which there is titled the *First Apocalypse of James.* Pages 59-66 preserve an untitled work, in which the figure Allogenes ("Stranger") appears. This tractate, which is quite fragmentary, does not appear to be related to the third tractate of Nag Hammadi's codex 11, which is titled *Allogenes.* And finally, a fragment not related to these four tractates has surfaced recently, on which may appear the page number "108." If so, then we may infer that at least forty-two pages of Codex Tchacos are missing.

THE CONTENTS OF THE *GOSPEL OF JUDAS*

The *Gospel of Judas* begins with these words: "The secret account of the revelation that Jesus spoke in conversation with Judas Iscariot" (p. 33, lines 1-3). The tractate concludes with the words: "The Gospel of Judas" (p. 58, lines 28-29).[4] These lines are stunning enough, but what happens in between is what has given rise to most of the controversy.

In the *Gospel of Judas,* Judas Iscariot is singled out as Jesus' greatest disciple. He alone is able to receive Jesus' most profound teaching and revelation. Jesus laughs at the other disciples' prayers and sacrifices. They do not fully grasp who Jesus really is and from whom and where he has come. But Judas is able to stand before Jesus (p. 35, lines 8-9). "I know who you are and from where you have come. You are from the immortal realm of Barbelo. And I am not worthy to utter the name of the one who has sent you" (p. 35, lines 15-21). After this confession Jesus teaches Judas in private.

At the conclusion of this private teaching, in which Judas is invited to enter the cloud (and be transformed?), Jesus utters his most startling instruction: "You will exceed them all. For you will sacrifice the man who clothes me" (p. 56, lines 18-20). That is, while the other disciples are wasting time in inferior worship and activity (sacrificing animals in the Jewish fashion, presumably), Judas will carry out the sacrifice that truly counts, the sacrifice that will result in salvation: He will sacrifice the physical body of Jesus, thus allowing Jesus to complete his mission. In this way Judas does indeed become the greatest of the disciples.

Accordingly, the narrative concludes with the handing over of Jesus to the ruling priests:

> The ruling priests murmured because he [Jesus] had gone into the guest room to pray. But some scribes were there watching carefully, in order to arrest him during the prayer, for they were afraid of the people, for Jesus was regarded by all as a prophet. They approached Judas and said to him, "What are you doing here? You are the disciple of Jesus." Judas answered them as they wished; and Judas received some money and handed him (Jesus) over to them. (p. 58, lines 9-26)[5]

There is no mention of a trial, execution or resurrection. The *Gospel of Judas* has related what it wanted to relate: The obedience of Judas and how that obedience assisted Jesus in fulfilling his salvific mission. Judas has been transformed from villain to hero, from traitor to saint.

THE MEANING OF THE *GOSPEL OF JUDAS*

Writing in A.D. 180 Irenaeus inveighs against a group he and others call the Cainites, evidently because this group makes heroes out of biblical villains, from Cain, who murdered his brother Abel, to Judas, who handed Jesus to his enemies. Irenaeus has this to say:

> Others again declare that Cain derived his being from the Power above, and acknowledge that Esau, Korah, the Sodomites, and all such persons, are related to themselves. On this account, they add, they have been assailed by the Creator, yet no one of them has suffered injury. For Sophia was in the habit of carrying off that which belonged to her from them to herself. They declare that Judas the traitor was thoroughly acquainted with these things, and that he alone, knowing the truth as no others did, accomplished the mystery of the betrayal; by him all things, both earthly and heavenly, were thus thrown into confusion. They produce a fictitious history of this kind, which they style the *Gospel of Judas*. (*Against Heresies* 1.31.1)

In other words, the so-called Cainites identify with the villains of the Old Testament. They do this because they believe that the god of this world, in stark contrast to the God of light above, is evil. Accordingly, anyone that the god of this world hates and tries to destroy—such as Cain, Esau or the people of Sodom—must be good people, people on the side of the God of light. The *Gospel of Judas* shares this perspective.

The *Gospel of Judas* makes a meaningful contribution to our understanding of second-century Christianity, especially with regard to the question of diversity. We have here what may be an early exemplar of Sethian Gnosticism, a form of Gnosticism that may have roots in Jewish pessimism that emerged in the aftermath of the disastrous wars in A.D. 66-70 and 115-117.[6]

It is highly unlikely that the *Gospel of Judas* preserves for us authentic, independent material, material that supplements our knowledge of Judas and his relationship to Jesus. No doubt some popular writers will produce some fanciful stories about the "true story," but that is all that they will produce— fanciful stories. Even James Robinson, who is no traditional Christian by any stretch, dismisses the *Gospel of Judas* as having no value for understanding the historical Judas.[7] He is undoubtedly correct.

Father Donald Senior, a Roman Catholic priest, stated that in his opinion the *Gospel of Judas* will have no impact on Christian theology or on Christian understanding of the gospel story. Again, I have no doubt that he is correct.

The only thing that the *Gospel of Judas* has made me wonder about is the interesting statement we find in the Gospel of John, where Jesus says to Judas, "What you are going to do, do quickly" (Jn 13:27). The other disciples don't understand what Jesus has said.

What is interesting about this is that we have at least two other instances where Jesus evidently made a private arrangement with a few disciples that the other disciples know nothing about. We see this in the securing of the animal for entry into Jerusalem (Mk 11) and in the finding of the upper room (Mk 14). Exegetes and historians may rightly wonder if the episode in John 13 is a third example of a private arrangement Jesus had with a disciple that was not known to the others. It could be that, as the disciples speculated, Jesus was sending Judas to accomplish some task, perhaps relating to Jesus' security later that evening. If so, then Judas's appearance in the company of armed men, who seize Jesus and deliver him to the ruling priests, was a betrayal indeed.

It may be that what we have in the *Gospel of Judas* is a greatly developed, tendential, unhistorical and imaginative expansion of this theme. Yes, Jesus had a private understanding with Judas, and yes, Judas handed Jesus over to his enemies. But no, that was not a betrayal; it was what Jesus wanted him to do. So contends the *Gospel of Judas*.

Of course, whatever arrangement Jesus may have had with Judas (and John does seem to be a witness that he may have had some sort of arrangement), Jesus did not instruct Judas to hand him over to the ruling priests. Accordingly, the *Gospel of Judas* may provide us with a clue that will lead us to ask new questions about why Judas betrayed Jesus and exactly how he did so.[8]

Writings outside the New Testament and even later than the New Testament sometimes offer important assistance in going about the task of New Testament interpretation. The *Gospel of Judas* does not provide us with an account of what the historical Judas really did or what the historical Jesus really taught this disciple, but it may preserve an element of tradition—however greatly distorted and misrepresented—that could serve exegetes and historians as we struggle to understand better this enigmatic disciple.[9]

GLOSSARY

agnostic. a person who is not sure whether God exists

agrapha. independent sayings of Jesus "not written" in the New Testament

Antiochus IV. (215-163 B.C.) ruler of the Hellenistic Seleucid Empire

apocrypha. texts from the New Testament era that are not accepted as Scripture

canon. the texts accepted by the church as authoritative Scripture; the Bible

canonical Gospels. the four Gospels (Matthew, Mark, Luke, John) of the New Testament

Christology. the theological study of and doctrines related to who Jesus is and what he accomplished through his life, death and resurrection

codex. an ancient book produced on leather (vellum or parchment) or papyrus pages

Cynicism. an ancient philosophy founded by Diogenes (c. 412-321 B.C.) that rejected the social values of its time

Dead Sea Scrolls. an important collection of ancient Jewish texts found in caves near the Dead Sea between 1947 and 1956

docetism. an ancient view, deemed as a heresy in the early church, that Jesus only seemed to have a body

Ebionites. an ancient form of Jewish Christianity that tended to enhance the status of the law and minimize the divine nature of Jesus

eschatology. the study of final or last things; God's final accomplishment of his purposes

Essenes. a sect within ancient Judaism that zealously contended for Jewish faith and life, and seems to have viewed themselves as the true Israel; they are probably connected to the Dead Sea Scrolls

Evangelist. an author of a canonical Gospel

extracanonical Gospels. texts outside of the New Testament that relate stories about or sayings of Jesus

gloss. words added to a text by someone other than the author

Gnosticism. a religious orientation that focused more on the supposed secret knowledge (*gnōsis*) Jesus revealed to an elite for their salvation, and less on faith in Jesus as redeemer

Gospel of Thomas. an esoteric writing purporting to record the secret (or "hidden") teachings of Jesus to Thomas and to his other disciples

inerrancy. the belief that the original writings (autographs) of the Bible contained no errors or internal inconsistencies

Jesus Seminar. a research team of New Testament scholars who, through historical and textual evidence, attempt to reconstruct what Jesus did or did not actually say and do

Johannine tradition. the texts of the New Testament that are related to the apostle John—the Gospel of John, 1-3 John, and Revelation

logia. a collection of sayings attributed to Jesus

messianism. a term referring to the hope of a coming "anointed" descendant of David to restore Israel

Nag Hammadi. a town in Egypt where thirteen leather-bound books, including some of the Gnostic Gospels, dating to about A.D. 350-380, were found sometime near the end of 1945

Oxyrhynchus. an archaeological site in Egypt, first discovered at the end of the nineteenth century, where thousands of papyri and fragments, mostly Greek, have been found, including Old and New Testament documents and apocryphal texts

Pastoral Letters. the New Testament letters 1-2 Timothy and Titus

Q. a hypothetical sayings source containing material common to Matthew and Luke but not found in Mark

Synoptic Gospels. the canonical Gospels of Matthew, Mark and Luke

triple tradition. material common to Matthew, Mark and Luke

ABBREVIATIONS

The following abbreviations are used in the notes.

AB	*Anchor Bible*
ABD	*Anchor Bible Dictionary*
ABRL	Anchor Bible Reference Library
AGJU	Arbeiten zur Geschichte des antiken Judentums und des Urchristentums
ANRW	*Aufstieg und Niedergang der römischen Welt*
BA	*Biblical Archaeologist*
BBR	*Bulletin for Biblical Research*
BETL	Bibliotheca ephemeridum theologicarum lovaniensium
Bib	*Biblica*
BJRL	*Bulletin of the John Rylands University Library of Manchester*
BZNW	Beihefte zur Zeitschrift für die Neutestamentliche Wissenschaft
CBQ	*Catholic Biblical Quarterly*
CRINT	Compendia rerum iudaicarum ad novum testamentum
CSR	*Christian Scholar's Review*
CTM	*Concordia Theological Monthly*
DSD	*Dead Sea Discoveries*
ExpT	*Expository Times*
GNS	Good News Studies
HTS	Harvard Theological Studies
JBL	*Journal of Biblical Literature*
JETS	*Journal of the Evangelical Theological Society*
JR	*Journal of Religion*
JSHJ	*Journal for the Study of the Historical Jesus*
JSNTSup	*Journal for the Study of the New Testament* Supplement Series

JTS	*Journal of Theological Studies*
MTS	Marburger theologische Studien
Neot	*Neotestamentica*
NHC	Nag Hammadi Codices
NHS	Nag Hammadi Studies
NICNT	New International Commentary on the New Testament
NIGTC	New International Greet Testament Commentary
NovT	*Novum Testamentum*
NovTSup	Supplement to *Novum Testamentum*
NTAbh	Neutestamentliche Abhandlungen
NTS	*New Testament Studies*
NTTS	New Testament Tools and Studies
SBLRBS	SBL Resources for Biblical Study
SBLSBS	SBL Sources for Biblical Study
SBLSP	Society of Biblical Literature Seminar Papers
SecCent	*Second Century*
SFSHJ	South Florida Studies in the History of Judaism
SNTSMS	Society for New Testament Studies Monograph Series
SPB	Studia postbiblica
TLZ	*Theologische Literaturzeitung*
TSAJ	Texte und Studien zum antiken Judentum
TU	Texte und Untersuchungen
VC	*Vigiliae christianae*
VCSup	Supplements to *Vigiliae christianae*
WUNT	Wissenschaftliche Untersuchungen zum Neuen Testament
YJS	Yale Judaica series
ZNW	*Zeitschrift für die neutestamentliche Wissenschaft*

NOTES

For readers who are interested, a fuller set of notes may be found by accessing InterVarsity Press's website at www.ivpress.com, typing in *Fabricating Jesus,* and following the links provided there.

Chapter 1: Misplaced Faith and Misguided Suspicion: Old and New School Skeptics

[1]FOR THE QUOTATION FROM FUNK: See Robert W. Funk, *Honest to Jesus* (San Francisco: Harper-Collins, 1996), pp. 4-5. The title of Funk's book recalls the title of Bishop John Robinson's *Honest to God* (London: SCM Press, 1963).

[2]FOR THE QUOTATIONS FROM ROBINSON: See James M. Robinson, "Theological Autobiography," in *The Craft of Religious Studies,* ed. Jon R. Stone (New York: St. Martin's, 1998), pp. 117, 121, 145; reprinted in James M. Robinson, *The Sayings Gospel Q,* BETL 189 (Leuven: Peeters and Leuven University Press, 2005), pp. 3, 7, 31. The ellipsis is the author's.

[3]ON ROBINSON'S ASSESSMENT OF THE HISTORICAL JESUS: See James M. Robinson, *The Gospel of Jesus* (San Francisco: HarperCollins, 2005).

[4]BOOKS BY ROBERT PRICE: Robert M. Price, *Deconstructing Jesus* (Amherst, N.Y.: Prometheus Books, 2000); *The Incredible Shrinking Son of Man* (Amherst, N.Y.: Prometheus Books, 2003).

[5]ON EHRMAN'S VIEWS OF SCRIPTURE: See Bart D. Ehrman, *Misquoting Jesus: The Story Behind Who Changed the Bible and Why* (San Francisco: HarperSanFrancisco, 2005), pp. 5, 11, 12. See also the discussion on pp. 210-12. For an earlier, more learned version of this book, see Bart D. Ehrman, *The Orthodox Corruption of Scripture* (New York: Oxford University Press, 1993).

[6]FOR A CRITICAL ASSESSMENT OF BART EHRMAN'S INTERPRETATION OF THE NEW TESTAMENT MANUSCRIPT EVIDENCE: See J. Ed Komoszewski, M. James Sawyer and Daniel B. Wallace, *Reinventing Jesus* (Grand Rapids: Kregel, 2006).

[7]ON NOT RESTING ON THE FAITH OF PETER AND THE FAITH OF PAUL: See Funk, *Honest to Jesus,* p. 304.

[8]ON THE IMPORTANCE OF THE EARLY CHRISTIAN WITNESSES: See Richard J. Bauckham, *Jesus and the Eyewitnesses* (Grand Rapids: Eerdmans, 2006).

Chapter 2: Cramped Starting Points and Overly Strict Critical Methods: The Question of Authenticity

[1]ON THE MINIMALIST RESULTS OF THE JESUS SEMINAR: See Robert W. Funk and Roy W. Hoover, eds., *The Five Gospels: The Search for the Authentic Words of Jesus* (Sonoma: Polebridge; New York: Macmillan, 1993); Robert W. Funk, ed., *The Acts of Jesus: What Did Jesus Really Do?* (San

Francisco: HarperCollins, 1998). The Seminar caught the attention of the press with its system of color-coding the sayings of Jesus in the following manner: red = something Jesus said; pink = something approximating what Jesus said; gray = doubt that Jesus said it; black = something that Jesus very probably or definitely did not say.

[2]FOR RECENT PUBLICATIONS ARGUING THAT JESUS WAS ILLITERATE: See Funk and Hoover, *Five Gospels,* p. 27; John Dominic Crossan, *Jesus: A Revolutionary Biography* (San Francisco: HarperCollins, 1994), p. 25; Robert W. Funk, *Honest to Jesus* (San Francisco: HarperCollins, 1996), p. 158; Pieter F. Craffert and Pieter J. J. Botha, "Why Jesus Could Walk on the Sea But He Could Not Read and Write," *Neot* 39 (2005): 5-35.

[3]FOR RECENT PUBLICATIONS ARGUING THAT JESUS WAS LITERATE: See Craig A. Evans, "Context, Family and Formation," in *The Cambridge Companion to Jesus,* Cambridge Companions to Religion, ed. Markus Bockmuehl (Cambridge: Cambridge University Press, 2001), pp. 11-24; Paul Foster, "Educating Jesus: The Search for a Plausible Context," *JSHJ* 4 (2006): 7-33. Foster's study shows mastery of the relevant primary and secondary literature and is argued with precision and nuance.

[4]ON JOHN 7:53–8:11: Most Bibles recognize that this passage was probably not original to John's Gospel. For example, prior to John 7:53, the NIV says, "The earliest and most reliable manuscripts and other ancient witnesses do not have John 7:53–8:11," and NASB says, "John 7:53–8:11 is not found in most of the old mss."

[5]ON LITERACY IN THE ROMAN EMPIRE AND ISRAEL IN LATE ANTIQUITY: See William V. Harris, *Ancient Literacy* (Cambridge, Mass.: Harvard University Press, 1989), who concludes that literacy rates were very low; and Alan R. Millard, *Reading and Writing in the Time of Jesus* (New York: New York University Press, 2000), who concludes that literacy rates were higher, especially among Jewish men.

[6]ON THE TERMINOLOGY OF "TEACHER" AND "DISCIPLE": For examples of "rabbi" see Mk 9:5; 11:21; 14:45. For examples of "rabbouni" see Mk 10:51; Jn 20:16. For examples of "teacher" see Mt 8:19; 9:11; 12:38; Mk 4:38; 5:35; 9:17; 10:17, 20; 12:14, 19, 32; Lk 19:39; Jn 1:38; 3:2. For examples of "disciples" see Mk 2:15, 16, 18, 23; 3:7, 9; 4:34; 5:31; Lk 6:20; 10:23; 12:22; 14:26, 27 (all with parallels in Matthew).

[7]ON JESUS' USE OF SCRIPTURE: See the helpful tabulation in R. T. France, *Jesus and the Old Testament* (London: Tyndale, 1971), pp. 259-63. For a more recent investigation, see Bruce D. Chilton and Craig A. Evans, "Jesus and Israel's Scriptures," in *Studying the Historical Jesus,* NTTS 19, ed. B. D. Chilton and C. A. Evans (Leiden: Brill, 1994), pp. 281-335.

[8]THE PROPHETS AND WRITINGS QUOTED OR ALLUDED TO BY JESUS: *Prophets:* Hosea, Joel, Amos, Jonah, Micah, Zephaniah, Zechariah and Malachi. *Omitted* are Obadiah, Nahum, Habakkuk and Haggai. *Writings:* Psalms, Proverbs, Job, Daniel and Chronicles. *Omitted* are Song of Solomon, Ruth, Lamentations, Ecclesiastes, Esther, Ezra and Nehemiah.

[9]ON JESUS' "CANON" OF SCRIPTURE: See Craig A. Evans, "The Scriptures of Jesus and His Earliest Followers," in *The Canon Debate,* ed. Lee Martin McDonald and James A. Sanders (Peabody, Mass.: Hendrickson, 2002), pp. 185-95.

[10]QUOTATIONS OF SCRIPTURE IN THE DEAD SEA SCROLLS: In the nonbiblical scrolls of Qumran and the region of the Dead Sea, the book of Deuteronomy is quoted some 22 times, Isaiah some 35 times and the Psalter some 31 times. See James C. VanderKam, "Authoritative Lit-

erature in the Dead Sea Scrolls," *DSD* 5 (1998): 382-402; James C. VanderKam, "Question of Canon Viewed through the Dead Sea Scrolls," in *The Canon Debate*, ed. Lee Martin McDonald and James A. Sanders (Peabody, Mass.: Hendrickson, 2002), pp. 91-109.

[11]ON THE JESUS SEMINAR'S UNDERSTANDING OF ESCHATOLOGY AND THE KINGDOM OF GOD: See Burton L. Mack, "The Kingdom Sayings in Mark," *Forum* 3 (1987): 3-47; James R. Butts, "Probing the Poll: Jesus Seminar Results on the Kingdom Sayings," *Forum* 3 (1987): 98-128. Butts asserts, "For Jesus, the kingdom of God was *not* an eschatological nor an apocalyptic phenomenon" (p. 112). This, of course, is quite mistaken and rests on an egregious misunderstanding of eschatology and the kingdom of God. Mack's attempt to interpret the expression "kingdom of God" without reference to Hebrew and Aramaic sources is especially misleading.

[12]ON THE VIEWS OF BORG AND CROSSAN: See Marcus J. Borg, *Conflict, Holiness, and Politics in the Teachings of Jesus* (1984; reprint, Harrisburg, Penn.: Trinity Press International, 1998); Marcus J. Borg, "A Temperate Case for a Non-Eschatological Jesus," *Forum* 2 (1986): 81-102; John Dominic Crossan, *The Historical Jesus: The Life of a Mediterranean Jewish Peasant* (San Francisco: HarperCollins, 1991).

[13]ON THE JESUS SEMINAR'S PROFOUND MISUNDERSTANDING OF ESCHATOLOGY AND THE MEANING OF THE EXPRESSION "KINGDOM OF GOD": See Bruce Chilton, "The Kingdom of God in Recent Discussion," in *Studying the Historical Jesus*, NTTS 19, ed. Bruce D. Chilton and Craig A. Evans (Leiden: Brill, 1994), pp. 255-80.

[14]ON JESUS AS THE SON OF MAN FIGURE IN DANIEL 7: Here again the Jesus Seminar is confused. Not only does the Seminar translate "son of man" (Greek: *ho huios tou anthrōpou*) as "son of Adam," which is anything but clarifying, the Seminar denies that the historical Jesus was alluding to Daniel 7. Jesus' consistent reference to the "son of man" as "*the* Son of Man" indicates that he has in mind a specific figure. The only figure that will serve is the figure of Daniel 7. When this is recognized, many important features in Jesus' teaching and activities fall into place.

[15]FOR ASSESSMENTS OF THE CRITERIA OF AUTHENTICITY: See Craig A. Evans, "Authenticity Criteria in Life of Jesus Research," *CSR* 19 (1989): 6-13; John P. Meier, *A Marginal Jew: Rethinking the Historical Jesus*, ABRL (New York: Doubleday, 1991), 1:167-95.

[16]ON THE MISAPPLICATION OF THE CRITERION OF DISSIMILARITY: Long ago in a doctoral seminar on the historical Jesus I questioned the historical validity of "double dissimilarity" as a criterion of authenticity. James Robinson, who was leading the seminar, responded that the criterion was necessary to rule out sayings that may have originated in either Jewish or Christian circles. I found this puzzling. This thinking was greatly at odds with my studies in history (in which I had majored). Eventually I learned that many scholars engaged in the study of the historical Jesus have studied Bible and theology, but not history. These Jesus scholars *are not historians at all*. This lack of training is apparent in the odd presuppositions, methods and conclusions that are reached. I dare say that if all New Testament scholars exercised proper historical methods, there would have been no need to write this book.

Chapter 3: Questionable Texts—Part I: The *Gospel of Thomas*

[1]ON THE USE OF EXTRACANONICAL SOURCES FOR NEW TESTAMENT INTERPRETATION: see Craig A.

Evans, *Ancient Texts for New Testament Studies* (Peabody, Mass.: Hendrickson, 2005); and Darrell L. Bock and Gregory J. Herrick, *Jesus in Context* (Grand Rapids: Baker Academic, 2005). On the contribution of the Dead Sea Scrolls to New Testament interpretation, see John J. Collins and Craig A. Evans, eds., *Christian Beginnings and the Dead Sea Scrolls,* Acadia Studies in Bible and Theology (Grand Rapids: Baker Academic, 2006).

[2]ON ISSUES OF DATING CANONICAL AND EXTRACANONICAL SOURCES: see Donald Harman Akenson, *Saint Paul* (Oxford: Oxford University Press, 2000), pp. 89-94; and Philip Jenkins, *Hidden Gospels: How the Search for Jesus Lost Its Way* (New York: Oxford University Press, 2001), pp. 90-106.

[3]ON PRIVILEGING EXTRACANONICAL SOURCES: D. Moody Smith said, "I think it is not unfair to suggest that we are seeing now a willingness or propensity to credit the independence and antiquity of the apocryphal Gospels that is somewhat surprising in view of what is allowed in the case of the canonicals" ("The Problem of John and the Synoptics in Light of the Relation Between Apocryphal and Canonical Gospels," in *John and the Synoptics,* BETL 101, ed. Adelbert Denaux [Leuven: Peeters and Leuven University Press, 1992], p. 151).

[4]ON THE RESULTS OF THE JESUS SEMINAR: See Robert W. Funk, Roy W. Hoover and the Jesus Seminar, *The Five Gospels: The Search for the Authentic Words of Jesus* (New York: Macmillan, 1993).

[5]THE HISTORICAL JESUS BOOKS BY CROSSAN AND MEIER: John Dominic Crossan, *The Historical Jesus: The Life of a Mediterranean Jewish Peasant* (San Francisco: HarperCollins, 1991); John P. Meier, *A Marginal Jew: Rethinking the Historical Jesus,* ABRL (New York: Doubleday, 1991). Meier's is the first of four volumes. The first volume deals with sources and historical context. The second and third volumes deal with the life and ministry of Jesus. The fourth volume is still in preparation. Crossan has written a more popular version in *Jesus: A Revolutionary Biography* (San Francisco: HarperCollins, 1994).

[6]ON MEIER'S ASSESSMENT OF THE EXTRACANONICAL SOURCES: See Meier, *Marginal Jew,* pp. 140-41 (full assessment, pp. 112-66).

[7]ON HELMUT KOESTER'S ASSESSMENT OF THE EXTRACANONICAL SOURCES: See Helmut Koester, *Introduction to the New Testament* (New York: de Gruyter, 1982), 2:13; and Helmut Koester, *Ancient Christian Gospels* (Philadelphia: Trinity Press International, 1990). Koester believes that some of the extracanonical sources do indeed contain traditions that can be traced back to the very origins of Christianity.

[8]ON REFERENCES TO THE *GOSPEL OF THOMAS* IN EARLY CHURCH FATHERS: See Hippolytus *De Haeresibus* 5.7.20; Origen *Homilies on Luke* 1.5.13-14; Jerome *Commentary on Matthew,* prologue; and Ambrose *Exposition of the Gospel of Luke* 1.2.10.

[9]ON BEING PROPERLY ATTIRED IN GNOSTIC THOUGHT: See *Gospel of Thomas* 21 ("They will undress in their presence"); *The Dialogue of the Savior* 51-52 ("the garments of life"); *Manichaean Psalm Book* 54.19-30 ("they wore me as a garment upon them").

[10]SCHOLARS WHO BELIEVE THAT THE *GOSPEL OF THOMAS* CONTAINS PRIMITIVE, PRE-SYNOPTIC TRADITION: Gilles Quispel, "the Gospel of Thomas and the New Testament," *VC* 11 (1957) 189-207; Helmut Koester, "Q and Its Relatives," in *Gospel Origins & Christian Beginnings,* ed. James E. Goehring et al. (Sonoma, Calif.: Polebridge, 1990), pp. 49-63; R. D. Cameron, "The Gospel of Thomas: A Forschungsbericht and Analysis," *ANRW* 2.25.6 (1988): 4195-251.

Stevan L. Davies makes the astonishing claim that the *Gospel of Thomas* "may be our best source for Jesus's teachings" ("Thomas: The Fourth Synoptic Gospel," *BA* 46 [1983]: 9; see also Stevan L. Davies, *The Gospel of Thomas and Christian Wisdom* [New York: Seabury, 1983]. Davies dismisses too quickly the possible Gnostic orientation of many of the sayings; it is surely inaccurate to report that scholars have concluded that the *Gospel of Thomas* is Gnostic *only because it was found among Gnostic documents.* Most scholars are persuaded that the *Gospel of Thomas* is Gnostic in its final form, though to what degree is debated.

[11] FOR A SYNOPSIS OF PARALLELS BETWEEN THE NEW TESTAMENT WRITINGS AND THE *GOSPEL OF THOMAS:* See Craig A. Evans, Robert L. Webb and Richard A. Wiebe, *Nag Hammadi Texts and the Bible,* NTTS 18 (Leiden: Brill, 1993), pp. 88-144. Scholars who think *Thomas* is dependent on the New Testament writings include Craig L. Blomberg, "Tradition and Redaction in the Parables of the Gospel of Thomas," in *The Jesus Tradition Outside the Gospels,* Gospel Perspectives 5, ed. David Wenham (Sheffield: JSOT Press, 1984), pp. 177-205; Raymond E. Brown, "the Gospel of Thomas and St John's Gospel," *NTS* 9 (1962-1963): 155-77; Boudewijn Dehandschutter, "Recent Research on the Gospel of Thomas," in *The Four Gospels, 1992: Frans Neirynck Festschrift,* BETL 100, ed. Frans van Segbroeck et al. (Leuven: Peeters, 1992), pp. 2257-62.

[12] SEVERAL SCHOLARS HAVE CONCLUDED THAT THE *GOSPEL OF THOMAS* DRAWS UPON THE NEW TESTAMENT GOSPELS: See Robert M. Grant, *The Secret Sayings of Jesus* (Garden City, N.Y.: Doubleday, 1960), p. 113; and Bertil E. Gärtner, *The Theology of the Gospel According to Thomas* (New York: Harper, 1961), pp. 26-27, 34, 42-43. Similar conclusions have been reached by Harvey K. McArthur, "The Dependence of the Gospel of Thomas on the Synoptics," *ExpTim* 71 (1959-1960): 286-87; William R. Schoedel, "Parables in the Gospel of Thomas," *CTM* 43 (1972) 548-60; Klyne R. Snodgrass, "The Gospel of Thomas: A Secondary Gospel," *SecCent* 7 (1989-1990): 19-38; Christopher M. Tuckett, "Thomas and the Synoptics," *NovT* 30 (1988): 132-57, esp. p. 157; Meier, *Marginal Jew,* pp. 130-39. According to Charles E. Carlston "many readings of the Gospel of Thomas and a considerable amount of time spent with the secondary literature . . . have not yet convinced me that any of the parabolic material in Thomas is clearly independent of the Synoptic Gospels" (*The Parables of the Triple Tradition* [Philadelphia: Fortress, 1975], p. xiii).

[13] ON THE VIEW THAT THE *GOSPEL OF THOMAS* 65 REPRESENTS AN OLDER FORM OF THE PARABLE OF THE WICKED TENANT FARMERS: See John Dominic Crossan, "The Parable of the Wicked Husbandmen," *JBL* 90 (1971): 451-65; and his *Historical Jesus,* pp. 351-52.

[14] ON THE VIEW THE VERSION IN *THOMAS* IS AN EDITED AND ABRIDGED FORM OF LUKE'S VERSION: See Boudewijn Dehandschutter, "La parabole des vignerons homicides (Mc., XII, 1-12) et l'évangile selon Thomas," in *L'Évangile selon Marc: Tradition et rédaction,* BETL 34, ed. Maurits Sabbe (Leuven: Peeters, 1974), pp. 203-19; Jean-Marie Sevrin, "Un groupement de trois paraboles, contre les richesses dans l'Evangile selon Thomas. *EvTh* 63, 64, 65" in *Le paraboles évangéliques: Perspectives nouvelles,* ed. Jean Delorme (Paris: Cerf, 1989), pp. 425-39, esp. pp. 433-34.

[15] ON THE APOSTLE THOMAS IN SYRIAN CHRISTIAN TRADITION: See Henri-Charles Puech, "The Gospel of Thomas," in *The New Testament Apocrypha,* ed. Edgar Hennecke and Wilhelm Schneemelcher (London: SCM Press; Philadelphia: Westminster, 1963), 1:278-307; John

Dominic Crossan, *Four Other Gospels* (Sonoma, Calif.: Polebridge, 1992), pp. 9-11; Stephen J. Patterson, *The Gospel of Thomas and Jesus* (Sonoma, Calif.: Polebridge, 1993), pp. 118-20; and Patterson "Understanding the Gospel of Thomas Today," in *The Fifth Gospel,* ed. Stephen J. Patterson, James M. Robinson, and Hans Gebhard Bethge (Valley Forge, Penn.: Trinity Press International, 2000), pp. 37-40.

[16]ON THE PROPOSAL THAT THE *GOSPEL OF THOMAS* DATES TO THE FIRST CENTURY: See Davies, *Gospel of Thomas,* pp. 146-47; Crossan, *Historical Jesus,* 427-30; Patterson, *Gospel of Thomas and Jesus,* 118-20; Patterson, "Understanding the Gospel of Thomas Today," pp. 40-45. The editors of the Greek fragments of the *Gospel of Thomas* (that is, P.Oxy. 1, 654, 655) suggested that the original Greek text probably dated to A.D. 140, a date that Crossan, Patterson and others find too late and based on untested and unwarranted assumptions.

[17]ON THE ARGUMENT THAT THERE IS NO COMPOSITIONAL ORDER TO THE *GOSPEL OF THOMAS*: See Crossan, *Four Other Gospels,* pp. 11-18.

[18]ON TATIAN'S DIATESSARON: The *Diatessaron* (from Greek, meaning "through the four [Gospels]") blends together the four New Testament Gospels, plus some material from a fifth Gospel source. See Samuel Hemphill, *The Diatessaron of Tatian* (London: Hodder & Stoughton, 1888); William L. Petersen, *Tatian's Diatessaron,* VCSup 25 (Leiden: Brill, 1994); William L. Petersen, "Tatian's Diatessaron," in *Ancient Christian Gospels,* by Helmut Koester (Philadelphia: Trinity Press International, 1990), pp. 403-30. The latter essay provides a very helpful overview. In a comprehensive study Gilles Quispel observed that, in comparison with the Greek New Testament Gospels, the *Gospel of Thomas* and Tatian's *Diatessaron* share a large number of textual variants. Indeed, almost half of the sayings in *Thomas* give evidence of at least one such variant. See Gilles Quispel, *Tatian and the Gospel of Thomas* (Leiden: Brill, 1975). Tatian (c. 120-185), a disciple of Justin Martyr (c. 100-165), composed the *Diatessaron,* probably in Syriac and probably in Syria, sometime between 172 and 185. The *Diatessaron* relies heavily on Matthew and may have been inspired by the earlier harmony of the Synoptic Gospels produced by Justin Martyr.

[19]ON CATCHWORDS IN THE *GOSPEL OF THOMAS* AND SYRIAC AS THE ORIGINAL LANGUAGE: See Nicholas Perrin, *Thomas and Tatian,* Academia Biblica 5 (Atlanta: Society of Biblical Literature, 2002); and Nicholas Perrin, "NHC II,2 and the Oxyrhynchus Fragments (P.Oxy 1, 654, 655): Overlooked Evidence for a Syriac *Gospel of Thomas,*" VC 58 (2004): 138-51.

[20]ON THE WORK CALLED *RECOGNITIONS*: Several apocryphal writings circulated in the second, third and fourth centuries attributed to Clement of Rome (who flourished in the late first century). Among these are the *Apostolic Constitutions,* the *Clementine Homilies,* the *Clementine Recognitions,* an *Apocalypse of Clement* and other writings. The *Clementine Recognitions* originated in Greek in the first half of the third century. The Greek is lost, but the work survives in Latin and Syriac translation.

[21]ON CROSSAN'S ANALYSIS OF THE BEATITUDE IN THE *GOSPEL OF THOMAS* 54: See Crossan, *Four Other Gospels,* p. 19 (see pp. 18-19). See also the analysis in Patterson, *Gospel of Thomas and Jesus,* pp. 42-44. The source-critical and exegetical arguments of Crossan and Patterson lose all force in view of the Syrian evidence.

[22]ON THE ARGUMENT THAT THE SAYINGS GENRE OF THE *GOSPEL OF THOMAS* IS EVIDENCE OF AN EARLY DATE: See James M. Robinson, "LOGOI SOPHON: On the Gattung of Q," in *Trajectories Through Early Christianity,* by James M. Robinson and Helmut Koester (Philadelphia: Fortress,

1971), pp. 71-113; James M. Robinson, "On Bridging the Gulf from Q to the Gospel of Thomas (or *vice versa*)," in *Nag Hammadi, Gnosticism, and Early Christianity*, ed. Charles W. Hedrick and Robert Hodgson Jr. (Peabody, Mass.: Hendrickson, 1986), pp. 127-55; Davies, *Gospel of Thomas*, p. 145; Patterson, *Gospel of Thomas and Jesus*, pp. 113-18.

Chapter 4: Questionable Texts—Part II: The *Gospel of Peter*, the *Egerton Gospel*, the *Gospel of Mary* and the *Secret Gospel of Mark*

[1]ON THE PUBLICATION OF THE NINTH-CENTURY AKHMÎM GREEK TEXT: The Gospel fragment was published five years after its discovery, in Urban Bouriant, "Fragments du texte grec du livre d'Enoch et de quelques écrits attribués à Saint Pierre," in *Mémoires publiés par les membres de la Mission archéologique française au Caire* 9.1 (Paris: Libraire de la Société asiatique, 1892), pp. 137-42. Edited and corrected editions of the text can also be found in J. Armitage Robinson and Montague Rhodes James, *The Gospel According to Peter, and The Revelation of Peter* (London: C. J. Clay, 1892); Hans von Schubert, *The Gospel of St. Peter* (Edinburgh: T & T Clark, 1893).

[2]ON THE DIVERGENT ASSESSMENTS OF THE RELATIONSHIP BETWEEN THE ALLEGED *GOSPEL OF PETER* AND THE SYNOPTIC GOSPELS: Those who argue that the newly discovered Gospel fragment depends on the Synoptic Gospels include Henry Barclay Swete, *Euangelion kata Petron: The Akhmîm Fragment of the Apocryphal Gospel of St. Peter* (New York: Macmillan, 1893), pp. xiii-xx, and J. Armitage Robinson, who speaks of "the unmistakable acquaintance of the author with our Four Evangelists. . . . He uses and misuses each in turn" (*Gospel According to Peter*, pp. 32-33). Percival Gardner-Smith argues that the fragment is independent of the Synoptic Gospels in "The Gospel of Peter," *JTS* 27 (1925-1926): 255-71; and "The Date of the Gospel of Peter," *JTS* 27 (1925-1926): 401-7.

[3]ON THE OXYRHYNCHUS FRAGMENTS THAT MIGHT BE PART OF THE *GOSPEL OF PETER*: For reconstruction of P.Oxy. 2949 (vol. 41) see Revel A. Coles, "Fragments of an Apocryphal Gospel (?)," in *The Oxyrhynchus Papyri*, Vol. 41, ed. Gerald M. Browne et al. (London: Egypt Exploration Society, 1972), pp. 15-16 (+ pl. II). P.Oxy. 2949 may date as early as the late second century. The second fragment, P.Oxy. 4009, also probably dates to the second century. See Dieter Lührmann and P. J. Parsons, "4009. Gospel of Peter?" in *The Oxyrhynchus Papyri*, vol. 60, ed. Peter J. Parsons et al. (London: Egypt Exploration Society, 1993), pp. 1-5 (+ pl. I).

[4]ON RECENT SCHOLARLY SUPPORT OF THE ANTIQUITY OF THE *GOSPEL OF PETER*: See Helmut Koester, *Introduction to the New Testament* (New York: de Gruyter, 1982), 2:163; Ron D. Cameron, ed. *The Other Gospels: Non-Canonical Gospel Texts* (Philadelphia: Westminster Press, 1982), p. 78. Another Koester student, Benjamin A. Johnson has argued that Peter's empty tomb tradition is not based on the canonical Gospels, but on an older tradition (*The Empty Tomb Tradition in the Gospel of Peter*, Ph.D. dissertation [Cambridge, Mass.: Harvard University Press, 1966]).

[5]ON THE THEORY THAT AN EARLY FORM OF THE *GOSPEL OF PETER* LIES BEHIND THE PASSION NARRATIVES OF THE NEW TESTAMENT GOSPELS: John Dominic Crossan says, "This book has argued for the existence of a document which I call the *Cross Gospel* as the single known source for the Passion and Resurrection narrative. It flowed into Mark, flowed along with him into Matthew and Luke, flowed along with the three synoptics into John, and finally flowed along with the intracanonical tradition into the pseudepigraphical *Gospel of Peter*. I cannot find persuasive

evidence of anything save redactional modification being added to that stream once it departs its *Cross Gospel* source" (*The Cross That Spoke* [San Francisco: Harper & Row, 1988], p. 404).

[6]CITING THE GOSPEL FRAGMENT: The division of the Akhmîm fragment (a.k.a. *Gospel of Peter*) into sections is anomalous. One scholar divided the work into fourteen paragraphs (or chapters) and another scholar divided it into sixty verses. It is conventional to cite both systems together. This is done in the translation that has been provided.

[7]ON THE LATE AND SECONDARY NATURE OF THE AKHMÎM GOSPEL FRAGMENT (OR GOSPEL OF PETER): See T. W. Manson, "The Life of Jesus: A Study of the Available Materials," *BJRL* 27 (1942-1943): 323-37; C. H. Dodd, "A New Gospel," in *New Testament Studies,* by C. H. Dodd (Manchester, U.K.: Manchester University Press, 1953), pp. 12-52; and Edouard Massaux, *The Influence of the Gospel of Saint Matthew on Christian Literature Before Saint Irenaeus,* NGS 5.1-3, ed. Arthur J. Bellinzoni (Macon: Mercer University Press, 1990-1993), 2.202-14. Dodd concludes that the Akhmîm fragment (which he accepts as the *Gospel of Peter*) "depends on all four canonical Gospels, and probably not on any independent tradition" (p. 46). On the secondary nature of the guard tradition in the Akhmîm fragment, see Susan E. Schaeffer, "The Guard at the Tomb (*Gos. Pet.* 8:28-11:49 and Matt 27:62-66; 28:2-4, 11-16): A Case of Intertextuality?" in *Society of Biblical Literature 1991 Seminar Papers,* SBLSP 30, ed. Eugene H. Lovering (Atlanta: Scholars, 1991), pp. 499-507; and Massaux, *Influence of the Gospel of Saint Matthew,* 2.202-4.

[8]ON THE FANTASTIC ELEMENTS IN THE AKHMÎM GOSPEL FRAGMENT: The Akhmîm Gospel fragment describes the risen Jesus as so tall that his head extended above the heavens and that the cross on which Jesus had been crucified exited the tomb with him. These are the details of late, not early, tradition. On the great height of Jesus, see *Shepherd* of Hermas *Parables* 83.1 ("a man so tall that he rose above the tower"). The *Shepherd* of Hermas was composed sometime between A.D. 110 and 140. The mid-second century addition to 4 Ezra (that is, 2 Esdras 1-2) describes the "Son of God" as possessing "great stature, taller than any of the others" (2:43-47). The Akhmîm Gospel fragment's description of Jesus' head extending *above the heavens* probably represents a further and much later embellishment of these traditions. The Akhmîm Gospel fragment's description of the cross that exits the tomb with the risen Jesus, accompanied by angels, parallels late Ethiopic tradition, attested in two works, whose original Greek compositions probably dated no earlier than the middle of the second century. According to the *Epistula Apostolorum* (or *Letter of the Apostles*) 16, Jesus assures his disciples "I will come as the sun which bursts forth; thus will I, shining seven times brighter than it in glory, while I am carried on the wings of the clouds in splendor with my cross going on before me, then to earth to judge the living and the dead" (J. K. Elliott, *The Apocryphal New Testament* [Oxford: Oxford University Press, 1993], p. 566). This tradition, with some variation, is repeated in the Ethiopic *Apocalypse of Peter* 1: "with my cross going before my face will I come in my majesty; shining seven times brighter than the sun will I come in my majesty with all my saints, my angels" (p. 600).

[9]MORE INDICATIONS OF THE LATENESS AND SECONDARY NATURE OF THE AKHMÎM GOSPEL FRAGMENT: See Jerry W. McCant, "Gospel of Peter: Docetism Reconsidered," *NTS* 30 (1984): 258-73; David F. Wright, "Apocryphal Gospels: The 'Unknown Gospel' (Pap. Egerton 2) and the *Gospel of Peter,*" in *The Jesus Tradition Outside the Gospels,* Gospel Perspectives 5, ed. David

Wenham (Sheffield: JSOT Press, 1984), pp. 207-32, esp. 221-27; Raymond E. Brown, "The Gospel of Peter and Canonical Gospel Priority," *NTS* 33 (1987): 321-43; Joel B. Green, "The Gospel of Peter: Source for a Pre-Canonical Passion Narrative?" *ZNW* 78 (1987): 293-301; Frans Neirynck, "The Apocryphal Gospels and the Gospel of Mark," in *The New Testament in Early Christianity*, BETL 86, ed. Jean-Marie Sevrin (Leuven: Peeters, 1989), pp. 123-75; Susan E. Schaeffer, *The Gospel of Peter, the Canonical Gospels, and Oral Tradition*, Ph.D. dissertation (New York: Union Theological Seminary, 1991); John P. Meier, *A Marginal Jew: Rethinking the Historical Jesus*, ABRL (New York: Doubleday, 1991), pp. 117-18; Charles L. Quarles, "The Gospel of Peter: Does It Contain a Precanonical Resurrection Narrative?" in *The Resurrection of Jesus: John Dominic Crossan and N. T. Wright in Dialogue*, ed. Robert B. Stewart (Minneapolis: Fortress, 2006), pp. 106-20; D. Moody Smith, "The Problem of John and the Synoptics in Light of the Relation Between Apocryphal and Canonical Gospels," in *John and the Synoptics*, BETL 101, ed. Adelbert Denaux (Leuven: Peeters and Leuven University Press, 1992), p. 150.

[10]ON ALLEGED DOCETIC GNOSTICISM IN THE AKHMÎM GOSPEL FRAGMENT: In 4.10 it says that Jesus "himself was silent, as having no pain." This does not say that Jesus in fact felt no pain; it implies that he was silent even though the experience was indeed painful. Also the cry from the cross—"My power, [my] power, you have abandoned me!" (5.19)—is taken by some to indicate docetism. But what we have here is probably no more than influence from a variant form of Ps 22:1, where one of the Greek recensions reads "strength" (or "power"), instead of "God." For further discussion on this issue, see McCant's "Gospel of Peter." There really is no compelling basis for seeing docetic tendencies in the Akhmîm Gospel fragment.

[11]ON THE PROBLEM OF IDENTIFYING THE EARLY GREEK FRAGMENTS WITH THE AKHMÎM GOSPEL FRAGMENT: See Paul Foster, "Are There Any Early Fragments of the So-Called *Gospel of Peter*?" *NTS* 52 (2006): 1-28. Foster shows that it is far from certain that the small Greek fragments P.Oxy. 2949, P.Oxy. 4009 and P.Vindob. G 2325 are from the *Gospel of Peter* mentioned by Bishop Serapion. Foster rightly warns of the circular reasoning in the interpretation of the evidence, where the ninth-century Akhmîm fragment is assumed at the outset to be the *Gospel of Peter* and then the early third-century papyri are reconstructed on the basis of the Akhmîm fragment, which in turn confirms the assumption that the Akhmîm fragment is indeed the *Gospel of Peter*.

[12]FOR THE GREEK TEXT OF THE LONDON FRAGMENTS OF EGERTON PAPYRUS 2: See H. Idris Bell and T. C. Skeat, *Fragments of an Unknown Gospel and Other Early Christian Papyri* (London: British Museum, 1935), pp. 8-15, 26; H. Idris Bell and T. C. Skeat, *The New Gospel Fragments* (London: British Museum, 1951), pp. 29-33. The superscript numbers in the English translation indicate approximate line breaks.

[13]ON ENUMERATING THE LINES IN THE EGERTON AND KÖLN PAPYRI: Lines 22a and 23a, which are based upon Papyrus Köln 255, are so designated, in order to distinguish them from lines 22 and 23 of Papyrus Egerton 2, frag. 1 recto. The same is done with lines 42a-44a, which also are based on Papyrus Köln 255, at the end of the same fragment, in order to distinguish them from lines 42-44 of Papyrus Egerton 2, frag. 2 recto.

[14]ON CLAIMS THAT THE EGERTON PAPYRUS IS EARLY AND INDEPENDENT OF THE NEW TESTAMENT GOSPELS: See John Dominic Crossan, *Four Other Gospels* (Sonoma, Calif.: Polebridge, 1992), p. 183. Helmut Koester, *Ancient Christian Gospels* (Philadelphia: Trinity Press International,

1990), p. 207; cf. Joachim Jeremias, "Papyrus Egerton 2," in *The New Testament Apocrypha,* ed. Edgar Hennecke and Wilhem Schneemelcher (London: SCM Press; Philadelphia: Westminster, 1963), 1:96; Koester, *Ancient Christian Gospels,* p. 215. Crossan argues that Mark is actually "directly dependent on the [Egerton] papyrus text" (*Four Other Gospels,* p. 86).

[15]ON THE INFANCY GOSPEL OF THOMAS: The translation is from Montague R. James, *The Apocryphal New Testament* (Oxford: Clarendon, 1953), p. 63. The *Infancy Gospel of Thomas* may have originated as early as the late second century; cf. Oscar Cullmann, "Infancy Gospels," in *The New Testament Apocrypha,* ed. Edgar Hennecke and Wilhelm Schneemelcher (Philadelphia: Westminster, 1963), 1:419. The *Infancy Gospel of Thomas* should not be confused with the *Gospel of Thomas,* found complete at Nag Hammadi and in three fragments at Oxyrhynchus. See also J. K. Elliott, *A Synopsis of the Apocryphal Nativity and Infancy Narratives,* NTTS 34 (Leiden: Brill, 2006).

[16]ON THE EXTANT GOSPEL OF MARY MANUSCRIPTS: The *Gospel of Mary* is preserved in the Rylands Papyrus 463 (Greek; published in 1938), Berlin Gnostic Papyrus 8052,1 (Coptic; published in 1955), and P.Oxy. 3525 (Greek, published in 1983). The Berlin Gnostic Papyrus (or Berolinensis Gnosticus) was discovered in 1896. Besides the *Gospel of Mary,* this manuscript also included the *Apocryphon of John,* the *Sophia of Jesus Christ* and the *Acts of Peter.* It was first published in Walter C. Till, *Die gnostischen Schriften des koptischen Papyrus Berolinensis 8502,* TU 60 (Berlin: Akademie, 1955; rev. ed., ed. Hans-Martin Schenke, 1972). See George W. MacRae and Robert McL. Wilson, "The Gospel according to Mary. BG 1:7.1–19.5," in *Nag Hammadi Codices V 2-5; VI with Pap. Berol. 8502, 1 and 4,* NHS 11, ed. Douglas M. Parrott (Leiden: Brill, 1979), pp. 453-71. For P.Rylands 463, see Colin H. Roberts, *Catalogue of the Greek Papyri in the John Rylands Library* (Manchester: Manchester University Press, 1938), 3:18-23. For P.Oxy. 3525 see *Oxyrhynchus Papyri,* vol. 50 (London: Egypt Exploration Society, 1983), pp. 12-14. For English translations of the Greek and Coptic fragments, see Henri-Charles Puech, "The Gospel of Mary," in *The New Testament Apocrypha,* ed. Edgar Hennecke and Wilhelm Schneemelcher (London: SCM Press; Philadelphia: Westminster, 1963), 1:392-95; Karen L. King, "The Gospel of Mary," in *The Complete Gospels,* ed. Robert J. Miller (Sonoma, Calif.: Polebridge, 1992), pp. 355-60.

[17]FOR SCHOLARLY TREATMENTS OF THE GOSPEL OF MARY: See Richard Atwood, *Mary Magdalene in the New Testament Gospels and Early Tradition* (New York: Peter Lang, 1993); Esther A. de Boer, *Mary Magdalene* (Harrisburg, Penn.: Trinity Press International, 1997), pp. 74-117; Ann Graham Brock, *Mary Magdalene, the First Apostle,* HTS 51 (Cambridge, Mass.: Harvard University Press, 2003); Karen L. King, *The Gospel of Mary of Magdala* (Sonoma, Calif.: Polebridge, 2003); Holly E. Hearon, *The Mary Magdalene Tradition* (Collegeville, Minn.: Liturgical Press, 2004); Marvin W. Meyer, with Esther A. de Boer, *The Gospels of Mary* (San Francisco: HarperCollins, 2004); Bruce Chilton, *Mary Magdalene* (New York: Doubleday, 2005).

[18]ON THE DATE OF THE GOSPEL OF MARY: The Gnosticizing orientation of the *Gospel of Mary,* among other things, suggests a date no earlier than mid-second century. Nevertheless, scholars will sometimes attempt to smuggle the *Gospel of Mary* or its tradition into the first century. An early date of the tradition lying behind Mary seems to be implied in this statement: "the reader may well agree with Andrew's complaint that Mary's teachings are strange. Strange to us, perhaps. But *in the first* and second centuries, *they were firmly embedded in Christian debates*

about the meaning of Jesus' teaching" (cf. King, *Gospel of Mary,* p. 351, emphasis added). There is no evidence that the teachings of Mary Magdalene, as presented in the *Gospel of Mary,* "were firmly embedded in Christian debates" as early as the first century. Debates about the role of women in the church no doubt took place in the first century, especially if the Pastoral Letters date to the first century. But the perspectives distinctive to the *Gospel of Mary* reflect a much later time. Hans-Josef Klauck remarks: "The contents point to a date in the second half of the second century. An early date between 100 and 150 has been proposed by some scholars, but is not convincing" (*Apocryphal Gospels* [London and New York: T & T Clark International, 2003], p. 160).

[19]FOR A SAMPLING OF SCHOLARSHIP CONCERNED WITH THE SECRET GOSPEL OF MARK: See Morton Smith, *Clement of Alexandria and a Secret Gospel of Mark* (Cambridge, Mass.: Harvard University Press, 1973); Morton Smith, *The Secret Gospel: The Discovery and Interpretation of the Secret Gospel According to Mark* (New York: Harper & Row, 1973); F. F. Bruce, *The Secret Gospel of Mark,* Ethel M. Wood Lecture (London: Athlone, 1974); Marvin W. Meyer, *Secret Gospels: Essays on Thomas and the Secret Gospel of Mark* (Harrisburg, Penn.: Trinity Press International, 2003). For a recent monograph, see Scott G. Brown, *Mark's Other Gospel: Rethinking Morton Smith's Controversial Discovery* (Waterloo, Ont.: Canadian Corporation for the Studies in Religion, 2005). An early and outstanding critical review of Smith's books was written by Quentin Quesnell, "The Mar Saba Clementine: A Question of Evidence," *CBQ* 37 (1975): 48-67. Quesnell's probing review raised many troubling questions about the authenticity of the Clementine letter.

[20]FOR GOOD QUALITY COLOR PHOTOGRAPHS OF THE CLEMENTINE LETTER: See Charles W. Hedrick, "Secret Mark: New Photographs, New Witnesses," *The Fourth R* 13, no. 5 (2000): 3-16. Hedrick thought that his photographs supplied evidence supporting the authenticity of the Clementine letter. As it turns out, they had the opposite effect.

[21]FOR CONVINCING EVIDENCE THAT THE CLEMENTINE LETTER THAT CONTAINS QUOTATIONS AND DISCUSSION OF SECRET MARK IS A HOAX: See Stephen C. Carlson, *The Gospel Hoax: Morton Smith's Invention of Secret Mark* (Waco, Tex.: Baylor University Press, 2005). In his essay "The Question of Motive in the Case Against Morton Smith," *JBL* 125 (2006): 351-83, Scott Brown attempts to cast doubt on Carlson's proposals. The question of motive—apart from the discovery of a confession—will remain the most uncertain feature of this strange case. But the handwriting evidence, along with several other pieces of circumstantial evidence, allows for much less doubt.

[22]AN "OUTSIDER'S" ASSESSMENT OF THE HIGH VALUE PLACED BY SOME ON THE EXTRACANONICAL GOSPELS: Philip Jenkins, *Hidden Gospels: How the Search for Jesus Lost Its Way* (New York: Oxford University Press, 2001), pp. 105-6.

Chapter 5: Alien Contexts: The Case Against Jesus as Cynic

[1]ON THE DIVERSE PORTRAITS OF JESUS IN ANCIENT WRITINGS: See Craig A. Evans, *Life of Jesus Research: An Annotated Bibliography,* NTTS 24 (Leiden: Brill, 1996), pp 278-300; Robert E. Van Voorst, *Jesus Outside the New Testament,* Studying the Historical Jesus (Grand Rapids: Eerdmans, 2000).

[2]ON THE DIVERSE PORTRAITS OF JESUS IN MODERN SCHOLARSHIP: See Claude G. Montefiore, *Some Elements of the Religious Teaching of Jesus* (London: Macmillan, 1910); Joseph Klausner, *Jesus*

of Nazareth, 3rd ed. (1925; reprint, London and New York: Macmillan, 1952); Asher Finkel, *The Pharisees and the Teacher of Nazareth* (1964; reprint, Leiden: Brill, 1974); Geza Vermes, *Jesus the Jew* (London: Collins, 1973); Geza Vermes, *Jesus in His Jewish Context* (London: SCM Press, 2003); Morton Smith, *Jesus the Magician* (San Francisco: Harper & Row, 1978); Hyam Maccoby, *Jesus the Pharisee* (London: SCM Press, 2003).

[3]ON COMPARING JESUS WITH BUDDHA: See the remark in John Dominic Crossan, *In Parables: The Challenge of the Historical Jesus* (San Francisco: Harper & Row, 1985), p. 77: "But it must be emphasized that Jesus' use of proverbs and parables is far closer to that of Zen Buddhism than it is to conventional Hebrew wisdom." This is very misleading. Jesus' use of proverbs and parables is far closer to that of the early rabbis, who in turn derived much of their material and style from Hebrew Scripture itself. For parallels between Jesus and the proverbs and parables of the rabbis, see Craig A. Evans, *Jesus and His Contemporaries*, AGJU 25 (Leiden: Brill, 1995), pp. 251-97. For a convenient presentation of the parallels between Jesus and the Buddha, see Marcus Borg, *Jesus and Buddha* (Berkeley, Calif.: Ulysses Press, 1997).

[4]ON JESUS AS JEWISH CYNIC: See John Dominic Crossan, *The Historical Jesus: The Life of a Mediterranean Jewish Peasant* (San Francisco: HarperCollins, 1991), p. 421.

[5]ON THE DRESS AND BEHAVIOR OF CYNICS: See the comments in ancient writers, such as Epictetus 3.22.50; cf. Lucian *Peregrinus* 15; Diogenes Laertius *Lives of Eminent Philosophers* 6.13; Ps.-Diogenes 30.3. The quotation is from Epictetus.

[6]ON THE CYNIC LIVING ACCORDING TO NATURE: See Julian *Orations* 6.193D.

[7]ON CYNIC CRUDENESS: See Cicero *De officiis* 1.128; Diogenes Laertius *Lives of Eminent Philosophers* 6.69; Epictetus *Discourses* 2.20.10: Cynics "eat and drink and copulate and defecate and snore."

[8]FOR THE QUOTATION ON WHICH END THE NOISE COMES FROM: See Seneca *Moral Epistles* 91.19.

[9]FOR STUDIES BY SCHOLARS WHO FIND THE CYNIC HYPOTHESIS UNCONVINCING: See David E. Aune, "Jesus and Cynics in First-Century Palestine: Some Critical Considerations," in *Hillel and Jesus*, ed. James H. Charlesworth and Loren L. Johns (Minneapolis: Fortress, 1997), pp. 176-92; Hans Dieter Betz, "Jesus and the Cynics: Survey and Analysis of a Hypothesis," *JR* 74 (1994): 453-75; Christopher M. Tuckett, "A Cynic Q?," *Bib* 70 (1989): 349-76; Christopher M. Tuckett, *Q and the History of Early Christianity* (Edinburgh: T & T Clark, 1996), pp. 368-91; Ben Witherington III, *Jesus the Sage* (Minneapolis: Fortress, 1994), pp. 123-43.

[10]FOR A COLLECTION OF PARALLELS BETWEEN JESUS AND CYNICS: See F. Gerald Downing, *Christ and the Cynics*, JSOT Manuals 4 (Sheffield: JSOT Press, 1988).

[11]ON THE LACK OF PIG BONES IN PRE-A.D. 70 SEPPHORIS: According to Old Testament law, pigs are unclean animals that are not to be eaten by Jews.

[12]ON THE JEWISH CHARACTER OF GALILEE AND SEPPHORIS IN THE TIME OF JESUS: See James F. Strange, "First Century Galilee from Archaeology and from the Texts," in *Archaeology and the Galilee*, ed. Douglas R. Edwards and C. Thomas McCollough (Atlanta: Scholars Press, 1997), pp. 39-48; Mark A. Chancey, *The Myth of a Gentile Galilee*, SNTSMS 118 (Cambridge: Cambridge University Press, 2002); Mark A. Chancey, *Greco-Roman Culture and the Galilee of Jesus*, SNTSMS 134 (Cambridge: Cambridge University Press, 2005).

[13]ON JEWISH REVOLTS AND ZEAL FOR THE JEWISH LAW AND WAY OF LIFE: See Martin Hengel, *The Zealots: Investigations into the Jewish Freedom Movement in the Period from Herod I until 70 A.D.* (Edinburgh: T & T Clark, 1989).

[14]ON THE SABBATH IN THE TEACHING OF THE RABBIS: See J. Z. Lauterbach, *Mekilta de-Rabbi Ishmael* (Philadelphia: Jewish Publication Society, 1933), 3:198.

Chapter 6: Skeletal Sayings: Maxims Without a Context

[1]FOR EXAMPLES OF WORK IN WHICH THE GOSPEL CONTEXTS OF THE SAYINGS OF JESUS ARE DISCOUNTED: See John Dominic Crossan, *In Fragments: The Aphorisms of Jesus* (San Francisco: Harper & Row, 1983); John Dominic Crossan, *In Parables: The Challenge of the Historical Jesus* (New York: Harper & Row, 1973); and, representative of the work of the Jesus Seminar, Robert W. Funk and Roy W. Hoover, eds., *The Five Gospels: The Search for the Authentic Words of Jesus* (Sonoma, Calif.: Polebridge, 1993).

[2]ON THE ASSUMPTION THAT THE SAYINGS OF JESUS MEAN MANY THINGS: Some scholars speak of the *polyvalent* (or multimeanings) dimension of Jesus' sayings. This, they say, is actually a good thing. There was no single, original meaning but an almost unlimited range of meanings. What we have here is modern (or, better, postmodern) theory, not the reality of teaching and communication in the world of Jesus and his contemporaries.

[3]ON THE FACTS OF JESUS' LIFE AND MINISTRY: See E. P. Sanders, *Jesus and Judaism* (London: SCM Press, 1985). The list of facts is found on p. 11.

[4]ON THE FAITHFUL PRESERVATION OF JESUS' TEACHING IN THE EARLY CHURCH: See especially Birger Gerhardsson's works: *Memory and Manuscript: Oral Tradition and Written Transmission in Rabbinic Judaism and Early Christianity,* Biblical Resource Series (1961; reprint, Grand Rapids: Eerdmans, 1998); "Narrative Meshalim in the Synoptic Gospels," *NTS* 34 (1988): 339-63; "If We Do Not Cut the Parables Out of Their Frames," *NTS* 37 (1991): 321-35; "Illuminating the Kingdom: Narrative Meshalim in the Synoptic Gospels," in *Jesus and the Oral Gospel Tradition*, JSNTSup 64, ed. Henry Wansbrough (Sheffield: JSOT Press, 1991), pp. 266-309; and Rainer Riesner, "Jesus as Preacher and Teacher," in *Jesus and the Oral Gospel Tradition*, ed. Henry Wansbrough (Sheffield: JSOT Press, 1991), pp. 185-210.

See also Shemaryahu Talmon, "Oral Tradition and Written Transmission, or the Heard and the Seen Word in Judaism of the Second Temple Period," in *Jesus and the Oral Gospel Tradition*, ed. Henry Wansbrough (Sheffield: JSOT Press, 1991), pp. 121-58, with quotation from p. 158. The quoted phrase, "contradictory and mutually exclusive," comes from Werner Kelber, in his *The Oral and Written Gospel* (Philadelphia: Fortress, 1983). There are many problems with Kelber's understanding of orality. See Larry W. Hurtado, "Greco-Roman Textuality and the Gospel of Mark: A Critical Assessment of Werner Kelber's *The Oral and the Written Gospel,*" *BBR* 7 (1997): 91-106.

[5]ON THE PROPOSAL THAT THE PARABLE OF THE WICKED VINEYARD TENANTS DOES NOT DERIVE FROM JESUS AND THAT ITS CONTEXT IN MARK 12 IS NOT ORIGINAL: See Charles E. Carlston, *The Parables of the Triple Tradition* (Philadelphia: Fortress, 1975), pp. 178-90.

[6]ON THE CLAIM THAT THE PARABLE OF THE WICKED VINEYARD TENANTS PROVIDES NO IDENTIFICATION: See Bernard Brandon Scott, *Hear Then the Parable* (Minneapolis: Fortress, 1989), pp. 252-53.

[7]ON THE PROPOSAL THAT THE PARABLE OF THE WICKED VINEYARD TENANTS IS A WARNING TO LANDOWNERS EXPROPRIATING AND EXPORTING THE PRODUCE OF THE LAND: See Bruce J. Malina and Richard L. Rohrbaugh, *Social-Science Commentary on the Synoptic Gospels* (Minneapolis: Fortress, 1992), p. 255.

[8]ON THE JESUS SEMINAR'S INTERPRETATION OF THE PARABLE OF THE WICKED VINEYARD TENANTS: See Funk and Hoover, *Five Gospels,* p. 101.

[9]ON THE PARABLE OF THE WICKED VINEYARD TENANTS AS A STORY OF MURDER: See Crossan, *Parables,* p. 96. In the course of his work on the parable, Crossan has put forward a number of interpretations. Nothing seems to work.

[10]ON THE "BLESSED IDIOCY OF GRACE": See Carlston, *Parables of the Triple Tradition,* p. 185.

[11]FOR QUESTIONS ABOUT THE AUTHENTICITY OF THE PARABLE OF THE WICKED VINEYARD TENANTS DUE TO THE ABSURDITY OF THE CHARACTERS: See Carlston, *Parables of the Triple Tradition,* pp. 183-84.

Chapter 7: Diminished Deeds: A Fresh Look at Healings and Miracles

[1]ON THE SUBJECT OF MIRACLES IN TODAY'S THINKING: See Colin Brown, *Miracles and the Critical Mind* (Grand Rapids: Eerdmans, 1984).

[2]ON THE JESUS SEMINAR'S ASSESSMENT OF JESUS' ACTIVITIES, INCLUDING HIS MIGHTY DEEDS: See Robert W. Funk, ed., *The Acts of Jesus: What Did Jesus Really Do?* (San Francisco: HarperCollins, 1998). Note the odd assertion on p. 34: "stories in which Jesus is represented as other than a laconic sage are not likely to be historical."

[3]ON CROWDS FOLLOWING JESUS BECAUSE OF HIS MIRACLES OF EXORCISM AND HEALING: See E. P. Sanders, *Jesus and Judaism* (London: SCM Press, 1985), pp. 157-73. There are aspects of Sanders's discussion with which I disagree. But I think he is basically correct in reasoning as follows: "The more natural [view] seems to be that Jesus found that he could heal; that he thus attracted crowds and special followers; that he complemented his healing of the needy in Galilee by promising the kingdom to the poor and the outcasts" (p. 164). Sanders does not engage in a philosophical or scientific discussion of what constitutes "miracles" or how Jesus performed them.

[4]ON SAYINGS OF JESUS IN THE Q SOURCE THAT PRESUPPOSE MIRACLES IN JESUS' MINISTRY: See Mt 11:2-6 = Luke 7:18-23; Mt 10:8 = Lk 10:9; Mt 11:21-23 = Lk 10:13-15; Mt 13:16-17 = Lk 10:23-24; Mt 12:43-45 = Lk 11:24-26.

[5]ON THE DISTINCTIVENESS OF JESUS' MIRACLES: See Anton Vögtle, "The Miracles of Jesus Against Their Contemporary Background," in *Jesus in His Time,* ed. Hans Jürgen Schultz (Philadelphia: Fortress, 1971), pp. 96-105; and Colin Brown, "Synoptic Miracle Stories: A Jewish Religious and Social Setting," *Forum* 2, no. 4 (1986): 55-76.

[6]FOR RECENT STUDIES THAT SUPPORT THE HISTORICITY OF THE ACCOUNTS OF JESUS' MIRACLES: See David Wenham and Craig Blomberg, eds., *The Miracles of Jesus,* Gospel Perspectives 6 (Sheffield: JSOT Press, 1986); Graham H. Twelftree, *Jesus the Exorcist* (1993; reprint, Peabody, Mass.: Hendrickson, 1993); *Jesus the Miracle Worker* (Downers Grove, Ill.: InterVarsity Press, 1999); Barry Blackburn, "The Miracles of Jesus," in *Studying the Historical Jesus,* NTTS 19, ed. Bruce Chilton and Craig A. Evans (Leiden: Brill, 1994), pp. 353-94.

[7]FOR RECENT STUDIES ON THE LINK OF EXORCISM AND HEALING WITH THE ANNOUNCEMENT OF THE RULE OF GOD: See Craig A. Evans, "Defeating Satan and Liberating Israel: Jesus and Daniel's Visions," *JSHJ* 1 (2003): 161-70; "Inaugurating the Kingdom of God and Defeating the Kingdom of Satan," *BBR* 15 (2005): 49-75.

[8]FOR STUDIES ON 4Q521: See John J. Collins, "The Works of the Messiah," *DSD* 1 (1995): 98-

112; Craig A. Evans, "Jesus and the Dead Sea Scrolls," in *Eschatology, Messianism, and the Dead Sea Scrolls,* Studies in the Dead Sea Scrolls and Related Literature 1, ed. Craig A. Evans and Peter W. Flint (Grand Rapids: Eerdmans, 1997), pp. 91-100, esp. pp. 96-97; "The New Quest for Jesus and the New Research on the Dead Sea Scrolls," in *Jesus, Mark, and Q,* JSNTSup 214, ed. Michael Labahn and Andreas Schmidt (Sheffield, U.K.: Sheffield Academic Press, 2001), pp. 16-83, esp. pp. 171-73.

[9]FOR MORE ON THE DEEDS OF JESUS AND THE FULFILLMENT OF PROPHECY: See Ben F. Meyer, "Appointed Deed, Appointed Doer: Jesus and the Scriptures," in *Authenticating the Activities of Jesus,* NTTS 28/2, ed. Bruce Chilton and Craig A. Evans (Leiden: Brill, 1999), pp. 155-76. Meyer states: "Jesus is saying that his own public activity in Israel must be read as the superabundant fulfillment of eschatological promises" (p. 159).

[10]ON THE FAME OF SOLOMON AS HEALER AND EXORCIST: In the time of Jesus, King Solomon was famous as healer and exorcist. The fictitious *Testament of Solomon,* probably composed at the end of the first century, is dedicated to Solomon's legendary skills in thwarting evil spirits.

[11]FOR NOTES AND ENGLISH TRANSLATION OF THE GREEK MAGICAL PAPYRUS: See Hans Dieter Betz, ed., *The Greek Magical Papyri in Translation, Including the Demotic Spells,* 2nd ed. (Chicago: University of Chicago Press, 1992), 1:96.

Chapter 8: Dubious Uses of Josephus: Understanding Late Antiquity

[1]ON THE LIFE AND WRITINGS OF JOSEPHUS: See Henry St. J. Thackeray, *Josephus* (New York: Jewish Institute of Religion Press, 1929); Shaye J. D. Cohen, *Josephus in Galilee and Rome,* Columbia Studies in the Classical Tradition 8 (Leiden: Brill, 1979); Tessa Rajak, *Josephus* (Philadelphia: Fortress, 1984); Louis H. Feldman, *Josephus and Modern Scholarship* (New York: de Gruyter, 1984); Bruce D. Chilton, *The Temple of Jesus: His Sacrificial Program Within a Cultural History of Sacrifice* (University Park: Penn State Press, 1992), pp. 69-87; Steve Mason, *Josephus and the New Testament* (Peabody, Mass.: Hendrickson, 1992); Cleon L. Rogers Jr., *The Topical Josephus* (Grand Rapids: Zondervan, 1992); Louis H. Feldman, *The Importance of Jerusalem as Viewed by Josephus* (Ramat Gan, Israel: Bar-Ilan University, 1998).

[2]ON JOHN THE BAPTIST: See Charles H. H. Scobie, *John the Baptist* (Philadelphia: Fortress, 1964); Walter Wink, *John the Baptist in the Gospel Tradition,* SNTSMS 7 (Cambridge: Cambridge University Press, 1968); Robert L. Webb, *John the Baptizer and Prophet,* JSNTSup 62 (Sheffield: JSOT Press, 1991); Carl R. Kazmierski, *John the Baptist* (Collegeville, Minn.: Liturgical Press, 1996); Joan E. Taylor, *The Immerser: John the Baptist Within Second Temple Judaism,* Studying the Historical Jesus (Grand Rapids: Eerdmans, 1997).

[3]ON THE DEAD SEA SCROLLS AND MARRIAGE: See also other Dead Sea Scrolls, such as 4Q416 frag. 2, col. 4, line 5; and 4Q524 frags. 15-22, line 2.

[4]ON HEROD ANTIPAS: See Arnold H. M. Jones, *The Herods of Judaea* (Oxford: Clarendon Press, 1938), pp. 176-83; and Harold W. Hoehner, *Herod Antipas,* SNTSMS 17 (Cambridge: Cambridge University Press, 1972).

[5]ON THE THESIS THAT THE GOSPELS PORTRAY PILATE INACCURATELY: See John Dominic Crossan, *The Historical Jesus* (San Francisco: HarperCollins, 1991), pp. 373-83; and his *Who Killed Jesus? Exposing the Roots of Anti-Semitism in the Gospel Story of the Death of Jesus* (San Francisco: HarperCollins, 1995), pp. 147-59.

[6]ON PHILO OF ALEXANDRIA: See David T. Runia, *Philo in Early Christian Literature,* CRINT 3.3 (Minneapolis: Fortress, 1993); Peder Borgen, *Philo of Alexandria,* NovTSup 86 (Leiden: Brill, 1997); Francesca Calabi, *The Language and the Law of God: Interpretation and Politics in Philo of Alexandria,* SFSHJ 188 (Atlanta: Scholars Press, 1998); Maren Niehoff, *Philo on Jewish Identity and Culture,* TSAJ 86 (Tübingen: Mohr Siebeck, 2001).

[7]ON PILATE'S VIOLENCE AGAINST HIS SUBJECTS: See James S. McLaren, *Power and Politics in Palestine: The Jews and the Governing of Their Land 100 BC-AD 70,* JSNTSup 63 (Sheffield: JSOT Press, 1991), pp. 81-87; Raymond E. Brown, *The Death of the Messiah,* ABRL (New York: Doubleday, 1994), 698-705; Helen K. Bond, *Pontius Pilate in History and Interpretation,* SNTSMS 100 (Cambridge: Cambridge University Press, 1998), pp. 24-93. Raymond Brown provides a convenient summary of six incidents involving Pilate and his Jewish subjects.

[8]ON PILATE'S BEHAVIOR AS CONSISTENT WITH THE PORTRAIT FOUND IN THE NEW TESTAMENT GOSPELS: See Brian C. McGing, "Pontius Pilate and the Sources," *CBQ* 53 (1991): 416-38; Brown, *Death of the Messiah,* p. 704. Brown concludes that the portrait of Pilate found in the Gospels is not inconsistent with what we know of the former governor of Judea, especially in reference to the incident of the standards. See also Bond, *Pontius Pilate,* pp. 119, 205.

[9]FOR RESEARCH THAT SUPPORTS THE HISTORICITY OF PILATE'S OFFER OF A PASSOVER PARDON: See Charles B. Chaval, "The Releasing of a Prisoner on the Eve of Passover in Ancient Jerusalem," *JBL* 60 (1941): 273-78; Robert L. Merritt, "Jesus Barabbas and the Paschal Pardon," *JBL* 104 (1985): 57-68. Bond remarks that "Pilate, and possibly other governors, may have occasionally released lesser criminals as a gesture of Roman goodwill, especially during such a potentially volatile festival as the Passover" (*Pontius Pilate,* p. 199). For concise summaries of the scholarly positions on the pardon, see Bond, *Pontius Pilate,* pp. 199-200; and McLaren, *Power and Politics,* p. 93 n. 2.

[10]ON MOCKERY OF THE CONDEMNED IN ANTIQUITY: See Brown, *Death of the Messiah,* pp. 873-77.

Chapter 9: Anachronisms and Exaggerated Claims: Christianities Lost and Otherwise

[1]ON THE IDEA THAT THERE WERE MANY "CHRISTIANITIES": See Bart D. Ehrman's works *Lost Christianities* (New York: Oxford University Press, 2003); *Lost Scriptures: Books That Did Not Make It into the New Testament* (New York: Oxford University Press, 2003); and *The New Testament and Other Early Christian Writings,* 2nd ed. (New York: Oxford University Press, 2004).

[2]ON THE DATE OF JESUS' DEATH: Most historians opt for either A.D. 30 (perhaps April 7) or 33 (perhaps April 3). For further discussion of the date of Jesus' death, see Harold W. Hoehner, *Chronological Aspects of the Life of Christ* (Grand Rapids: Zondervan, 1977), pp. 65-93; and Jack Finegan, *Ancient World and Problems of Chronology in the Bible,* rev. ed. (Peabody, Mass.: Hendrickson, 1998), pp. 353-69.

[3]ON LUKE 24:12: Verse 12 in Luke's resurrection narrative reads: "But Peter arose, and ran to the tomb; and stooping and looking in, he sees the linen cloths by themselves; and he returned to his home, wondering at what had happened." This verse is found in most old Greek texts (but it is omitted in some). Scholars suspect that it is an early addition to Luke's Gospel, inspired by Jn 20:3-10.

[4]ON THE NAMES OF SIMON PETER: Jesus gave to Simon the name "Rock" (Mk 3:16; cf. Mt

16:18). In Greek the name is *Petros* (or Peter), while in Aramaic it is *Kepha* (or Cephas).

[5]ON THE ORIGIN OF THE NAME CHRISTIAN: The first Christians were not, in fact, called "Christians." Initially they were simply followers of or believers in Messiah Jesus, and their movement (or "sect") was called "The Way" (Acts 9:2; 19:9, 23; 24:14, 22), probably alluding to Is 40:3 ("Prepare the way of the Lord"). We are told that some years later, in the city of Antioch, believers in Jesus began to be called "Christians" or Messianists (Acts 11:26).

[6]ON THE LIST OF WITNESSES WHO SAW THE RISEN JESUS: See Gordon D. Fee, *The First Epistle to the Corinthians*, NICNT (Grand Rapids: Eerdmans, 1987), pp. 728-34.

[7]ON THE CONVERSION OF JAMES, THE BROTHER OF JESUS: According to Jn 7:5, the brothers of Jesus did not believe in him. Hints in Mk 3:20-35 of strained relations with family and in Mk 6:1-6 a less-than-welcome reception in hometown Nazareth probably also reflect this lack of belief and support in Jesus and his ministry. James suddenly appears in Acts (see Acts 12:17: "tell this to James and the brothers"; 15:13: "Brothers, listen to me") not only as a believer but as leader of the church. Interpreters plausibly surmise that it was the appearance of the risen Jesus to James (and to his brother Jude also?) that led to the conversion of James.

[8]ON WOMEN AS APOSTLES IN THE FIRST GENERATION OF THE CHURCH: Experts in the study of the Greek New Testament, Greek manuscripts and the early Greek church fathers believe that *Junia* (not *Junias*) in Rom 16:7 is a woman's name. The verse reads: "Greet Andronicus and Junia, my kinsmen and my fellow prisoners, who are of note among the apostles, who also were in Christ before me." Unfortunately, some versions translate this verse as though only men are in view. On the contrary, the name Junia in the first two or three centuries of the church was *always* a female name. There is no justification for reading the masculine form Junias in Rom 16:7 (as in the RSV). Accordingly, at least one woman was numbered among the apostles. For more on this issue, see Eldon Jay Epp, *Junia: The First Woman Apostle* (Minneapolis: Fortress Press, 2005).

[9]ON THE DATE OF PAUL'S CONVERSION TO CHRISTIAN FAITH: See Jack Finegan, *Handbook of Biblical Chronology* (Peabody, Mass.: Hendrickson, 1998), pp. 395-96; Bo Reicke, *The New Testament Era: The World of the Bible from 500 B.C. to A.D. 100* (Philadelphia: Fortress, 1968), p. 191.

[10]ON THE ROLE OF THE "PILLARS" IN THE JERUSALEM CHURCH: The role of the "pillars" of the early church in Jerusalem was to examine and validate new developments in the rapidly expanding Christian community. For example, "Now when the apostles at Jerusalem heard that Samaria had received the word of God, they sent to them Peter and John" (Acts 8:14). In Acts 10–11 Peter witnesses and testifies to the conversion of the Roman centurion and his family, thus showing that Gentiles, as well as Samaritans, can be saved.

[11]ON THE CLAIM THAT PAUL'S UNDERSTANDING OF THE CHRISTIAN MESSAGE DIFFERED SIGNIFICANTLY FROM THE TEACHING OF JESUS' FIRST FOLLOWERS: This claim has found a new voice in James D. Tabor, *The Jesus Dynasty* (New York and London: Simon & Schuster, 2006), pp. 259-71. In my view Tabor is not fair to Paul, suggesting that he was dishonest and disingenuous in his communications with the pillars of the Christian community in Jerusalem. What Paul states in his letters, especially in Galatians, a circulating and therefore very public letter, makes quite clear his position. Paul held nothing back.

[12]ON THE CONTINUITY OF JESUS' TEACHING BEFORE EASTER AND CHRISTIAN THEOLOGY AFTER EASTER: See James D. G. Dunn, *Jesus Remembered*, Christianity in the Making 1 (Grand Rapids:

Eerdmans, 2003), esp. pp. 210-54. Dunn plausibly concludes that the process of remembering and assembling the teaching and actions of Jesus began during Jesus' lifetime itself. This activity did not spring into action years after Easter, as some critics have assumed. Dunn also rightly argues that the reason the sayings source Q, used by Matthew and Luke, does not emphasize Jesus' death and resurrection, is because it represents the teaching of Jesus *before* Passion Week. On this also see James D. G. Dunn, *A New Perspective on Jesus,* Acadia Studies in Bible and Theology (Grand Rapids: Baker Academic, 2005), p. 121: "The character [of Q] was already impressed in and on the Jesus tradition as it was orally circulated already during the mission of Jesus."

[13]ON PAUL'S TURNING TO NON-JEWS: In his letters Paul says that he takes the gospel message "to the Jew first then to the Greek" (for example, Rom 1:16). We see this in the book of Acts. When Paul enters a city, he preaches the gospel first in the synagogue. As long as he is welcome, he continues in the synagogue. When the welcome is withdrawn, he preaches to the Gentiles. When he enters another city, he repeats the process.

[14]ON THE PHARISEES: See Anthony J. Saldarini, *Pharisees, Scribes and Sadducees in Palestinian Society* (Wilmington: Glazier, 1988); Steve Mason, *Flavius Josephus on the Pharisees,* SPB 39 (Leiden: Brill, 1991); and Stephen Westerholm, "Pharisees," in *Dictionary of Jesus and the Gospels,* ed. Joel B. Green, Scot McKnight and I. Howard Marshall (Downers Grove, Ill.: InterVarsity Press, 1992), pp. 609-14.

[15]ON PLURAL "CHRISTIANITIES" AND "JUDAISMS": In recent years it has become quite fashionable in academic circles to speak of "Christianities" and "Judaisms." Perhaps this is a reflection today of the West's preoccupation with multiculturalism and other aspects of political correctness. Apart from the awkwardness of this language, I think it reflects a misunderstanding of the reality of diversity that normally occurs within any given system of belief and practice. Though not all Jews or Christians think the same way or follow the same practices, this does not justify speaking of Judaisms or Christianities. The real question is: Is it Christian or is it not? If the distinctive core is missing (or much of it is missing), then it is not. But if the core is present, then it is. Christian theologians and church historians have given this a lot of thought, especially in reference to "Christian cults."

[16]ON THE PROBLEM OF THE ROLE OF THE LAW OF MOSES IN CHURCH CONGREGATIONS THAT WERE PRIMARILY MADE UP OF NON-JEWISH PEOPLE: See Markus N. A. Bockmuehl, *Jewish Law in Gentile Churches* (Edinburgh: T & T Clark, 2000).

[17]ON THE AUTHENTICITY AND ANTIQUITY OF THE LETTER OF JAMES: See Peter H. Davids, *The Epistle of James,* NIGTC (Grand Rapids: Eerdmans, 1982); Luke Timothy Johnson, *The Letter of James,* AB 37A (Garden City, N.Y.: Doubleday, 1995); William F. Brosend II, *James and Jude,* New Cambridge Bible Commentary (New York: Cambridge University Press, 2004).

[18]ON JAMES AND HIS RELATIONSHIP TO PETER AND PAUL: See Bruce Chilton and Craig A. Evans, eds., *James the Just and Christian Origins,* NovTSup 98 (Leiden: Brill, 1999); Bruce Chilton and Craig A. Evans, eds., *The Missions of James, Peter, and Paul,* NovTSup 115 (Leiden: Brill, 2004).

Chapter 10: Hokum History and Bogus Findings: Jesus Between the Lines

[1]ON READING THE SCROLLS AND THE NEW TESTAMENT AS CODE: Thiering bases her method of interpretation on the model of *pesher* interpretation found in some of the Scrolls (such as the

commentaries on the Prophets and Psalms) and in a few passages in the New Testament. *Pesher* is an Aramaic word (also used in Hebrew) that means "solution" or "meaning." As practiced in the Scrolls it can be a very subjective, allegorical-like method of interpretation. Thiering takes this method to new levels and applies it to Scrolls and New Testament writings where there is no reason at all to think hidden meaning, in any form, is present.

[2]ON BARBARA THIERING'S METHODS AND CONCLUSIONS: Most scholars have ignored Barbara Thiering's work because it is so subjective and idiosyncratic. Fortunately, one scholar has given her work the criticism it deserves; see N. T. Wright, *Who Was Jesus?* (Grand Rapids: Eerdmans, 1992), pp. 19-36. At this point brief mention needs to be made of Robert Eisenman, who in *James the Just in the Habakkuk Pesher* (1986) and other writings, has argued that James the brother of Jesus is Qumran's Teacher of Righteousness. So here we have another theory that argues that the Dead Sea Scrolls are either Christian writings, or refer to Christians. Virtually no one has followed Eisenman, but compared to Thiering's views, Eisenman's are pretty tame.

[3]ON THE INTERPRETATION OF RENAISSANCE ART: Jeannine O'Grody, the curator of European Art at the Birmingham Museum of Art, in Alabama, lectured on "The Da Vinci Code and Renaissance Art," at the Art Gallery of Nova Scotia, in Halifax, on June 2, 2006. She commented: "The long hair and lack of beard was how Renaissance artists portrayed youth." Later she said that the figure to the right of Jesus in Leonardo's "Last Supper" is not Mary Magdalene but the Beloved Disciple, a youthful man. Because Brown has so much wrong about art, O'Grody added, she doubts the accuracy of much of his church history.

[4]ON THE ROLE OF MARY MAGDALENE AS A DISCIPLE OF JESUS: See Karen L. King, *The Gospel of Mary of Magdala* (Santa Rosa, Calif.: Polebridge, 2003), pp. 55-56.

[5]FOR BOOKS THAT DEBUNK THE *DA VINCI CODE*: See Richard Abanes, *The Truth Behind the Da Vinci Code* (Eugene, Ore.: Harvest House, 2004); Darrell L. Bock, *Breaking the Da Vinci Code* (Nashville: Thomas Nelson, 2004); Carl E. Olson, *The Da Vinci Hoax* (San Francisco: Ignatius Press, 2004); Ben Witherington III, *The Gospel Code* (Downers Grove, Ill.: InterVarsity Press, 2004). There are many others.

[6]ON THE STATIONS OF THE CROSS: There are fourteen stations of the cross, a tradition established in the Middle Ages. The stations are based on details from the Gospels, as well as later traditions, and depict Jesus' progress from Pilate's hall of judgment to the cross and to the tomb. These stations are marked in Jerusalem, along the Via Dolorosa, and are depicted in paintings and stone reliefs in many churches, such as the church at Rennes le Château.

[7]ON THE PLACE OF EGYPT IN THE LIFE OF JESUS: Matthew's story of the holy family fleeing to Egypt has occasioned a great deal of speculation through the ages. Besides Baigent's *Jesus Papers,* we also have Anne Rice, of vampire fame, guessing what Jesus might have done in Egypt, in her *Christ the Lord* (New York: Alfred Knopf, 2005).

[8]ON PAPYRI SURVIVING OUTSIDE OF ARID CLIMATES: Technically speaking, there are a few exceptions. Papyri from Greece, Italy (that is, Pompeii and Herculaneum) and a few other places have been recovered, but in *carbonized* form. Had these papyri not been subjected to intense heat, they would have decomposed and have been lost.

[9]ON DOUBTS ABOUT THE PANTERA LEGEND: Scholars who have studied the inscription doubt that Pantera was old enough to have impregnated Mary or anyone else in 5 or 6 B.C. Pantera may have been born no earlier than 10-12 B.C.

[10]FOR CRITICISM OF *THE JESUS DYNASTY*: See the appendix in Ben Witherington III, *What Have They Done with Jesus?* (San Francisco: HarperSanFrancisco, 2006).

[11]ON HARPUR: See Tom Harpur, *The Pagan Christ* (Toronto: Thomas Allen, 2004).

[12]ON THE IDEA THAT THE JESUS OF THE GOSPELS DERIVES FROM EGYPTIAN TRADITIONS: Harpur, *Pagan Christ,* p. 10. Much of what Harpur claims on this page is simply not true.

[13]FOR TRENCHANT CRITICISM OF *THE PAGAN CHRIST*: See Stanley E. Porter and Stephen J. Bedard, *Unmasking the Pagan Christ* (Toronto: Clements, 2006).

Chapter 11: Will the Real Jesus Please Stand Up? Unfabricating His Aims and Claims

[1]FOR A NEW LOOK AT JESUS IN THE CONTEXT OF JUDAISM: See E. P. Sanders, *Jesus and Judaism* (Philadelphia: Fortress, 1985). For an earlier and broader criticism of Christian misinterpretation of first-century Judaism, see Sanders, *Paul and Palestinian Judaism* (Philadelphia: Fortress, 1977).

[2]ON JESUS AND THE SYNAGOGUE: See Bruce Chilton, *A Galilean Rabbi and His Bible,* GNS 8 (Wilmington, Del.: Michael Glazier, 1984).

[3]ON THE TEXT AND MEANING OF 4Q521: See John J. Collins, "The Works of the Messiah," *DSD* 1 (1994): 98-112.

[4]ON JESUS SITTING ON THE DIVINE THRONE: In later Christian tradition the idea of Jesus sharing God's throne is expressed explicitly, as seen in Rev 3:21: "He who conquers, I will grant him to sit with me on my throne, as I myself conquered and sat down with my Father on his throne."

[5]ON THE QUESTION OF WHAT CONSTITUTED CAPITAL BLASPHEMY IN THE TIME OF JESUS: Whether or not it was blasphemous in the technical sense of the discussion of capital blasphemy in the Mishnah tractate *Sanhedrin* 6–7, where the name of God has to be pronounced and in a vain or obscene context, is an open question. Even if Jesus had uttered the divine name ("You will see the Son of Man seated at the right hand of Yahweh"), it is not clear that that in itself would have constituted blasphemy according to *Sanhedrin* 6–7. But in the first century the word *blasphemy* was used in a more informal sense and could apply much more broadly than what is allowed in the Mishnah. On this topic, see Darrell L. Bock, *Blasphemy and Exaltation in Judaism and the Final Examination of Jesus* (1998; reprint, Grand Rapids: Baker, 2000).

[6]FOR AN ENGLISH TRANSLATION OF SOME OF REIMARUS'S WORK: See Charles H. Talbert, ed., *Reimarus* (Philadelphia: Fortress, 1970).

[7]FOR THE CLASSIC SURVEY OF THE EIGHTEENTH-CENTURY "OLD QUEST" OF THE HISTORICAL JESUS: See Albert Schweitzer, *The Quest of the Historical Jesus* (London: Black, 1910).

[8]ON THE THIRD QUEST OF THE HISTORICAL JESUS: See N. T. Wright, *Who Was Jesus?* (Grand Rapids: Eerdmans, 1992); Ben Witherington III, *The Jesus Quest* (Downers Grove, Ill.: InterVarsity Press, 1995).

[9]ON THE AUTHENTICITY OF THE WORDING OF THE PLACARD: Most scholars accept the placard (or *titulus*) as authentic. They reason, and I think cogently, that if Christians had invented the *titulus*, the wording would have been different. Christians did not regard Jesus as the "King of the Jews." They regarded him as the Lord of the church, as the Savior of the world, as the Son of God, and as the Messiah.

[10]ON THE RESURRECTION OF JESUS: See N. T. Wright, *The Resurrection of the Son of God,* Christian Origins and the Question of God 3 (Minneapolis: Fortress Press, 2003); and Dale C. Allison Jr., *Resurrecting Jesus* (New York: T & T Clark, 2005).

Appendix 1: Agrapha: Free-floating Sayings of Jesus

[1]On the agrapha attributed to Jesus: See Joachim Jeremias, *The Unknown Sayings of Jesus*, 2nd ed. (London: SPCK, 1964); Wilhelm Schneemelcher, ed., *New Testament Apocrypha*, rev. ed. (Louisville: Westminster/John Knox, 1991), 1:88-91; J. K. Elliott, *The Apocryphal New Testament* (Oxford: Clarendon Press, 1993), pp. 26-30; William D. Stroker, *Extracanonical Sayings of Jesus*, SBLRBS 18 (Atlanta: Scholars, 1989); "Agrapha," *ABD* 1 (1992): 92-95; Marvin W. Meyer, *The Unknown Sayings of Jesus* (San Francisco: HarperCollins, 1998). In *Extracanonical Sayings* Stroker provides the text of 266 sayings attributed to Jesus. Meyer assembles 200 sayings and provides brief but very useful commentary.

[2]On the conclusions of Jeremias and Hofius: See Jeremias, *Unknown Sayings*, p. 44; Otfried Hofius, "Unknown Sayings of Jesus," in *The Gospel and the Gospels*, ed. Peter Stuhlmacher (Grand Rapids: Eerdmans, 1991), pp. 336-60.

[3]On the limited value of the agrapha: See Hofius, "Unknown Sayings of Jesus," p. 357. See also Robert H. Stein, "A Critique of Purportedly Authentic Agrapha," *JETS* 18 (1975): 29-35.

Appendix 2: What Should We Think About the Gospel of Judas?

[1]On the Coptic language: Coptic is the Egyptian language that in the time after Alexander's fourth-century-B.C. conquest of the Middle East came to adopt the Greek alphabet (along with a few additional letters). The Nag Hammadi books are also written in Coptic.

[2]On the discovery of the codex containing the *Gospel of Judas:* The convoluted and fascinating history of the codex, now called Codex Tchacos, is narrated by Herb Krosney in his richly documented and insightful book *The Lost Gospel* (Washington, D.C.: National Geographic Society, 2006). The story is also featured in Andrew Cockburn, "The Judas Gospel," *National Geographic* 209, no. 9 (2006): 78-95.

[3]For the published *Gospel of Judas:* See Rodolphe Kasser, Marvin Meyer, and Gregor Wurst, *The Gospel of Judas*, with additional commentary by Bart D. Ehrman (Washington, D.C.: National Geographic Society, 2006). The English translation and photographs of the Coptic text are available on National Geographic's website <www.nationalgeographic.com/lostgospel>.

[4]On the word gospel: The word translated *Gospel* is actually the Greek loan word *euangelion*. We should also note that the explicit text reads "Gospel *of* Judas," not "Gospel *according to* Judas," as we have in the New Testament Gospels and in many of the Gospels outside the New Testament. The composer of the *Gospel of Judas* may be implying that Judas should not be understood as the *author* of the Gospel; rather, the *Gospel of Judas* is *about* Judas.

[5]On the English translation of the *Gospel of Judas:* The translations are based on Kasser, Meyer and Wurst, *Gospel of Judas.*

[6]On the origin of Gnosticism: For more on this interesting hypothesis, see Carl B. Smith II, *No Longer Jews: The Search for Gnostic Origins* (Peabody, Mass.: Hendrickson, 2004).

[7]On Robinson's negative assessment of the value of the *Gospel of Judas:* See James M. Robinson, *From the Nag Hammadi Codices to the Gospel of Mary and the Gospel of Judas*, Institute for Antiquity and Christianity Occasional Papers 40 (Claremont, Calif.: Institute for Antiquity and Christianity, 2006).

[8]On the motives of Judas Iscariot: The motives of Judas for handing Jesus over to the authorities are not clear. Was it greed (as in Matthew and John), or was it Satan (as in Luke and

John)? But were these the primary factors or only contributing factors? Indeed, the New Testament provides two accounts of Judas's fate (see Mt 27:3-10, where Judas commits suicide and the priests buy the field of blood, and Acts 1:15-20, where Judas buys the field and then suffers a fatal fall). Judas is indeed a man of mystery.

[9]A CORRECTION: I need to offer a correction to what otherwise I think is a fine piece of journalism. In Andrew Cockburn's "Judas Gospel," the author summarizes my assessment of the *Gospel of Judas* in these words: "this tale is meaningless fiction" (p. 91). No, it is not meaningless fiction; far from it. The *Gospel of Judas* is loaded with meaning, especially for second-century mystics and Gnostics, who understood the world and mission of Jesus in very different terms. My point, given in my words, which Cockburn faithfully records, is summed up here: "There is nothing in the *Gospel of Judas* that tells us anything we could consider historically reliable" (also p. 91). I stand by that statement, but not by Cockburn's interpretation of my comment. What I have suggested in this brief study is that the imaginative tale in *Judas* may in fact reflect an authentic tradition, in which it was remembered that Judas was an important disciple and that Jesus had given him a private assignment of some sort. This is what may be hinted at in Jn 13. The *Gospel of Judas* alerts us to this possibility, even if we judge its narrative to be wholly fictional.

Recommended Reading

Allison, Dale C., Jr. *Resurrecting Jesus: The Earliest Christian Tradition and Its Interpreters*. London and New York: T & T Clark, 2005.

Bock, Darrell L. *Jesus According to Scripture: Restoring the Portrait from the Gospels*. Grand Rapids: Baker Academic, 2002.

Chilton, Bruce, and Craig A. Evans. *Jesus in Context: Temple, Purity, and Restoration*. AGJU 39. Leiden: Brill, 1997.

Chilton, Bruce, and J. Ian H. McDonald. *Jesus and the Ethics of the Kingdom*. London: SPCK; Grand Rapids: Eerdmans, 1987.

Collins, John J., and Craig A. Evans, eds. *Christian Beginnings and the Dead Sea Scrolls*. Acadia Studies in Bible and Theology. Grand Rapids: Baker Academic, 2006.

Dunn, James D. G. *Jesus Remembered*. Christianity in the Making 1. Grand Rapids: Eerdmans, 2003.

Evans, Craig A. *Jesus and His Contemporaries: Comparative Studies*. AGJU 25. Leiden: Brill, 1995.

————. *Jesus and the Ossuaries: What Jewish Burial Practices Reveal About the Beginning of Christianity*. Waco, Tex.: Baylor University Press, 2003.

Green, Joel B., Scot McKnight and I. Howard Marshall, eds. *Dictionary of Jesus and the Gospels*. Downers Grove, Ill.: InterVarsity Press, 1992.

Komoszewski, J. Ed, M. James Sawyer and Daniel B. Wallace. *Reinventing Jesus*. Grand Rapids: Kregel, 2006.

Stein, Robert H. *Jesus the Messiah: A Survey of the Life of Christ*. Downers Grove, Ill.: InterVarsity Press, 1996.

————. *The Method and Message of Jesus' Teachings*. Rev. ed. Louisville: Westminster John Knox, 1994.

————. *Studying the Synoptic Gospels: Origin and Interpretation*. Grand Rapids: Baker, 2001.

Wilkins, Michael J., and J. P. Moreland, eds. *Jesus Under Fire: Modern Scholarship Re-*

invents the Historical Jesus. Grand Rapids: Zondervan, 1995.

Witherington, Ben, III. *The Christology of Jesus.* Minneapolis: Fortress, 1990.

———. *The Jesus Quest: The Third Search for the Jew of Nazareth.* 2nd ed. Downers Grove, Ill.: InterVarsity Press, 1997.

———. *What Have They Done with Jesus?* San Francisco: HarperSanFrancisco, 2006.

Wright, N. T. *The Challenge of Jesus: Rediscovering Who Jesus Was and Is.* Downers Grove, Ill.: InterVarsity Press, 1999.

———. *Jesus and the Victory of God.* Christian Origins and the Question of God 2. London: SPCK; Minneapolis: Fortress, 1996.

———. *The Resurrection of the Son of God.* Christian Origins and the Question of God 3. Minneapolis: Fortress Press, 2003.

Author Index

Subject Index

Scripture Index

Index of Extracanonical Ancient Sources

Page numbers for major discussions are highlighted in bold.